A NEW PARADIGM FOR GLOBAL SCHOOL SYSTEMS

Education for a Long and Happy Life

SOCIOCULTURAL, POLITICAL, AND HISTORICAL STUDIES IN EDUCATION

JOEL SPRING, EDITOR

Spring
The Cultural Transformation of a Native American Family and Its Tribe 1763–1995

Peshkin
Places of Memory: Whiteman's Schools and Native American Communities

Nespor
Tangled Up in School: Politics, Space, Bodies, and Signs in the Educational Process

Weinberg
Asian-American Education: Historical Background and Current Realities

Lipka/Mohatt/The Ciulistet Group
Transforming the Culture of Schools: Yu'pik Eskimo Examples

Benham/Heck
Culture and Educational Policy in Hawai'i: The Silencing of Native Voices

Spring
Education and the Rise of the Global Economy

Pugach
On the Border of Opportunity: Education, Community, and Language at the U.S.-Mexico Line

Hones/Cha
Educating New Americans: Immigrant Lives and Learning

Gabbard, Ed.
Knowledge and Power in the Global Economy: Politics and The Rhetoric of School Reform

Glander
Origins of Mass Communications Research During the American Cold War: Educational Effects and Contemporary Implications

Nieto, Ed.
Puerto Rican Students in U.S. Schools

Benham/Cooper, Eds.
Indigenous Educational Models for Contemporary Practice: In Our Mother's Voice

Spring
The Universal Right to Education: Justification, Definition, and Guidelines

Peshkin
Permissible Advantage?: The Moral Consequences of Elite Schooling

DeCarvalho
Rethinking Family-School Relations: A Critique of Parental Involvement in Schooling

Borman/Stringfield/Slavin, Eds.
Title I: Compensatory Education at the Crossroads

Roberts
Remaining and Becoming: Cultural Crosscurrents in an Hispano School

Meyer/Boyd, Eds.
Education Between State, Markets, and Civil Society: Comparative Perspectives

Luke
Globalization and Women in Academics: North/West – South/East

Grant/Lei, Eds.
Global Constructions of Multicultural Education: Theories and Realities

Spring
Globalization and Educational Rights: An Intercivilizational Analysis

McCarty
A Place to Be Navajo: Rough Rock and The Struggle for Self-Determination in Indigenous Schooling

Hones, Ed.
American Dreams, Global Visions: Dialogic Teacher Research with Refugee and Immigrant Families

Benham/Stein, Eds
The Renaissance of American Indian Higher Education: Capturing the Dream

Ogbu
Black American Students in an Affluent Suburb: A Study of Academic Disengagement

Books, Ed.
Invisible Children in the Society and Its Schools, Second Edition

Spring
Educating the Consumer-Citizen: A History of the Marriage of Schools, Advertising, and Media

Hemmings
Coming of Age in U.S. High Schools: Economic, Kinship, Religious, and Political Crosscurrents

Heck
Studying Educational and Social Policy: Theoretical Concepts and Research Methods

Lakes/Carter, Eds.
Global Education for Work: Comparative Perspectives on Gender and the New Economy

Spring
How Educational Ideologies are Shaping Global Society: Intergovernmental Organizations, NGOs, and the Decline of the Nation-State

Shapiro/Purpel, Eds.
Critical Social Issues in American Education: Democracy and Meaning in a Globalizing World, Third Edition

Books
Poverty and Schooling in the U.S.: Contexts and Consequences

Reagan
Non-Western Educational Traditions: Indigenous Approaches to Educational Thought and Practice, Third Edition

Bowers/Apffel-Marglin, Eds.
Rethinking Freire: Globalilzation and the Environmental Crisis

Sidhu
Universities and Globalization: To Market, To Market

Spring
Political Agendas for Education: From the Religious Right to the Green Party, Third Edition

Spring
Pedagogies of Globaliztion: The Rise of the Educational Security State

A NEW PARADIGM FOR GLOBAL SCHOOL SYSTEMS

Education for a Long and Happy Life

Joel Spring

Queens College
City University of New York

LEA
LAWRENCE ERLBAUM ASSOCIATES, PUBLISHERS
2007 Mahwah, New Jersey London

Lawrence Erlbaum Associates, Inc., Publishers
10 Industrial Avenue
Mahwah, New Jersey 07430
www.erlbaum.com

Cover design by Tomai Maridou

Library of Congress Cataloging-in-Publication Data

Spring, Joel H. A new paradigm for global school systems : education for a long and happy life / Joel Spring.
p. cm.
Includes bibliographical references and index.

ISBN 0-8058-6123-8 (cloth : alk. paper)
ISBN 0-8058-6124-6 (pbk. : alk. paper)
1. Education–Social aspects. 2. Education–Economic aspects.
3. Globalization. I. Title.
LC191.S6865 2007
306.43'2—dc22

2006026891

Books published by Lawrence Erlbaum Associates are printed on acid-free paper, and their bindings are chosen for strength and durability.

Printed in the United States of America
10 9 8 7 6 5 4 3 2 1

Contents

Preface

Educating workers for global economic competition is the prevailing goal of most national school systems. Around the globe from China to Japan to the United States and the European Union, educational policymakers try to match the school curriculum and instruction to what they perceive are the needs of the global workplace. As economists and social psychologists have found in international studies of the social factors that support subjective well-being and longevity, in its current global form education does not increase happiness except when it leads to a better paying job! Is education only valuable for preparing students for employment?

The findings on the current contribution of education to happiness and longevity should be considered a call to arms to change education policy. The current educational paradigm assumes that economic growth is positive and that the good life is achieved by increasing one's ability to consume new products. In this industrial-consumer paradigm, equality of educational opportunity means giving everyone an equal chance to be educated for participation in the global economy through work and consumption. Equality of opportunity means having an equal chance to earn income for the purchase of an endless stream of products spewing from global enterprises. Global schools are factories for processing raw human materials and approving them with tests and certificates to become global workers and consumers.

This book offers a new paradigm for global school systems. In Chapter 1, "Goals for a Global School System," I analyze prevailing global economic goals for schools and I discuss research on social conditions that support a long life and happiness. In Chapter 2, "Basic Educational Principles for a Long Life and Happiness," I develop guidelines for a global core curriculum, methods of instruction, and school organization based on research on the social factors that support happiness and a long life. I translate these guidelines into "A New Paradigm for a Global Curriculum" in Chapter 3, which includes discussions of progressive, human rights, and environmental education traditions.

Any discussion of global schooling requires an understanding of cultural differences. In Chapter 4, "Ways of Seeing and a Global Core Curriculum," I contrast differing ways of seeing and knowing among indigenous, Western, and Confucian-based societies. Based on this comparison, I propose that global teaching and learning involve a particular form of holistic knowing and seeing.

Integrating the previously analyzed research on subjective being and longevity with my discussion of a global core curriculum and holistic knowing and seeing, I propose in Chapter 5 "A Prototype for a Global School: Humanity Flag Certification." This school design incorporates factors that support the happiness and well-being of the school staff, students, and the immediate community. It is an eco-school site which functions to protect the biosphere and human rights and well-being. Model lessons and instruction are provide in Chapter 6, "Humanity: A Prototype Textbook for a Global Core Curriculum." The model textbook's lessons are holistic, utilizing reading and vocabulary skills while integrating knowledge and methodologies from science, math, geography, geology, history, economics, sociology, and politics. Chapters in this model textbook provide a holistic picture of issues related to health, the environment, social relations, consumer economics, human rights, and politics. One goal of this textbook is to teach through student activism an ethical responsibility to protect the longevity and happiness of all the world's peoples. Chapter 7 concludes the book with a retelling of Plato's parable of the cave-in which educators break the chains that bind them to the industrial-consumer paradigm and rethink their commitment to humanity's welfare.

Chapter 1

Goals for a Global School System

Currently, global educational policy is centered on economic growth and preparation of workers for the world's labor market. Economic growth is considered the measure of social progress. But these policies are increasingly criticized because of their negative effects on the quality of life. For instance, Nobel economist Amartya Sen is concerned about development policies that focus solely on economic growth. In *Development As Freedom,* he uses longevity rates as a guide to the quality of human life.[1] Sen stresses that

> since life expectancy variations relate to a variety of social opportunities that are central to development (including epidemiological policies, health care, educational facilities and so on), an income-centered view is in serious need of supplementation, in order to have a fuller understanding of the process of development.[2]

Criticizing modern development plans for failing to improve the quality of life in Africa, Paul Wangoola, leader of Uganda's African Multiveristy argues that modern development plans attempt to discard traditional ways of life for industrialization, urbanization, and large-scale commercial farming. The results for the quality of human life, he argues, are disastrous. Against a background of an Africa mired in the consequences of European colonialism and postcolonial development plans, Wangoola complains that "the modernization development paradigm … tended to regard comfort, well-being, and material and capital acquisition as the central goals of life. Thus poverty was perceived to be the central enemy, and development its antidote."[3]

I am proposing a new global educational paradigm as an alternative to the increasingly criticized emphasis on education for economic growth and meeting labor market needs. In the new paradigm, educational policy is focused on longevity and subjective well-being rather than economic success. These will serve as common global objectives, with other educational goals determined at the local level. These two objectives, while taking on different meanings in different cultures and religions, can be measured. They can be given concrete and objective meaning that can be used to guide public policy. There exists a vast literature of research studies on these topics, with a growing interest in research on happiness, as evidenced by the 2000 launching of the *Journal of Happiness Studies.*[4] The goals of protecting human life and happiness can guide the selection of part of the subject matter for standard school courses, such as science, history, civics, health, mathematics, environmental studies, and physical training. Moreover, these goals can be used to plan the organization for schools, curricula, and methods of instruction.

This new paradigm is to replace the current dominant global educational goals, which focus on economic growth, military development, and citizenship in the nation-state. By dominant global educational goals, I refer to the education policies of most nation-states, which directly link education to economic and military planning.[5]

By a global school system, I am referring to the similarity of school structures. More than 90% of the world's children and 20% of the world's population are enrolled for varying lengths of time in national school systems sharing a common structure of age-graded classrooms divided into primary and secondary education.[6] One group of researchers claims that the spread of mass education, with similar school organization, teaching methods, and curricula, resulted when the Western model of the nation-state was globally adopted. When the terms "Western" and "West" are used in this volume, they refer to nations of the European Union and North America. The aforementioned researchers assert:

> Mass education spread around the world with the spread of the Western system, with its joined principles of national citizenship and state authority. ... Once mass education appeared, it was likely to expand toward universality. Both the rates of appearance of mass education and the rates of expansion accelerated sharply around World War II.... The logic of universal modern schooling is one that links the individuals who are conceived as making up the modern nation with the unified collective that is represented by the modern state.[7]

The spread of Western-style schooling was accompanied by a belief that progress meant adopting Western industrial models. In this model, schools existed to educate workers who would ensure continued economic growth.

As I explain in more detail later in this chapter, nation-states currently share similar educational goals to establish, maintain, and protect an industrial-consumer economy, an industrial consumer society in which success is measured by economic development and the consumption of new products.

In recent years, some people have questioned the use of economic growth and consumption as measures of human development. One group of economists and sociologists is calling for the use of human happiness or, as some researchers refer to it, "subjective well-being" as a goal of public policy. In 2005, well-known British economist Richard Layard in *Happiness: Lessons From a New Science* pondered the question of why British citizens are no happier, according to objective measurements, than they were 50 years ago despite increasing personal incomes. As Layard writes, "Happiness is an objective dimension of all our experience. And it can be measured. We can ask people how they feel; ... we can now take measurements of the electrical activity in the relevant parts of a person's brain. ... All of these different measurements give consistent answers about a person's happiness."[8]

Layard proposes that happiness serves both as a guide to public policy and as a social unifier. He argues, "Modern society desperately needs a concept of the common good around which to unite the efforts of its members. Here is the right concept. We want to increase the general happiness and we commit ourselves to that end."[9]

In her pioneering book, *Happiness and Education,* philosopher Nel Noddings, after reviewing philosophical arguments for the importance of happiness as a life goal, argues, "Today, with recent changes in social thought and massive changes in technology, it is more important than ever to consider why we are promoting certain goals in schooling and why we continue to neglect education for personal life and for happiness in our occupations."[10]

"The relevance of happiness as a goal of social policy is growing," argues Ruut Veenhoven of Erasmus University. Veenhoven organized the Worlddatabase of Happiness: Continuous Register of Scientific Research on Subjective Appreciation of Life.[11] He asserts, "The better we succeed in eliminating pressing problems such as hunger and plagues, the more we move to abstract goals such as happiness. One of the manifestations of this development is the growing emphasis on 'quality-of-life', rather than mere quantity of life years, in health care."[12] Veenhoven provides the following justification for investigating happiness:

> Happiness is a highly valued matter. Most people agree that it is better to enjoy life than to suffer, and endorse public policies that aim at creating greater happiness for a greater number of people. Though not everybody accepts the utilitarian axiom that happiness is ultimately the only value, the desirability of happiness as such is almost undisputed. This appears in high ranks for happiness in survey studies about value priorities.[13]

Veenhoven contends: "Overall happiness is the degree to which an individual judges the overall quality of his/her own life-as-a-whole favorably. In other words: how much one likes the life one leads."[14]

Concern about human survival and happiness is present in most religious and ethical systems, and it sometimes is referred to as "compassion." For instance, Confucianism, which might be the ethical system affecting the largest number of the world's population, considers compassion an innate human drive. Mencius, Confucius's greatest disciple, declared, "All men have a mind which cannot bear *to see the sufferings of* others."[15] Mencius explained:

> If men suddenly see a child about to fall into a well, they will without exception experience a feeling of alarm and distress. They will feel so, not as a ground on which they may gain the favor of the child's parents, nor as a ground on which they may seek the praise of their neighbors and friends, nor from a dislike to the reputation of having been unmoved by such a thing. From this case we may perceive that the feeling of commiseration is essential to man.[16]

Also, Mencius believed the innate impulse of compassion supported the principle of benevolent rulers, and that it was through the practice of benevolence that rulers found happiness.

> Mencius another day saw King Hûi of Liang. The king went and stood with him by a pond and, looking round at the large geese and deer, said, "Do wise and good princes also find pleasure in these things?"
>
> Mencius replied, "Being wise and good, they have pleasure in these things. If they are not wise and good, though they have these things, they do not find pleasure."[17]

In discussing "The Ten Evils" afflicting humanity, Buddha said, "Cleanse your heart of malice and cherish no hatred, not even against your enemies; but embrace all living beings with kindness."[18] Charity is a central tenet of Islam. The Qur'an states, "O believers, give in charity what is good of the things you have earned, and of what you produce from the earth; and do not choose to give what is bad as alms, that is, things you would like to accept yourself except with some condescension."[19]

Of course, some of these ethical systems, such as Buddhism, Islam, and Christianity, consider the exercise of human compassion as the pathway to a metaphysical form of happiness such as heaven or nirvana. In the case of these religions, earthly happiness is only a chimera. However, these religious traditions, in different ways, do call for compassion toward others. Global goals based on protection of human life and happiness could not be repudiated easily by most of the world's religions. However, important differences in interpretation become evident when these goals are translated into local actions. Issues of abortion and euthanasia divide religions over interpretations of the meaning of life and death. If it is believed that life begins at conception, then abortion is viewed as seriously limiting the life of the human. Euthanasia, although it might help a person avoid a slow and painful death, does shorten the individual's life. Religious issues have had an important effect on cloning and stem cell research, with Christian societies being swept up in debates about the right to life while Buddhist and Confucian researchers are not bothered. Consequently, Asia, according to Robert Paarlberg writing in the 2005 July/August issue of *Foreign Policy*, is taking the lead in cloning and stem cell research. A summary of an article appearing in the *New York Times* states: "In Confucian and Buddhist societies, there are fewer religious inhibitions to the destruction of microscopic embryos. Throughout Roman Catholic Europe and in much of Christian America, religious authorities teach that a fertilized egg is already a person. In Confucian tradition, the defining moment of life is birth, not conception, and Buddhists view life not as beginning with conception but as a cycle of reincarnations."[20] Or, as a Korean researcher stated, "Cloning is a different way of thinking about the recycling of life. It's a Buddhist way of thinking."[21]

Most religions will not accept the goal of happiness if it means pure hedonism. Most of them cast moral strictures around the path to happiness. The goal of a long and happy life can have an ethical dimension: everyone has the responsibility to protect human life and happiness. What studies have found is that showing compassion does increase a person's happiness. Economist Layard declares, "The secret is compassion towards oneself and others, and the principle of the Greatest Happiness is essentially the expression of this ideal."[22]

The goals of protecting of human life and maximizing human satisfaction are quite different from the traditional goals of national school systems, which have focused on educating good citizens, able workers, and socially controlled populations. Much has been written about national school goals. The United States' educator Horace Mann, important because of the global influence of U.S. education, set the 19th century standard by arguing that the goals of public schooling should include controlling social interaction by teaching a common morality, enhancing economic growth through educating better workers, eliminating poverty by increasing community wealth and providing equality of opportunity, creating a common national culture, establishing a consensus of political values and thus reducing the possibility of political revolution, and eliminating class conflict. Added to these goals were patriotic school exercises designed to attach the emotions of students to symbols of the state.[23]

Of course, it could be argued that enhancement of the state's economic and political power by educating worker-citizens ultimately will protect the lives of citizens and enhance their satisfaction with their lives. Unfortunately, this has not always been the case. Extreme nationalism, often supported by the attitudes and knowledge taught in schools, has in the last several centuries been a source of war, one of the major dangers to survival of the human species. Education for work can be dysfunctional because the labor market changes, and students are educated for nonexistent jobs or for jobs that have an oversupply of skilled employees. Also, education for work may be for jobs that do not enhance human satisfaction with life. Most, if not all, government plans that combine educational and economic goals are concerned with economic growth and not job satisfaction.[24]

Given the traditional approach to national schooling, I argue that it is unique to plan a school system around the protection of the human species and the maximizing of human satisfaction with life, particularly as common global objectives for education. Of course, as I discuss, there are local educational issues such as culture, religion, and language. In other words, curricula and instructional methods should reflect the expression "Think globally, but act locally."

PROGRESS: EDUCATIONAL AND GLOBAL

Is there a global standard of progress that can be used to evaluate schools and other public institutions? In the latter part of the 20th century, concepts of progress born in the West during the 18th-century Enlightenment were criticized for being overly optimistic about the beneficial effects of science, technology, rationality, and mass education. The benefits of science and technology seemed dubious for a society faced with weapons of mass destruction. Technology seemed to be eroding the availability of natural resources and causing vast destruction to the biosphere. The Enlightenment belief in progress currently seems dubious with continued environmental destruction and war. Rationality can be used for war as well as for improving the conditions of human life.

In the framework of the Enlightenment, mass education held out the hope of progress for humanity. Then people began to realize that education, like science, could be both beneficial and destructive. During the 1930s and 1940s, Japan and Germany demonstrated the power of education to build nationalism and beliefs in racial superiority that would fuel a major world war. Throughout the world, schooling became another means of dividing social classes by providing the children of already privileged members of society with the credentials and social capital to ensure the continuation of their class advantages while ensuring that the poor remained poor by limiting their credentials and social capital. By the 21st century, the goals of most national school system were to educate workers for an industrial-consumer society, which, by exploiting natural resources, might doom the planet. Also, advertising drives the consumption and keeps people in a constant state of dissatisfaction. This could undermine their subjective well-being. As I detail in another book, current global educational discourse is limited by general acceptance of an industrial-consumer paradigm in which the major educational issues are economic growth and provision of equal access to consumer goods.[25]

International studies show that in nations already industrialized by World War II technological development, economic growth does not increase human happiness. There is a limit to the ability of currently organized industrial societies to contribute to human happiness. For instance, a study by Bureau of Economic Analysis of the U.S. Department of Commerce and the U.S. Bureau of the Census found that since World War II, there has been a marked decline in feelings of happiness concurrent with significant increases in gross domestic product.[26] Between approximately the early 1950s and 1990, the measured level of happiness in the United States declined while gross domestic product sharply increased. In the words of economists Bruno S. Frey and Alois Stutzer, "This … tremendous rise in average purchasing power was reflected in almost all households having an indoor toilet, a washing machine, telephone, color television as well as a car; … this tremendous rise in material well-being was accompanied by a modest *decrease* in average happiness."[27]

Is there a threshold for the contribution of education to happiness? Yes, such a threshold exists if education is defined by the current goals of national educational systems, to prepare students to fulfill the needs of the labor market in an industrial-consumer society. Ruut Veenhoven found that education was correlated to subjective well-being when it increased a person's ability to earn more money. Education, as currently organized, was not directly correlated with happiness. Education can increase income, but satisfaction from this increased income has a threshold level. In conclusion, Veenhoven stated: "Educationalists claim that school education paves the way to a more satisfying life. In Western nations its net effect appeared mostly small, however, and on the decline. Insofar as education contributed to happiness, it did so largely by opening doors to better-paying jobs."[28]

The United States is a good example of the apparent lack of relationship between national schooling and happiness. In the United States, the content and purpose of schooling has changed frequently from the 1950s to the present.[29] During the period of decline in subjective well-being since the early 1950s, the U.S. government's National Center for Education Statistics reports that between 1949 and 2001, there was an increase in the percentage of 5- to 17-year-olds enrolled in school: 1949 (83.1%), 1990

(90.9%), and 2001 (88.8%). Total school expenditures per capita of the total population increased from $289 (in 2000–2001 dollars) in 1949 to $1,462 in 2001, and annual teachers' salaries almost doubled from $22,253 (in 2000–2001 dollars) in 1949 to $43,400 during the same period.[30] While national levels of subjective well-being declined, school attendance and spending increased. I am not suggesting a casual relationship between the decline in happiness and the increase in school attendance and expenditures. However, I argue that, as currently organized, schooling in the United States does not contribute to individual happiness except as it provides an opportunity to earn more money, and that this effect is limited by the threshold level of the effect that income has on happiness.

Given these facts, the Enlightenment concept of progress should be changed to focus on human happiness and longevity. Francis Heylighen and Jan Bernheim argue that research identifies certain absolute conditions that contribute to happiness. One condition is physical well-being or health. "There may be a two-way relation," they write:

> Between health and happiness: on the one hand healthy people will suffer less physical discomfort and therefore be able to enjoy life more; on the other hand, there are indications that people who have many pleasant feelings are more likely to live a long and healthy life than people who feel bad, possibly because stress has a strong negative effect on health.[31]

They suggest using life expectancy and child mortality rates as measures of physical well-being.

Research on protection of human life and happiness demonstrates an inseparable link between the two: happiness contributes to a long life. Emory University Professor Abbott Ferriss asserts, "Almost universally, longevity is considered an indicator of the good life. Life expectancy, based upon age at time of death, provides a measure of health and related social and economic conditions that support the good life."[32]

What are the possibilities of creating global educational goals to promote human happiness and longevity?

GLOBAL GOALS AND GLOBAL SCHOOL SYSTEMS

As I mentioned earlier, most of the world's school systems already have similar organization. Adding common goals would be the next step in this process of educational globalization. The world's school systems share common features regarding school organization, curriculum, and instructional methods. In part, this is a result of Euro-American and Japanese imperialism, which imposed common models of schooling on colonized nations.[33] In addition, technological changes such as in communications, transportation, and information technology have contributed to the growing similarity between national school systems, making global schooling a possibility.[34] Social anthropologist Kathryn Anderson–Levitt summarizes the work of world cultural theorists: "A single global model of schooling has spread around the world as part of the diffusion of a more general cultural model of the nation-state, a model that also includes templates for organizing government, health systems, the military, and other institutions."[35] I have detailed the evolution of these common school features in another volume.[36]

Currently, most of the world's school systems are organized around some variation of an educational ladder, with age-graded classrooms leading from primary grades to intermediate to secondary to higher education. The common structure of the world's school systems is highlighted in United Nations' statistical reports, which assume the global existence of schools labeled as primary and secondary. In fact, it is just assumed in United Nations' reports that readers of these reports, no matter what their nationality, will know the difference between primary and secondary education. The United Nations' global literacy campaign, Education for All, provides in its Global Monitoring Report statistical information divided between primary and secondary schooling for each of the world's nations.[37] United Nations' educators just assume that the world's nations share a common educational ladder. In addition, most of the world's educational systems are governed by national examinations and, except for differing religious emphases and national historical concerns, they use a similar curriculum designed to support national economic interests. Also, English, the unofficial world language, is taught in most national school systems and serves as the world's common academic language.[38]

> Although a common global model of schooling exists, there are many differences in school quality. The United Nations' 2005 Education for All: The Quality Imperative uses a net enrollment ratio (NER) as an indicator of school quality. Reflecting the globalization of a common educational ladder, NER is defined as "the extent to which children who are in the official age group for a specific level of schooling (e.g., primary) are enrolled."[39] Based on this definition of quality, the 2005 Global Monitoring Report reports the following differences in global schooling.
>
> Regional variations are stark. In many sub-Saharan African countries, several Arab States, and Pakistan, NERs are below 70%. Education systems in Central and Eastern Europe also stand out, with several NERs between 70% and 90%. Girls' participation in primary education remains substantially lower than boys' participation in 71 of 175 countries. With only three exceptions, all the countries with a gender parity index below 0.90 are in sub-Saharan Africa (notably West Africa), the Arab States, and South and West Asia.[40]

The advent of a common global school structure had an impact on cultural differences in childhood experiences and learning. Kathryn Anderson– Levitt asserts: "The spread of Western-style schooling means that children growing up around the globe have a more uniform experience of socialization than in the past. That is, because, varied as it is, schooling is a more uniform experience than family socialization.... In spite of local and national variability, classroom experience has roughly a single structure."[41] She catalogues the following contributions of global schooling to common childhood experiences:

1. All children are exposed to the concept of themselves as individual citizens of a nation.
2. Teachers assume an important role in influencing child development.
3. Age-graded classrooms expose children to the influence of a community of peers.
4. Aged-graded classrooms often expose children to a gender-mixed world.
5. Schools as sorting devices for status and jobs replace traditional methods.
6. Maturity becomes defined by placement in a particular age-graded classroom.
7. A child's accomplishments become defined by scores on tests and grades.[42]

Although the structure of schooling, with its educational ladder, age-graded classrooms, and graded curriculum, is now global, there are important variations in the content of schooling related to language and cultural and religious values. These differences are explored throughout this volume. At this point in the book, I simply argue that a common global educational structure allows for the consideration of common global educational goals.

EQUALITY OF OPPORTUNITY AND EQUALITY OF EDUCATIONAL OPPORTUNITY

The global goal of increasing longevity and happiness changes the traditional meaning of equality of opportunity and equality of educational opportunity. In early national school ideology, as articulated by American public school advocate Horace Mann, a common education would give citizens equal skills to pursue the accumulation of property. The assumption was that an equal education would create a level playing field for competition for wealth. Mann believed that schools could keep a country from being torn apart by struggle between the rich and poor because all people would be taught that they had an equal opportunity to be rich or poor as a result of the knowledge and skills learned in school.[43]

In the 20th and 21st centuries, human capital economics makes equality of opportunity a central goal of schools. In the context of schooling, equality of opportunity is achieved by providing students with the ability to compete equally for jobs and income. Also, schools engage in a presorting of students for the labor market by determining their abilities through achievement and graduation examinations as well as placement in different curricula designed to prepare students for a particular part of the job market such as professional or clerical. Therefore, education takes on a dual function in human capital economics. First, it holds out the promise of providing graduates with the skills for an equal opportunity to compete in the labor market. Second, and possibly contradictory to the first goal, the school tries to enhance the process by matching student abilities with labor market needs. This meaning of equality of opportunity is used wherever schooling is dominated by human capital economics, as in communist countries such as the People's Republic of China; by social democracies, as in Singapore; by trading blocks, as in the European Union; and by republican governments, as in the United States.[44]

From the perspective of human capital economics, equality of educational opportunity is necessary to keep the system efficient and fair. Efficiency refers to the ability to identify and train all children for the labor market. If all children do not go to school, then their potential as human capital might not be developed. Ensuring that all children attend school guarantees that no talent is lost. Therefore, equality of educational opportunity ensures efficiency in the mobilization of talent for the economic system. It is economically inefficient if some children are not made available for testing and training because circumstances do not allow them to attend school. Compulsory education ensures the efficiency of schools in distributing talent in the economy.

In this volume, I am redefining equality of opportunity to mean an equal chance to live a long life and be happy. Research on subjective well-being finds that wealth and a high income are not factors in determining personal happiness unless a person is escaping poverty.[45] It is important to note that I am making a distinction between wealth and income. This distinction is important in recognizing the possibility of noncash economies, particularly among indigenous and alternative communities. Wealth comprises the material goods of a person or group, whereas income consists of the wages earned from work. It should be a global goal to bring everyone to the threshold level of wealth or income that supports happiness. Of course, this threshold may vary between cultures, religions, and individuals. A practicing Buddhist whose spiritual quest yields high levels of personal well-being might shun the accumulation of wealth, and he or she may require only a minimum of income. Or those wishing to maintain their indigenous culture may have different standards for determining wealth. I assert that if everyone is to have an equal opportunity to experience happiness, then every effort should be made to ensure that all people have the threshold income or wealth needed to maximize their happiness. In addition, other public policies should be initiated that increase the possibilities of an equal chance to live a long life and achieve happiness.

What is the role of education in achieving an equality of opportunity for all people to live a long and happy life? As previously stated, education-based human capital economics is weakly linked to happiness except as it helps a person reach the threshold of income needed for happiness.[46] However, an education that brings a person to the income threshold needed for happiness contributes to equality of opportunity. Also, education can influence feelings of control, self-esteem, and optimism, which in turn affect feelings of subjective well-being. Cummins provides this summary of research findings:

> Thus, the weak, but positive link between education and SWB [subjective well-being] can be viewed ... as due to two complementary influences. One is through higher education correlating with higher income. The other is through a direct effect of education to reinforce the internal strength of the three buffers [feelings of control, self-esteem, and optimism]. In sum, the essential quality of both income and education is that they reinforce the power of the three internal buffers, thereby providing insurance against circumstances likely to create a reduced level of SWB.[47]

Education can provide the knowledge that will help people have an equal opportunity to live longer and be happy. Definitely, education can contribute to "feelings of control, self-esteem, and optimism." Knowledge of nutrition and prevention of diseases can help to increase a person's life span. Knowledge of public health issues can result in the school graduate supporting public policies that will increase the life span of the general population. The same is true about knowledge that contributes to personal and public happiness. It is possible to teach what is known about the causes of longevity and happiness so that school graduates can guide their own lives and help others, thereby increasing their feelings of self-control. Also, school instruction can provide the skills and knowledge to implement public policies that will increase human happiness.

What about equality of educational opportunity? According to my definition, "everyone has a right to receive an education that will increase their chances to live a long life and be happy." Another facet of this definition is that "everyone has a right to a form of schooling that will enhance their happiness as a student." In other words, students have a right to be happy.

However, equality does not mean a uniform global education system! There are cultural differences affecting the subjective well-being of humans.

These cultural differences will affect the organization, curriculum, and methods of instruction of schools that help to provide equality of educational opportunity enabling individuals to achieve a long and happy life. In other words, for people to have an equal educational opportunity, there must be available schooling that reflects a person's cultural values regarding longevity and happiness. Possibly this would result in many different types of education with the same objective.

CULTURE, RELIGION, AND EQUALITY OF EDUCATIONAL OPPORTUNITY

Differences in culture and religion must be considered in the attempt to achieve equality of opportunity for an education that will increase students' chances to live a long life and be happy. Research finds that a person's culture influences her or his feelings of happiness. Most of this research focuses on differences between individualist and collectivist cultures. Which cultures are individualist and which are collectivist? Researchers often use the label "Western" to identify individualist cultures and "Asian," "Confucian," or "Islamic" to identify collectivist cultures. Seldom mentioned are others that might be termed "collective," such as the cultures of indigenous peoples and Hindus. However, most nations are now multicultural, which sometimes results in a tension between individualist and collectivist cultures and the development of hybrid cultures. This means that in the attempt to achieve the global goals of a long and happy life, there will be local variations based on cultural differences in school organization, curriculum, and methods of instruction.

Also, there has been considerable research on the contribution of religion to happiness. The major conclusion of this research is that a person's happiness is related to the nature and degree of individual involvement in religious practices. Religion increases subjective well-being when a person is spiritual and closely attends to religious practices. Also, religion improves happiness by providing a community of support that enhances an individual's social contacts. On the other hand, merely belonging to a religion with minimal attendance at religious ceremonies does not contribute to a person's happiness.[48] These conclusions suggest that schools will have to accommodate religious practices that enhance a person's subjective well-being. The differences between individualist and collectivist cultures center around personal orientation to self and others. In individualist cultures, behavior is determined primarily by personal attributes and feelings. People in these cultures focus on their own individual freedom and personal goals. Success in individualist societies entails individual self-fulfillment and accomplishment. Social psychologist Eunkook M. Suh writes: "Psychological characteristics [in individualist cultures] commonly associated with mental health ... portray the personal qualities of a highly independent, self-reliant individual who is capable of transcending the influences of others and the society."[49] This means that people in an individualist society use internal standards to judge their happiness.

In contrast, people in collectivist societies rely on their relationship to others to judge their own happiness. Success in a collectivist society is measured by fulfillment of one's duties and obligations toward one's in-group. In collectivist societies, Suh writes, "discussion of the individual starts with the Confucian assumption that the person exists in relationship to others. The individual is viewed as being fundamentally socially oriented, situation centered, interdependent, and inextricably bonded to others through emotional ties."[50]

"Hybridity" is the term often used to describe the cultural changes resulting from the intersection of two differing cultures. For example, many immigrants from collectivist cultures to the United States and Europe must undergo some adaptation to the individualist culture of the host society. Social psychologists Daphna Oyerman, Izumi Sakamoto, and Armand Lauffer write: "Hybridization involves the melding of cultural lenses or frames such that values and goals that were focused on in one context are transposed to a new context.... Cultural hybridization may be said to occur when an individual or group is exposed to and influenced by more than one cultural context."[51]

These researchers found that some immigrant cultures in the United States retained their parental culture in their private lives while taking on the values of the host culture in their public lives. Regarding hybridization, they found that among Asian American students, individualist cultural values were included in the in-group "without a loss of the social obligation that is built into collectivism."[52]

Also, in some cultures, there is a "hesitation" about people admitting that they are personally happy. In Japanese culture, happiness and unhappiness are believed to be bound together, resulting in a belief that unhappiness follows happiness and vice versa.[53] It is thought that to admit happiness is to invite unhappiness into one's life. In addition, collectivism forces many Japanese to become anxious about their relationships with others. The term "tight" is used to indicate cultures that can promote anxieties about social obligations, such as "Will I offend someone?" "Will I fulfill my social obligations?" "Have I forgotten some social obligation such as bringing a gift?" This anxiety about fulfilling social obligations possibly results in another problem with determining happiness. Some Japanese seek escape from social obligations by indulging in social drinking, which allows them to blame inappropriate actions on the influence of alcohol. Fantasy can be another escape. Most often, personal fantasies are pleasant and generate a low level of subjective well-being. Psychologist Harry

Triandis suggests that "if one has many pleasant fantasies, reality is likely to appear rather unpleasant. If it is true that people in tight cultures have more fantasies, then their SWB will be lower than the SWB of loose cultures."[54] However Triandis's suggestion has not been proved, and it does not mean that educators should try to eliminate personal fantasy to improve feelings of well-being. Triandis's comments do highlight some of the factors that can affect measurement of happiness.

Some studies group nations into individualist and collectivist cultures.[55] Unfortunately, these studies treat nations as if they had homogeneous cultures. For instance, two scales identify Peru as a collectivist society. But Peru has a large indigenous population. Is the Peruvian collectivist culture a result of the culture of the indigenous population or that of Peruvian–European culture? The same question can be asked of former European colonies in Africa rated as collectivist, such as Nigeria, Tanzania, and Zimbabwe. Moreover, because these nations have multiple indigenous groups, is the collectivist rating a result of all indigenous groups or only some? Also, is it religion that makes certain nations collectivist, or their ethnic cultures? For instance, Indonesia, a majority Muslim country with many different ethnic and indigenous groups, is rated as collectivist. Is Indonesia's collectivist culture a result of religious beliefs, ethnic cultures, or a combination of both?

Although these complex questions remain unanswered, international studies yield the following rankings between collectivist and individualist nations. These rankings indicate that it is wrong to think of collectivist societies as Asian or Confucian when many are in South America and Africa. I suspect that high collectivist ratings for countries in South America and Africa are a result of indigenous cultures.

The 10 most collectivist nations in rank order, beginning with the most collectivist, are as follows:

1. China
2. Columbia
3. Indonesia
4. Pakistan
5. Korea
6. Peru
7. Ghana
8. Nepal
9. Nigeria
10. Tanzania[56]

The following individualist nations are primarily Western. The one exception is South Africa, which despite the existence of indigenous peoples, might be considered as dominated by a European culture. The

10 most individualist nations in rank order, beginning with the most individualist, are as follows:

1. United States
2. Australia
3. Denmark
4. Germany
5. Finland
6. Norway
7. Italy
8. Austria
9. Hungary
10. South Africa[57]

The sources of subjective well-being vary according to cultural differences. The individualist characteristics of independence and autonomy were not associated with subjective well-being in collectivist countries including China, Columbia, Pakistan, Korea, Peru, Ghana, Tanzania, Bahrain, Singapore, Turkey, and Taiwan, whereas they were associated with subjective well-being in highly individualistic countries such as the United States, Australia, Germany, and Finland. One finding that is very important for social and economic policies along with educational policies is that competition and self-interest are negatively related to life satisfaction in both individualist and collectivist nations.[58]

These cross-national studies provide important guides for organizing global educational policies to enhance subjective well-being. First, the politically created boundaries of nations encompass a variety of cultures, with some that might be labeled individualist and some that may be seen as collectivist. In addition, there may exist forms of cultural hybridity. Therefore, global educational policy must be considered according to cultural groups and possibly religious groups rather than by nation-states. For instance, it appears from the data that a number of indigenous groups could be influenced by the collectivist ratings of some nations. It is possible to think of indigenous groups forming a global alliance to initiate school policies.

Second, all educational policies should recognize the possibility that competition and the pursuit of self-interest have a negative effect on happiness, even in highly individualist societies. One could conclude that school organizations and methods of instruction should avoid a reliance on competition in schooling if there is to be a concern about the well-being of students. However, it should be recognized that independence and autonomy, which are different from competition and self-interest, are important in individualist cultures in the planning of educational programs and organization.

Third, in relating educational policy to cultural standards, it is important to recognize a distinction between personal goals and cultural norms. In most countries, personal conformity to cultural norms is not related to subjective well-being. However, conformity to cultural norms is positively related to happiness in Columbia, Spain, and Hungary, but negatively related to happiness in Indonesia, Taiwan, South Africa, Puerto Rico, and Denmark. Researchers have no explanation for why it is positively and negatively related in these few countries.

There can be a conflict between personal goals and cultural norms when personal goals are not congruent with cultural expectations. In an example used by researchers, Aki, a Japanese corporate employee, does not have personal goals that are in conformity with cultural norms. She does not like helping others, and is primarily concerned about getting her own work completed. Despite the fact that her personal goals are not congruent with Japanese cultural norms, she still experiences "good feelings" when she does help others and fulfills cultural expectations. In other words, despite the difference between cultural norms and personal goals, a "good feeling" still is generated when Aki acts according to cultural expectations. On the other hand, Aki still feels good when achieving her personal goal of completing her work.[59] Achievement of personal goals that are in opposition to cultural norms still can yield personal satisfaction.

In summary, the overwhelming majority of research on culture and happiness focuses on differences between collectivist and individualist societies. There are, of course, other possible cultural differences that might affect feelings of subjective well-being. These will have to be accounted for in using global goals at the local level. On the basis of existing research, differences in culture and religion have the following effects on providing equality of opportunity for an education that will increase student chances for a long and happy life.

Cultural and Religious Differences Affecting Equality of Educational Opportunity

1. Factors promoting happiness in individualist cultures
   a. Achievement of personal goals
   b. Self-fulfillment
   c. Independence

2. Factors promoting happiness in collectivist cultures
   a. Achievement of collective goals
   b. Fulfillment of duty and obligations to one's in-group
   c. Interdependence

3. Hybridity of cultures in a globalizing world
   a. Individual or group exposed to and influenced by more than one cultural context

b. Varying forms of cultural hybridity experienced by most people because of the global migration of populations and global media
c. Retention of parental culture in private lives while the values of the host culture are adopted in public lives

4. Religion and factors promoting of happiness
   a. Spirituality
   b. Commitment to religious practice

5. Negative effect of competition and pursuit of self-interest on happiness even in individualist cultures

6. Personal goals and cultural norms
   a. Conformity through coercion to cultural norms negatively correlated with happiness
   b. Anxiety about achieving cultural expectations created in tight societies
   c. Fulfillment of cultural norms positively related to happiness
   d. Fulfillment of personal goals positively related to happiness

BHUTAN'S GROSS NATIONAL HAPPINESS INDEX: AN IMPOSED CONCEPT OF HAPPINESS AND CULTURE

The country of Bhutan provides an important example of an attempt to legislate happiness on the basis of particular cultural and religious values. This legislated concept of happiness is embodied in the country's Gross National Happiness Index. In addition, the government has imposed a single cultural standard to counter the increasing multicultural nature of its society. Both the Gross National Happiness Index and the single cultural standard are attempts to mediate the influence of globalization and economic development.

Nestled in the Himalaya mountains between India and China, Bhutan until 1950s remained somewhat isolated from the forces of globalization except for a small proportion of its elite. The lifestyle and the country's social structure for the overwhelming majority of the population had remained unchanged since about A.D. 1500. The country's cultural homogeneity began to change in the 1930s when political refugees began to arrive from Nepal, and then underwent a major change in 1959 when Chinese actions against Tibet caused Tibetan refugees to enter Bhutan. Also, China appeared interested in invading Bhutan. The threat of Chinese power caused Bhutan's government to seek closer ties with India and spurred the completion of a road link between the two nations. The result was a multicultural society composed of traditional Bhutanese Buddhists, Indian Hindus, and refugees from Nepal and Tibet.[60]

After China's actions in Tibet, Bhutan's reigning monarchy decided to open the country to gradual influences from the outside world. The hope was to spark development in medical care and education without undermining Bhutan's cultural and religious integrity. For instance, the monarchy did not allow television into Bhutan until 1999, and the government has restricted the number of visas issued to foreign visitors. Telecommunications was restricted in part because of the remote population and the mountainous terrain. Between 1999 and 2003, the number of telephone subscribers, both fixed line and mobile, increased from 5 to 14 per 1,000 people. Internet service was introduced in 1999 by Durknet, which by 2005 had 120,000 subscribers. The Bhutan government in 2005 still did not have an accurate count of its populations, but estimates ranged from 700,000 to 2 million.[61]

To protect the cultural and religious traditions of Bhutan while improving health care and education and introducing aspects of global economic development and culture, the King introduced the concept of a Gross National Happiness Index in the late 1980s. In 1991, the Seventh Five-Year Plan issued by the Royal Government of Bhutan provided a framework for economic development which included: "ensuring the emotional well-being of the population, the preservation of Bhutan's cultural heritage and its rich and varied natural resources."[62]

The Gross National Happiness Index, according to the Stefan Priesner, Program Officer of the United Nations Development Program in Bhutan and a scholar who has written about development in Bhutan, "has organically evolved from the constituent features of Bhutanese society before 1959, a socioeconomic system based on a Buddhist and feudal set of values."[63] Although the Gross National Happiness Index did not appear until the 1980s, earlier pronouncements by the King on the goals of development always included a call for ensuring the happiness of the people.

Based on cultural traditions and Buddhism, the Gross National Happiness Index is an official government concept of what promotes happiness rather than a concept based on social research such as the work of Ruut Veenhoven or the World Database of Happiness. Illustrating that the Bhutan government's idea of happiness is based on government edict rather than social science, Lyonpo Jigmi Y. Thinley, Chairman of the Bhutan's Royal Council of Ministers, declared in 1998 that "His Majesty Jigme Singye Wangchuck ... has been the fountainhead of philosophy, concepts, and policies of our development for nearly three decades. His majesty has proclaimed that the ultimate purpose of government is to promote the happiness of the people."[64]

Chairman Thinley defended the national development goal of happiness by raising a series of important questions about economic development in countries such as Bhutan. These are legitimate questions about development plans of such organizations as the World Bank:

- How will shrinkage of biologic and cultural diversities affect the individual and collective potential for happiness?
- Will the particular scientific worldview of contemporary education and curricula undercut in the next century the culturally rich and value-full basis of daily life?
- Will the process of secularization and nuclearization of the family increase man's loneliness and self-enclosure in the midst of urban crowd?
- How will global capitalism and competitive international trade make people more vulnerable to the unhappiness and uncertainty of their lives?
- Does the rapid automation of society and the economy increase or decrease the prospects for the happiness of individuals?[65]

This is a very important set of questions regarding the future quality of human life. In addition, Chairman Thinley raised a fundamental concern of Bhutan's government about the preservation of its culture and religion in the development process: "We asked ourselves the basic question of how to maintain the balance between materialism and spiritualism, in the course of getting the immense benefits of science and technology."[66] Thinley worried about "the likelihood of loss of spiritualism, tranquillity, and gross national happiness with the advance of modernization."[67] Because of these questions and concerns, Bhutan's development program includes four goals that are fundamental to achieving the government's concept of happiness: environmental preservation, economic self-reliance, cultural promotion, and good governance. In addition, Bhutan's policies for increasing gross national happiness include free education and health care as well as other social services.

Bhutan's environmental policies are based on a Buddhist belief that the biosphere is composed of an interdependence of life forms, with no life form having an existence independent from other life forms. Also, Buddhism does not practice speciesism, in which one life form, such humans, is superior to other life forms. This belief is in sharp contrast to the Christian dogma that nature exists for the benefit of humans, who are thought of as the only creatures who can benefit from the Christian God's promise of salvation. Also, Buddhist belief in reincarnation makes human lives only one stage in an eternal cycle of rebirth.[68] As Tashi Wanchuk, a researcher at Bhutan's environmental ministry and a graduate of the Yale School of Forestry and Environmental Studies, told an observer from the *Chronicle of Higher Education,* "you don't want to kill a tiger if it might be your grandmother."[69]

The government of Bhutan passed the Forest Act of 1969 and the Land Act of 1979. In 1974, preservation policies were introduced, declaring parks and forest preserves protected areas. Currently, 26% of Bhutan's lands are national parks. Logging is banned, and forests are protected by squadrons of forest rangers.[70]

The goal of economic self-reliance is, in part, a reflection of Bhutan's rugged topography, which has created self-reliant isolated communities. Also, Bhutan's leaders are trying to mediate the influence of the global industrial-consumer paradigm. Chairman Tinley accepts that economic development can rid Bhutan and other parts of the world of "the harsh, brief, and brutal existence. "But,", Thinley argues, as do global researchers on subjective well-being, "beyond a level, an increase in material consumption is not accompanied by a concomitant rise in happiness. There is ample evidence to support this conclusion."[71] In 1959, the National Assembly affirmed that it wanted "to maintain the sovereignty of the kingdom through economic self-reliance."[72] Since that time, the Bhutan government has tried to avoid a cash crop agricultural economy and a dependency on foreign loans, and it has favored decentralization of decision making about development.[73]

The most difficult problem for Bhutan's government is the tension between free education, its multicultural population, and cultural preservation. From the perspective of Chairman Thinley, education for happiness should promote Buddhist's concepts of enlightenment. Thinley claims that schooling involves a "curriculum that tries to blend education in the Buddhist worldview with scientific studies."[74] However, the reality is that Bhutan's schools rely on global models of schooling and on foreign supervision of their school's curriculum.[75] Similar to India, the primary source of Bhutan's global educational ideas is England, where Bhutan's king was educated at the University of Cambridge. Priesner claims that

> In spite of attempts to adjust the programs to the needs of the Bhutanese students (e.g., NAPE, the New Approach to Primary Education attempts to provide primary students with a useful package of skills), this has to date hardly comprised the teaching of "culture." In a teaching environment, which is largely *based on the scientific worldview and on Western philosophy*, culture has been confined to some mythological aspects of Bhutan's history, in which Buddhism played an important role [my emphasis].[76]

Consequently, the introduction of the global model of schooling is causing cultural change, particularly, as in other parts of the world, in childrearing patterns. Diederik Prakke, a Bhutan resident speaking at a workshop organized by Bhutan's Planning Commission to relate the concept of gross national happiness to the United Nations Development Program's Human Development Index, complained about development policies: "Buddhism, once the ordering principle of society, now becomes no more than icing on the cake. Buddhist topping on an essentially Western pizza."[77]

As an example of global schooling, Bhutan's Sherubtse college, which began as a high school in 1968 under the leadership of a Jesuit priest, uses syllabi and course materials provided by the University of Delhi. Also, University of Delhi professors grade class work, which allows easy admission for Sherubtse's graduates into graduate institutions throughout India. Of course, the curriculum of the University of Delhi was strongly influenced by British traditions resulting from Great Britain's colonization of India. Writing for the *Chronicle of Higher Education*, David Wheeler stated that "the drawback of the Delhi affiliation is that it can limit the Sherubtse curriculum and the college's autonomy. The professors at Sherubtse sometimes disagree with the Delhi professors' assessments of their students on exams, which can include essay questions."[78]

Classroom instruction at Sherubtse is primarily in English, with students required to study Dzongkha, the national language. English, of course, is the language of global culture and the academic language of India. Classrooms devoted to English instruction are lined with pictures of the Bronte sisters, Joseph Conrad, Charles Darwin, and Abraham Lincoln. Buddhist influence is primarily outside the classroom, with the college having its own temple and with students attending a morning prayer. But the pull of global culture remains extremely strong. Many of Bhutan's students attend colleges in India, Australia, New Zealand, and the United States.[79]

The cultural homogeneity of Bhutan also is threatened by its multicultural population. This is causing Bhutan's government to adopt policies that could be viewed as leading to cultural genocide of its minority groups. Professor Michael Hutt of the Department of Nepali and Himalayan Studies of the University of London argues that in recent years Bhutan has engaged in ethnic cleansing, which has forced many Nepalese who had settled in Bhutan to flee back to refugee camps in Nepal. Hutt cites a transcript from the proceedings of the 1989 meeting of Bhutan's National Assembly, in which the Deputy Home Minister argued that multiculturalism might work in a large country, but that "in a small country like ours it would adversely affect the growth of social harmony and unity among the people. The Government has, for these reasons, promulgated a policy to promote Drigham Namzha as well as national dress and language among the people."[80] At the same meeting of the national assembly, the King reportedly "expressed his deep appreciation and happiness to our people of southern Bhutan [the most multicultural area of Bhutan] who ... have wholeheartedly endeavored to fulfill this important national policy of promoting a unique national identity for ensuring the well-being of our country."[81]

Government policy identifies Drigham Namzha as the official national culture, with minority cultures required to assimilate to it. In other words,

Bhutan's government requires assimilation of all minority cultures into a single national culture. Drigham Namzha includes architectural style, dress, manners, official etiquette, outward behavior, and inner attitudes.[82]

In keeping with its monocultural policies, the Bhutan government made Dzongkha its official national language, although English is widely used by government officials and the educated elite. The government's intention, as discussed previously, is for Dzongkha and English to be the languages of classroom instruction despite the fact that Hindi once served that purpose.[83]

In summary, Bhutan is trying to mediate the influence of global culture. Culture and language policies are designed to rid the country of multiple cultures and languages, and to create a single national identity. The Gross National Happiness Index is based on what government officials believe are the conditions that promote happiness, in contrast to the use of social science research to determine subjective well-being. Its environmental policies demonstrate how Buddhism can serve to protect the biosphere. On the other hand, the attempt to protect the population from the materialist attitudes of the industrial-consumer paradigm may be undermined by its educational policies. Will students who study abroad bring back the values of industrial consumerism? Can students escape these values in classrooms devoted to the study of British literature? Learning English provides access to a global culture, but will it undermine Bhutan's cultural traditions? Will the expansion of primary schooling undermine the traditional childrearing practices of people who have lived for many years in isolated and self-reliant communities?

There are some important lessons to be learned from the example of Bhutan. First, global educational goals must be considered in terms of cultural and religious groups rather than nation-states. Bhutan's attempt to mediate global influences by maintaining its historical cultural integrity is resulting in cultural genocide being practiced against minority groups. Second, it is important to consider the religious aspect of global goals as exemplified by the Buddhist underpinnings of Bhutan's environmental policies. Environmental education and protection are important, as I discuss later, for ensuring a long and happy life. Third, it is important to consider the contribution of local religious beliefs to subjective well-being. Finally, the basic elements of the Gross National Happiness Index do provide an alternative to the globally dominant industrial-consumer paradigm. A consideration of cultural traditions, similar to the process in Bhutan, can be used to consider local alternatives to the global industrial-consumer paradigm. This could provide a means of considering how a local culture might develop alternative economic systems to ensure a long and happy life. All these issues become important in considering how global educational objectives can be translated into local educational practices.

DEMOCRACY, FREEDOM, AND EDUCATION

Cross-national studies also have implications for the practice of democracy and freedom in educational institutions. Should schools be democratically controlled by students and teachers? Should students be free to choose what they learn and how they learn it? International studies of freedom and democracy find little relationship between subjective well-being and freedom and democracy. In fact, I was personally surprised to find a rather high sense of personal well-being expressed by citizens of the authoritarian nation of Singapore. The lack of relationship between democracy and happiness is supported by the work of Ronald Inglehart at the University of Michigan's Institute of Social Research and the work of Hans–Dieter Klingemann at Berlin's Social Science Research Center. The two researchers used Freedom House's definition of democracy to determine the relationship between national ratings of subjective well-being and democracy.

Freedom House's definition of democracy focuses on representative government as opposed to other definitions that might emphasize direct decisions by the people. In fact, some of the early leaders of the United States referred to democracy as "mobocracy" and advocated a republican form of government in which representatives interpreted the needs and desires of the people as they enacted legislation.[84] Therefore, surveys using the Freedom House definition are really about the effects of representative government. They do not include other possible definitions of democracy. The world surveys of democracy (or representative government) conducted by Freedom House use the following definition:

> The Freedom in the World survey provides an annual evaluation of the state of global freedom as experienced by individuals. Freedom is the opportunity to act spontaneously in a variety of fields outside the control of the government and other centers of potential domination. Freedom House measures freedom according to two broad categories: political rights and civil liberties. Political rights enable people to participate freely in the political process, including through the right to vote, compete for public office, and elect representatives who have a decisive impact on public policies and are accountable to the electorate. Civil liberties allow for the freedoms of expression and belief, associational and organizational rights, rule of law, and personal autonomy without interference from the state.[85]

On the basis of the preceding definition, Inglehart and Klingemann conclude regarding subjective well-being that

> society's level of democracy was only marginally significant.... Although democracy and well-being are strongly linked, the interpretation that democracy determines well-being does not stand up: other factors—particularly the

number of years of communist rule and the society's level of economic development—seem to play much more powerful roles.[86]

Democracy is linked to economic development, which does contribute to happiness. However, an authoritarian state can sustain economic development, as exemplified by China and Singapore. Providing a broader historical context for understanding why democracy does not determine, but only supports, subjective well-being, they write:

> Democratic institutions do not necessarily make a people happy: history furnishes compelling examples. Democratic institutions did not make the people of Weimar Germany happy—quite the contrary, there is ample evidence that they experienced desperation. Similarly subjective well-being has not risen since Russia adopted free elections in 1991.... Freedom House ranks China as the most authoritarian society. ... But, in fact, the Chinese show higher levels of well-being than less authoritarian societies, and they rank above some democracies.[87]

Ruut Veenhoven concluded that "freedom does not always contribute to happiness, but it does not destroy it either."[88] Veenhoven's definition of freedom includes economic, political, and personal freedoms, with economic freedom meaning free enterprise, low taxes, and ability to transfer money. He also used the Freedom House definition for political freedoms. His list of personal freedoms include religious practice, ability to travel, marriage, and sexuality. He found that postcommunist countries with increased freedoms have not experienced increases in subjective well-being. Like other researchers, he found that highly authoritarian countries such as China and Singapore have experienced higher levels of subjective well-being than some democracies. Do these cross-national studies suggest that democracy and freedom in schools will not contribute to the subjective well-being of students? The economic freedoms of free enterprise, low taxes, and ability to transfer money have little relevance for methods of instruction and school organization, although the argument could be stretched to say that applying free enterprise to schools systems with schools competing for students will not necessarily increase the subjective well-being of students and parents.

On the other hand, the finding that economic freedoms do not cause improvements in subjective well-being is important for the school curriculum. If economics appears in the curriculum, then students could be asked how economic systems might be organized to increase human happiness. Currently, economic discussions focus primarily on differences between capitalism, welfare capitalism, and communism, or as it is referred to in China, "socialist modernization." Are there possibly other ways of thinking about economic organization? Should student investigation and study focus on how economic organizations can cause a greater sense of subjective well-being?

The lack of causal effect of political freedoms on happiness according to the Freedom House's definition of democracy—the right to vote, compete for public office, and elect representatives—suggests that students should explore other political arrangements that might cause increases in human happiness. In fact, they might want to explore other definitions of democracy and their relationship to happiness. Schools should approach teaching about political institutions from the standpoint of their contribution to human happiness.

What about personal freedom for teachers and students in schools? As I have already noted, deeply felt religious practices can contribute to personal well-being and apparently, according to the previously discussed studies, it does not matter which religion, whether monotheistic, polythestic, or animistic. People gain a sense of personal well-being from spiritual acts and religious practices. However, the fact that superficial religious practices do not contribute to personal well-being raises questions about school systems in which secularized religious morals are included in the school curriculum as character or moral education, particularly in Christian and Islamic countries.

In summary, there needs to be further study investigating the relationship of freedom and democracy to education. First, there is the issue of institutional structure and learning. To date, studies of subjective well-being and its contribution to freedom and democracy have been limited to very specific definitions. What happens to subjective well-being if freedom means the freedom to pursue an individual lifestyle, including freedom for a student to choose how he or she wishes to be instructed? What happens to subjective well-being if democracy means direct control by citizens of the government and laws as contrasted to government by elected representatives. What about direct control by staff and students of school governance? At this point, research on the contribution of freedom and democracy to subjective well-being is so limited by the use of Freedom House definitions that they provide little guidance in the structuring of educational experiences. On the other hand, research on freedom and democracy does open an area of learning, discussion, and investigation for students.

GOING WITH THE FLOW: ACHIEVING OPTIMAL EXPERIENCE

Flow theory provides another way of thinking about how to structure social organizations such as schools to maximize the subjective well-being of students and staff. How can workers, students, and others achieve optimal experiences? As I discuss, a serious limitation of flow theory is the lack of extensive research on its applicability in different cultural settings. Flow theory refers to the optimal experience that humans achieve when performing a task. Most of us experience situations in which we lose a sense of time and surrounding events while concentrating on a work project, sports performance, hobby, artistic endeavor, or other physical or intellectual pursuit. During and after an optimal experience, an individual experiences a high level of subjective well-being.

Mihaly Csikszentmihalyi, the social psychologist who did the pioneering work on flow theory, provides the following description of the characteristics associated with an optimal experience:

> Concentration is so intense that there is no attention left over to think about anything irrelevant, or to worry about problems. Self-consciousness disappears, and the sense of time becomes distorted. An activity that produces such experiences is so gratifying that people are willing to do it for its own sake, and little concern for what they will get out of it, even when it is difficult, or dangerous.[89]

The full meaning of flow can be appreciated by understanding how Csikszentmihalyi arrived at the theory. As part of his research as a University of Chicago doctoral student in 1962, he watched and photographed artists at work. He noted that once a painter became fully immersed in her or his work, "the motivation to go on painting was so intense that fatigue, hunger, or discomfort ceased to matter. Why were these people so taken with what they were doing?"[90] At the time, popular behaviorist theory argued that human motivation was dependent on rewards. Behaviorist theory assumed that painters were motivated by the reward of a completed painting. However, Csikszentmihalyi said, "The artists I was observing almost immediately lost interest in the canvas they had just painted. Typically, they turned the finished canvas around and stacked it against the wall.... They could hardly wait to start on a new one."[91]

Initially, Csikszentmihalyi examined the nature of this intense experience by studying the play of children and adults. Traditional psychologists considered children's play as a means for them to learn to be adults. However, Csikszentmihalyi suggested that play among children and adults was simply for an enjoyable experience similar to that of the artists he studied. But the politics of funding at the time limited his ability to acquire money for research on play and enjoyment. Consequently, he chose a topic more likely to receive funding, namely worker satisfaction. Under the general idea of investigating worker satisfaction, his team of researchers first examined individuals who were self-motivated to seek activities that would provide them with optimal experiences, such as dancing, rock climbing, basketball, and chess. Also, they examined workers who had similar optimal experiences.

Researchers referred to activities that caused flow as "autotelic experiences," which meant "a self-contained activity, one that is done not with the expectation of some future benefit, but simply because the doing itself is the reward." In other words, it is the psychological experience of concentration and the accompanying loss of self-consciousness and a sense of time that people seek. The researchers decided to call this experience "flow." The internal experience of flow is different from acting because of an external reward. For instance doing a job just to earn money does not necessarily provide an optimal experience. However, doing a job for the sheer joy of the experience is an optimal experience. Appropriately for our concern about education, Csikszentmihalyi uses the example of teaching to distinguish between external reward–oriented activities and flow: "Teaching children in order to turn them into good citizens is not autotelic, whereas teaching them because one enjoys interacting with children is."[92]

The investigation of worker satisfaction uncovered many instances of flow experience caused by individual desire for the experience or by the challenges of the job. The flow experience, and this is important for education, often is dependent on the relationship between personal skills and the challenges of the task. The title of Csikszentmihalyi's first book, *Beyond Boredom and Anxiety*, reflects the boundaries of the flow experience. If a student or worker has a high level of skills and is asked to do a task that involves little challenge, then the worker or student will be bored. If the challenge of the task exceeds the skills of the worker or student, then the worker or student will feel anxiety. Neither boredom or anxiety will contribute to subjective well-being.

Intellectual flow is an important aspect of education (i.e., the pleasure of being lost in thought). According to Csikszentmihalyi, reading is the most widely mentioned flow experience in the world.[93] Reading can involve all the aspects of flow: concentration and loss of self-consciousness and time. People can experience intense pleasure when reading is a flow experience. In the same manner, a similar pleasure can be achieved through solving puzzles or theoretical problems involving numbers or words; experiencing works of art; conducting scientific research; theorizing about social, political, and economic issues; and exploring philosophical issues. All these activities, so crucial to schooling, can produce "the profound joy of the thinker."[94]

The issue of joy in work is important for maximizing the subjective well-being of humans. The industrial-consumer paradigm focuses on achieving satisfaction through the consumption of goods and not on the pleasure that might be gained from work. However, some people are motivated to try turning any type of work into a flow experience. These people have what Csikszentmihalyi calls "autotelic personalities." He provides numerous examples of people who make no distinction between work and free time, and who are able to turn work situations, when it is possible, into flow activities.

There are also "autotelic jobs" that maximize the opportunity for workers to experience flow. From the perspective of this book, social policy should emphasize organizing work so that it increases worker enjoyment. "The more a job inherently resembles a game," Csikszentmihalyi writes, "with variety, appropriate and flexible challenges, clear goals, and immediate feedback, the more enjoyable it will be regardless of the worker's level of development." In other words, the enjoyment results from organizing a job so that the balance of skills and challenges saves the worker from anxiety or boredom. Has work not always involved a degree of boredom and anxiety? Yes and no! Studies of nonindustrial and corporate work suggest a high degree flow and personal enjoyment in lives that integrate personal living and work such as the lives of subsistence farmers. This research was conducted with farmers living in small villages in the Italian Alps where there is no distinction between work and free time. From arising to bedtime, life for these villagers involves a constant series of challenges. When one of the subjects of the research was asked what she would do if she had all the time and money in the world, she replied that she would continue living the same way. When other older villagers were asked to reflect on the subjective satisfaction of their past lives, "none of them drew a sharp distinction between work and free time; all mentioned work as the major source of optimal experiences, and none would want to work less if given a chance."[95]

In contrast, the rise of industrial and corporate organizations created many jobs that were routine and boring. From the standpoint of social policy, there has been little interest in changing jobs into flow experiences. Managers are primarily interested in productivity and profit. Worker enjoyment is sacrificed to these two goals. "This is regrettable," Csikszentmihalyi argues, "because if workers really enjoyed their jobs, they would not only benefit personally, but sooner or later they would almost certainly produce more efficiently and reach all the other goals that now take precedence."[96]

What does the goal of maximizing worker enjoyment mean for the industrial-consumer paradigm? It means a transformation of thinking about the goals of technology. Currently, technological development often results from a desire to maximize profits and produce new goods. What would happen if the goal of increasing worker happiness was introduced into this mix? Then technological development might be directed at eliminating work that is boring and minimizes the opportunity for workers to have an optimal experience.

There are some important cultural conditions that must be investigated when the use of flow theory is considered to guide educational policy. First, it has been found that cultural differences exist regarding the attainment of an optimal experience.[97] Second, research on flow theory has been primarily limited to the United States, Europe, China, and Japan. Because culture is a variable in flow theory, more work needs to be done with other cultures, particularly those that are Islamic and indigenous. The cultural differences that have been found are interesting. In comparing U.S., Japanese, and Chinese students, the following variations were found:

1. Japanese college students optimize their enjoyment when the challenges match their skills. Autotelic Japanese students optimize their enjoyment when the challenges exceed their skills.[98]
2. For Chinese college students and U.S. 12th graders, enjoyment is optimized when their skills exceed the challenge. Autotelic Chinese students optimize their enjoyment when the challenges match their skills.[99]

Giovanni Moneta, who conducted research with Chinese college students, expressed surprise that these students reached flow when their skills exceeded the challenges. Originally, this low-challenge/high-skill condition was called the boredom/relaxation condition. At first, this did not make sense to Moneta because he thought of Chinese as very hard working. Moneta noted that for Westerners "work" and "relaxation" are dichotomous. However in Taoism and Confucianism, a "mental state, that can be conveniently called the tao state, is optimal for both work and relaxation, as well as for all other daily activities. The tao state is defined as a state of maximum efficiency and self-reward."[100] Moneta provides a series of Taoist quotes that illustrate that the "tao state resides in a prudent approach to challenges;" a condition supported by high-level skills confronting low-level challenges.[101] Similar to Moneta, Csikszentmihalyi argues that in Taoism and Confucianism, there is an emphasis on people finding the "way" or "path" in life, which is the same as a flow experience. In Taoism, this way or path is referred to as *Yu*. "Chuang Tzu [the Taoist scholar]," Csikszentmihalyi states, "believed that to *Yu* was the proper way to live—without concern for external rewards, spontaneously, with total commitment—in short, as a total autotelic experience."[102]

Although more research is needed on the cultural context of flow, particularly for Islamic and indigenous cultures, flow theory provides some useful guidelines for the organization of school work to maximize student happiness. School work should be planned so that students are helped to achieve an optimal experience. Students should desire to do their work because they want to experience the psychological state of flow instead of doing their work because of an external reward. There should be joy in learning.

CONCLUSION: NEW EDUCATIONAL PARADIGM

In summary, my goal is to replace current global educational objectives of economic growth and supplying workers for the world's labor market with policies that focus on a long life and happiness. There already exist global school structures and curricula. In proposing a new paradigm, I give a new direction to current global schooling. A continually expanding body of research on happiness can be used to formulate school policies. In the next chapter, I review the research on the social conditions that promote longevity and subjective well-being, and I use these findings to formulate guidelines for a global core curriculum, school organization, and methods of instruction.

NOTES

1 Amartya Sen, *Development as Freedom* (New York: Anchor Books, 2000).
2 Ibid., pp. 46–47.
3 Paul Wngoola, "Mpambo, the African Multiveristy: A Philosophy to Rekindle the African Spirit," in *Indigenous Knowledges in Global Contexts: Multiple Reading of our World* edited by George J. Sefa Dei, Budd L. Hall, and Dorothy Golden Rosenberg (Toronto: University of Toronto Press, 2000), p. 267.
4 *Journal of Happiness Studies* (Berlin: Springer Science+Business Media B.V., 2000 to present).
5 I make this argument in Joel Spring, *Pedagogies of Globalization: The Rise of the Educational Security State.* (Mahwah, NJ: Lawrence Erlbaum Associates, 2006).
6 These figures are reported by John W. Meyer, Francisco Rameriz, and Yawemin Nuhoglu Soysal in "World Expansion of Mass Education, 1870–1980. *Sociology of Education, 65*(2): April, 1992, p. 128.
7 Ibid., p. 146.
8 Richard Layard, *Happiness: Lessons From a New Science* (New York: The Penguin Press, 2005), p. 224.
9 Ibid., p., 225.
10 Nel Noddings, *Happiness and Education* (New York: Cambridge University Press, 2003), p. 93.
11 Ruut Veenhoven, *World Database of Happiness, Correlational Findings,* Chapter 1, p. 2, http://worlddatabaseofhappiness.eur.nl. Retrieved on August 22, 2005. Also see Ruut Veenhoven, "Worlddatabase of Happiness: Continuous Register of Scientific Research on Subjective Appreciation of Life," http://www1.eur.nl/fsw/happiness. Retrieved on August 22, 2005.
12 Ibid.
13 "Philosophy" as posted on the "Worlddatabase of Happiness: Continuous Register of Scientific Research on Subjective Appreciation of Life," http://www1.eur.nl/fsw/happiness; Retrieved on August 22, 2005.
14 Veenhoven elaborates on this definition: The key terms in this definition may be elucidated as follows.

Degree
The word "happiness" is not used to denote an optimal appreciation of life. It refers to a degree; like the concepts of "length" or "weight," it denotes more or less of something. When we say a person is happy, we mean that he or she judges his of her life favorably rather than unfavorably.

Individual
The term "happiness" is used to describe the state of an individual person only; it does not apply to collectivities. Thus, a nation cannot be said to be happy. At best, most of its citizens consider themselves happy.

Happiness denotes a subjective appreciation of life by an individual. So there is no given "objective" standard for happiness. A person who thinks he or she is happy, really is happy.

Judges
The word "happiness" is used where somebody has made an overall judgment about the quality of his or her life. This implies an intellectual activity. Making an overall judgmentimplies assessing past experiences and estimating both future experiences and average quality of life.
One consequence of this conceptualization is that the word "happiness" cannot be used for those who did not make up their mind. One cannot say whether a person is happy or not if that person is intellectually unable to construct an overall judgment. Thus, the concept cannot be used for animals or small children. Nor is the concept applicable to people who did not reflect on the quality of their life or could not reach a conclusion.

Overall
The evaluation of life aimed at is an overall judgment. It embodies all criteria for appreciation, which figure in the mind. In the past, hedonists used to equate happiness withsensory pleasures only. However, there are more modes of appreciation. Apart from the sensory system, cognition and affect also enable individuals to appraise their life. Thus,evaluations also involve cognitive appraisals based on aspirations, expectations, and values.The evaluation also draws on affective conditions, in particular, on average mood. The word "happiness" refers to a judgment, which integrates all the appreciation criteria used. Thus, the idea that one has all one has ever desired does not necessarily make one happy. Despite all material endowments, such a person may feel pain or be depressed. Similarly, the appraisal that one's life is "exciting" does not necessarily mark oneself as happyeither; life may be too exciting to be enjoyable. A Chinese curse says, "May you have interesting times."

Life-as-a-whole
We do not use the word "happiness" to characterize satisfaction with specific aspects of life,such as marriage or work. "Happiness" refers to satisfaction with life-as-a-whole. It coverspast, present, and anticipated experiences. This does not mean that all things everexperienced are given equal weight in the evaluation. As stated earlier, evaluation involves a sifting and ordering. In this process, some aspects may be emphasized and others ignored. Past life experiences, for example, seldom enter into the evaluation process in their original phenomenological Gestalt. What is taken into consideration is mostly a shallowrepresentation of what one tasted previously.

Own life
The term "happiness" concerns the evaluation of one's own life, not of life in general. Apessimistic "Weltanschauung" does not necessarily characterize someone as "unhappy."

Favorably
Evaluation always embodies appreciation, a conclusion as to whether one likes something or not. The term "happiness" refers only to judgments concerning this aspect. Happinessjudgments concern the dimension extending from appreciation to depreciation, from like to dislike. All humans are capable of appraisals of this kind, although not all humans can generalize all appraisals into a judgment of life-as-a-whole.
The criterion of "favorableness" is very close to what is called "pleasantness." However, it is not quite the same. The term "favorableness" concerns the appreciation involved in all evaluations, whereas the term "pleasantness" refers exclusively to direct affective experience.
As such, it is more characteristic of the affective component of happiness (to be discussed Later) than of overall happiness itself.
Veenhoven, *World Database of Happiness, Correlational Findings* ..., Chapter 2, pp. 3–4.

15 *The Works of Mencius,* translated by James Legge (New York: Dover Publications, 1970), p. 201.
16 Ibid., p. 202.
17 *The Works of Mencius* ..., p. 127.
18 Paul Carus, *The Gospel of Buddha* (Chicago: Open Court, 1894), p. 126.
19 Al-Qur'an: A Contemporary Translation, translated by Ahmed Ali (Princeton: Princeton University Press, 1984), p. 47.
20 See "Stem Cell Research and the 'Buddhist Way'," *New York Times on the Web* (19 June, 2005), http://www.nytimes.com/. Retrieved on June 6, 2005.
21 Ibid.
22 Layard, p. 235.
23 See Joel Spring, *The American School: 1642–2004 Sixth Edition* (New York: McGraw-Hill, 2005), pp. 73–130.
24 See Joel Spring, *Educating the Consumer–Citizen: A History of the Marriage of Schools, Advertising, and Media* (Mahwah: Lawrence Erlbaum Associates, 2003) and *Education and the Rise of the Global Economy* (Mahwah: Lawrence Erlbaum Associates, 1998).
25 See Joel Spring, *Pedagogies of Globalization: The Rise of the Educational Security State* (Mahwah: Lawrence Erlbaum Associates, 2006).
26 Bruno S. Frey and Alois Stutzer, *Happiness & Economics: How the Economy and Institutions Affect Human Well-Being* (Princeton: Princeton University Press, 2002), p. 77.
27 Ibid., p. 76.
28 Also see Ruut Veenhoven, *Conditions of Happiness and Databook of Happiness* (Dordrecht, Netherlands: Kluwer Academic, 1984), p. 388.
29 See Joel Spring, *The American School Sixth Edition* (New York: McGraw-Hill, 2005), pp. 375–472.
30 National Center for Education Statistics, *Digest of Education Statistics, 2003, Chapter 2. Elementary and Secondary Education,* Table 36 retrieved on September 12, 2005 from http://nces.ed.gov/programs/digest/d03/tables/dt036.asp.
31 Frances Heylighen and Jan Bernheim, p. 332.
32 Abbott L. Ferriss, "Religion and the Quality of Life," *Journal of Happiness Studies* 3: 2002, pp. 199-200.
33 John W. Meyer, Francisco Rameriz, and Yawemin Nuhoglu Soysal ..., p. 129. These researchers link colonialism to the spread of the Western model of the nation–state and, consequently, to the Western model of schooling.
34 For a statistical study of the globalization of the primary school curriculum, see John W. Meyer, David H. Kamens, and Aaron Benavot, *School Knowledge for the Masses: World Models and National Primary Curricular Categories in the Twentieth Century* (London: Falmer Press, 1992).
35 Kathryn M. Anderson–Levitt, "The Schoolyard Gate: Schooling and Childhood in Global Perspective," *Journal of Social History* (Summer 2005), p. 991.
36 See Spring, *Pedagogies of Globalization* ...
37 Global Monitoring Report 2005, *Education for All: The Quality Imperative.* Retrieved from UNESCO Web site for Education for All, http://www.unesco.org/education/efa/index.shtml, on August 22, 2005.
38 See Spring, *Pedagogies of Globalization* ...
39 Global Monitoring Report 2005, *Education for All* ..., p. 16.
40 Ibid., p. 16.
41 Kathryn Anderson–Levitt, p. 998.
42 Ibid., pp. 994–998.
43 See Spring, *The American School* ..., pp. 73–102.
44 See Spring, *Pedagogies of Globalization* ...
45 Cummins, p. 151.

46 Ibid., p. 134.
47 Ibid., p. 138.
48 William R. Swinyard, Ah-Keng Kau, and Hui-Yin Phua, "Happiness, Materialism, and Religious Experience in the U.S. and Singapore," *Journal of Happiness Studies* 2: 2001, pp. 27–28.
49 Eunkook M. Suh, "Self, the Hyphen Between Culture and Subjective Well-Being" in *Culture and Subjective Well-Being* edited by Ed Diener and Eunkook M. Suh (Cambridge: Massachusetts Institute of Technology Press, 2000), p. 64.
50 Ibid., pp 63–64.
51 Daphna Oyerman, Izumi Sakamoto, and Armand Lauffer, "Cultural Accommodation: Hybridity and the Framing of Social Obligation," *Journal of Personality and Social Psychology* 74: 1998, pp. 1606-1607.
52 Ibid., p. 1616.
53 Suh, p. 74.
54 Harry C. Triandis, "Cultural Syndromes and Subjective Well-Being" in *Culture and Subjective Well-Being* …, p. 23.
55 See Shigehiro Oishi, "Goals as Cornerstones of Subjective Well-Being: Linking Individuals and Cultures," in *Culture and Subjective Wel-Being* …, pp. 87–112.
56 Ibid., p. 100.
57 Ibid., p.100. Puerto Rico actually is listed as the sixth most individualist society. However, Puerto Rico is not a country, but a possession of the United States, and it has been influenced by U.S. culture since the early 20th century.
58 Ibid., p. 97.
59 Ibid., pp. 104–107. This work is based on the research of H. R. Markus and S. Kitayama, "The Cultural Construction of Self and Emotions: Implications for Social Behavior," in *Emotion and Culture: Empirical Studies of Mutual Influence* (Washington, D.C.: American Psychological Association, 1994).
60 Stefan Priesner, "Gross National Happiness—Bhutan's Vision of Development and Its Challenges," *Gross National Happiness: A Set of Discussion Papers* edited by Sonam Kinga, Karma Galay, Phuntsho Rapten, and Adam Pain (Thimphu, Bhutan: The Centre for Bhutan Studies, 1999), p. 25. These essays can be found on the official Bhutan government Web site for the center for Bhutan studies: http://www.bhutanstudies.org.bt/publications/gnh/gnh.htm. I retrieved these essays on September 25, 2005. At the time that Priesner wrote this essay, he was Program Officer, United Nations Development Program Thimpu, Bhutan. In part, the research findings of his essay were based on his doctoral thesis, "Gross National Happiness—The Dimensions of Bhutan's Unique Development Concept," competed in 1996 at Johns Hopkins University. For a description of the growth of Bhutan's multicultural society focused on the refugees from Nepal, see Michael Hutt, *Unbecoming Citizens: Culture, Nationhood, and the Flight of Refugees From Bhutan* (New Delhi: Oxford University Press, 2003), pp. 58–85.
61 For a discussion on the introduction of communications technology into Bhutan, see Stephen Herrera, "Healthy, Wealthy, and Wise," *Technology Review* (August 2005), pp. 60–63.
62 Quoted by Priesner, p. 26.
63 Priesner, p. 27.
64 Lyonpo Jigmi Y. Thinley, "Values and Development: Gross National Happiness," in *Gross National Happiness: A set of discussion papers* …, p. 12.
65 Ibid., p. 14.
66 Ibid., p. 15.
67 Ibid., p. 15.
68 Priesner, pp. 37–38.

69 David L. Wheeler, "Embracing Technology and Spirituality at the Top of the World," *Chronicle of Higher Education* (1/5/2001), p. 2.
70 Ibid. and Priesner, p. 38.
71 Thinley, p. 26.
72 Quoted by Priesner, p. 40.
73 Ibid., p. 40.
74 Thinley, p. 18.
75 For a description of Bhutan's educational ladder (primary, junior high, secondary, and college) and its curriculum, see P. P. Karan, *Bhutan: Environment, Culture and Development Strategy* (New Delhi: Intellectual Publishing House, 1990), pp. 52–54.
76 Priesner, p. 42.
77 Diederik Prakke, "Development With sparks: Placing the Hamburger in the Mandala," in *Gross National Happiness: A set of discussion papers …*, p. 64.
78 Wheeler, p. 3.
79 Ibid., pp. 2–3.
80 Hutt, p. 164.
81 Ibid., pp. 164–165.
82 Ibid., p. 165.
83 Ibid., pp. 178–183.
84 Democracy as mobocracy was an idea widely distributed in a 1798 edition of Noah Webster's *Spelling Book,* which contained his "Federal Catechism." The Federal Catechism contains the following question and answer to be memorized by the reader:

Q. What are the defects of democracy?
A. In democracy, where the people all meet for the purpose of making laws, there are commonly tumults and disorders. A small city may sometimes be governed in this manner; but if the citizens are numerous, their assemblies make a crowd or mob, where debates cannot be carried on with coolness and candor, nor can arguments be heard: therefore a pure democracy is generally a very bad government. It is often the most tyrannical government on earth; for a multitude is often rash, and will not hear reason. "noah webster's federal catechism (1798)" in *Education in the United States: a Documentary History* edited by sol cohen (new york: random house, 1974), pp. 769–770.

85 This definition of democracy and freedom was retrieved on September 9, 2005 from the Freedom House Web site under "Freedom in the World 2005 Survey Methodology," http:// www.freedomhouse.org/research/freeworld/2005/methodology.htm.
86 Ronald Inglehart and Hans–Dieter Klingemann, "Genes, Culture, Democracy, and Happiness," in *Culture and Subjective Well-Being …*, p. 181.
87 Ibid., p. 179.
88 Ruut Veenhoven, "Freedom and Happiness: A Comparative Study in Forty-Four Nations in the Early 1990s," in *Culture and Subjective Well-Being …*, p. 282.
89 Mihaly Csikszentmihalyi, *Flow: The Psychology of Optimal Experience* (New York: Harper Perennial, 1990), p. 71.
90 Mihaly Csikszentmihalyi, *Beyond Boredom and Anxiety: Experiencing Flow in Work and Play, 25th Anniversary Edition* (San Francisco: Jossey–Bass Publishers, 2000), p. xiv.
91 Ibid., p. xiv.
92 Csikszentmihalyi, *Flow …*, p. 67.
93 Ibid., p.
94 Ibid., p. 142.
95 Ibid., p. 146.
96 Ibid., p. 154.

97 Giovanni B, Moneta, "The Flow Experience Across Cultures," *Journal of Happiness Studies* 5: 2004, pp. 115–121.

98 Kiyoshi Asakawa, "Flow Experience and Autotelic Personality in Japanese College Students: How Do They Experience Challenges in Daily Life?" *Journal of Happiness Studies* 5: 2004, pp. 123–154.

99 Giovanni Moneta, "The Flow Model of Intrinsic Motivation in Chinese: Cultural and Personal Moderators," *Journal of Happiness Studies* 5: 2004, pp. 181–213.

100 Ibid., p. 212.

101 Ibid., p. 212.

102 Csikszentmihalyi, *Flow* …, p. 150.

Chapter 2

Basic Educational Principles for a Long Life and Happiness

In its current global form, education does not increase happiness except when it leads to a better paying job![1] Does this mean that schooling based on the principles of human capital and the industrial-consumer paradigm have stripped education of the possibility of helping people live a happy life other than just getting a better job? Does this mean that students in current human capital-oriented schooling are not finding pleasure in their studies except from the hope of getting a good-paying job? Do people today value education only as preparation for employment?

The findings on the current contribution of education to happiness should be considered a call to arms for a change in education policy. Even if the human capital model is accepted and it is believed that education should focus primarily on learning skills needed for employment in the global economy, there should be some concern that education does not enhance the individual's chances of being happy except through better employment. Should there not be something in the school structure, curriculum, and methods of instruction that will contribute to a person living a happy life other than just getting a job?

Findings from research on longevity and subjective well-being can provide guidelines for ensuring that education contributes to happiness and longevity. In turn, these guidelines can be used to formulate global principles for organizing schools, developing methods of instruction, and planning a global curriculum. The application of this research to schooling should consider the life of the student both as a student and as a future global citizen. The health and happiness of students should be a concern particularly with regard to school structures and methods of instruction. Students, like other world citizens, are entitled to school practices that promote their health and happiness. It would certainly be tragic if a student dying at an early age had been forced to endure a dull and punishing school experience for some unfulfilled career. In addition, the student, as a future global citizen, should be given the knowledge and ethical desire to protect the longevity and subjective well-being of the human species.

This chapter summarizes the research findings on longevity and subjective well-being as related to social inequalities. There is a close relationship between longevity and subjective well-being. Good health and the possibility of living a long life contribute to happiness. Research shows that economic inequality and status differences between individuals and nations have an impact on both happiness and health. In addition, there are thresholds in national and personal wealth beyond which any increases in wealth will not affect longevity or happiness. Besides social issues, longevity is affected by global environmental issues, such as the exploitation of natural resources in developing nations, the availability of health care, and pandemics. As with all research, these findings will probably change over time. Therefore, my proposals should be considered dynamic, and they should change as humans gain greater understanding of human biology and psychology, the biosphere, and the impact of social, political, and economic structures on humans.

MEASURING LONGEVITY AND SUBJECTIVE WELL-BEING

Unlike subjective well-being measurements, national longevity rates are quite straightforward as long as there is trust in the ability of governments to maintain accurate public records and summaries of vital statistics. There are startling differences in longevity between countries and within countries. Global data show dramatic differences in longevity; differences that cry out for a solution. Consider the life expectancy differences in Table 2.1, compiled from statistics provided by United Nations Educational, Scientific, and Cultural Organization's (UNESCO's) Global Monitoring Report 2005: *Education for All: The Quality Imperative.*

The dramatic differences in longevity between Zimbabwe (33.1 years) and Japan (81.6 years), and between Sierra Leone (34.2 years) and Sweden (80.1 years), along with the smaller differences between Bolivia and China, demonstrate that longevity is relative to particular national conditions.

Research on happiness requires a more subjective approach than the use of data from public records. Veenhoven's world happiness survey simply asks participants if they are satisfied with their lives. This is a relative question, which is answered according to how the participants evaluate

TABLE 2.1
Life Expectancy Between Selected Nations

Nation	*Life Expectancy at Birth (years) Male and Female 2000–2005*
Zimbabwe	33.1
Sierra Leone	34.2
Bolivia	63.9
China	71.0
Sweden	80.1
Japan	81.6

Source: "Annex," Global Monitoring Report 2005, *Education for All: The Quality Imperative,* pp. 254–261. Retrieved from UNESCO website for Education for All, http://www.unesco. org/education/efa/index.shtml, on August 22, 2005.

their own lives within their own cultural framework. The following are examples of questions asked in his survey:

- In the European Union (EU) nations, happiness was assessed by a single item on life satisfaction:
  "How satisfied are you with the life you lead?"
  - Very satisfied (4)
  - Fairly satisfied (3)
  - Not very satisfied (2)
  - Not at all satisfied (1)
- In Japan, a similar question on life satisfaction was used:
  "On the whole, are you satisfied with the life you lead?"
  - Fully satisfied (4)
  - Not fully, but to some extent satisfied (3)
  - As yet unsatisfied (2)
  - Very dissatisfied (1)
- In the United States, happiness has been assessed with several slightly different questions about happiness. The most commonly used question asks,
  "Taken all together, how would you say things are these days? Would you say you are…
  - Very happy (3)
  - Pretty happy (2)
  - Not too happy (1)[2]

Veenhoven analyzes the responses to these questions to determine the social causes of subjective well-being. Combining the results of his surveys with those of 156 other research projects, he discredits what he calls myths about happiness, for example, that people in underdeveloped countries or rural areas are happier than people in developed countries. Some of the findings that discredit myths about happiness, for example, that education contributes to happiness, can be summarized as follows:

1. Education does not increase happiness except when it leads to a better paying job.
2. People in developed nations are generally happier than people in underdeveloped countries.
3. People in the country are no more satisfied with life than people in towns.
4. Income is a factor in happiness if you are poor.
5. Women are just as happy as men.
6. Unemployment is not necessarily detrimental to a person's happiness, particularly if they did not like their former job.
7. Singles take less pleasure in life than those living with a steady partner.
8. A couple without children is just as happy as a couple with children.
9. Children without siblings are not predisposed to unhappiness.[3]

FOUR QUALITIES OF LIFE

Ruut Veenhoven's matrix, the Four Qualities of Life (Table 2.2) provides a useful method for discussing research findings on the causes of variations in longevity and happiness. One problem with using these research findings to guide education policy is the separation of the inner and outer conditions for happiness and their interrelationship with longevity. Education can encourage psychological conditions within individuals that will contribute to their personal happiness and longevity. Education also may be able to affect social, political, and economic conditions that affect the longevity and happiness of all people. Veenhoven's matrix represents the interplay between the inner and outer conditions of happiness. These various dimensions of satisfaction with life are described in the opening editorial in the first issue of the *Journal of Happiness Studies* written by the journal's editors, Ruut Veenhoven, Ed Diener, and Alex Michalos.

> This *Journal of Happiness Studies* is an interdisciplinary forum on subjective well-being. It covers both cognitive evaluations of life (e.g., life-satisfaction) and affective enjoyment of life (e.g., mood level). In addition to contributions on appraisal of life-as-a-whole, the journal accepts contributions on life domains (e.g., job-satisfaction) and life-aspects (e,g., perceived meaning of life).[4]

TABLE 2.2
The Four Qualities of Life

	Outer Qualities	*Inner Qualities*
Life chances	Livability of environment Examples: • Ecological • Social • Economic • Cultural	Life ability of the person Examples: • Physical health • Mental health • Skills • Lifestyle and taste

Life results	Objective utility of life
	Examples:
	• Effect on intimates such children, friends, etc.
	• Effect on society and the human species
		Subjective appreciation of life
		Examples:
		• Satisfaction of life aspects, such as satisfaction with job
		• Prevailing moods
		• Overall appraisals
		  • Affective: general mood level
		  • Cognitive: contentment with life

Adapted from Ruut Veenhoven (2000). The four qualities of life: Ordering concepts and measures of the good life. *Journal of Happiness Studies,* 1, 11.

Veenhoven's quality-of-life matrix encompasses the interplay of these factors by placing happiness in the general quality-of-life context. In his matrix, Veenhoven relates the outer and inner conditions of the quality of life to "life chances" and "life results." *Life chances* indicate the possibilities people have of achieving happiness, including outer qualities such as social, political, environmental, and economic conditions and inner qualities such as physical and mental health. For instance, life chances of achieving happiness are seriously limited if people experience famine and war and if they are mentally or physically ill. *Life results* include the impact of one's life on outer qualities such as how much one contributes to the happiness of other people.

In Veenhoven's matrix, personal happiness is located in the last quadrant, Subjective Appreciation of Life, and it is dependent on the first two quadrants: Livability of Environment and Life Ability of the Person. In other words, environmental, social, economic, and political conditions provide the outer framework that supports happiness, whereas personal mental and physical health, skills, and tastes provide the inner framework for supporting happiness. The first two quadrants can be the objects of public policies, including educational policies. The question for the creation of a global education objective is: What can schools do to improve the livability of the environment and the life ability of the person to help him or her achieve happiness?

The basis for a common global education in ethics is located in quadrant 3: Objective Utility of Life. Schools should prepare students to help other humans achieve happiness by teaching an ethical responsibility to improve the Livability of Environment and the Life Ability of the Person. In other words, students should be taught that they have an ethical obligation to ensure that environmental, social, political, and economic conditions support the happiness of all members of the human species, and that they should help others achieve the personal physical and mental conditions needed for happiness.

In summary, Veenhoven's matrix provides the following questions to guide the core teachings of a global school curriculum and instructional methods that will maximize subjective and physical well-being:

Questions for a Global Guide for School Curricula and Methods of Instruction That Support a Long Life and Happiness for the Human Species

1. What do current research findings indicate will improve the Livability of Environment" of the school including school organization and methods of instruction? In other words, what can be done to ensure that students have a school experience that promotes their sense of subjective well-being and longevity?
2. On the basis of current research findings, what should students be taught so that after graduation they will have knowledge, skills, and dispositions to support and improve environmental, social, political, and economic conditions that maximize the possibility that they and other humans will achieve long lives and happiness?

EQUALITY OF OPPORTUNITY AND EQUALITY OF EDUCATIONAL OPPORTUNITY

Veenhoven's matrix provides another way of expressing the definitions given for equality of opportunity and equality of educational opportunity in chapter 1: (a) everyone has an equal chance to live a long life and be happy; (b) everyone has a right to receive an education that will increase his or her chances to live a long life and be happy; and (c) everyone has a

TABLE 2.3
Equality of Opportunity, Equality of Educational Opportunity, and the Four Qualities of Life

	Outer Qualities	*Inner Qualities*
Life chances: Equality of opportunity	The livability of the environment, including ecological, social, economic, political, and cultural conditions, will provide humans with an equal chance to live a long and happy life.	The life ability of a person, including her/his physical and mental health, skills, and lifestyle, will give her/him an equal chance to live a long and happy life.
Life chances: Equality of educational opportunity	Everyone will have an equal chance to receive an education that will give them the knowledge and skills to ensure that ecological, social, economic, political, and cultural conditions support a long and happy life for all people.	Everyone will have an equal chance to receive an education that will give them the knowledge and skills to ensure that their own physical and mental health, skills, and lifestyles will enhance their personal abilities to live a long and happy life.
Life results: Equality of opportunity	Everyone will have the emotional desire and ethical beliefs that will cause them to act to ensure that others have an equal chance to live a long and happy life.	Everyone will have the same chance to experience a positive subjective appreciation of life.
Life results: Equality of educational opportunity	Everyone will have an equal chance to receive an education that will give them the desire, ethical beliefs, knowledge, and skills to help others live a long and happy life.	Everyone will have the same chance to receive an education that will improve their subjective appreciation of life.

right to a form of schooling that will enhance his or her happiness as a student. Table 2.3 illustrates how these concepts of equality can be integrated into Veenhoven's matrix. In the intersection of Outer Qualities and Life Chances: Equality of Educational Opportunity, everyone is offered the same chance to receive an education that gives them the knowledge and skills to ensure their contribution to environmental, political, social, and economic conditions that allow all people an equal opportunity to live a long and happy life. Similarly, the intersection of Inner Qualities and Life Chances: Equality of Educational Opportunity offers everyone the same chance to receive an education that gives them the knowledge and skills to ensure that their own physical and mental health, skills, and lifestyle support their chances for a long and happy life.

What I call the ethical imperative of education appears in the intersection of Outer Qualities and Life Results: Equality of Education Opportunity, where everyone is given an equal chance to acquire the desire, ethical beliefs, knowledge, and skills needed to help others live a long and happy life. In other words, schooling should inculcate a desire to protect the life and happiness of others and a belief system that values the life and happiness of others.

CATEGORIES OF RESEARCH FINDINGS

What does current research evidence tell us about improving the livability of environment and the life ability of a person? In *Global Progress I: Empirical Evidence for Ongoing Increase in Quality of Life*, Frances Heylighen and Jan Bernheim list five major categories of research findings:

1. Wealth and threshold effect
2. Longevity and health
3. Social equality, cooperation, and trust or lack of corruption in government, economic exchanges, and social relationships
4. Security from war, crime, terrorism, accidents, and political upheaval
5. Access to information.[5]

For the first category, "wealth and threshold effect," consistent research findings show that there is a threshold of personal and national wealth beyond which an increase in wealth will not improve longevity or subjective well-being. These findings, as I discuss, have important implications for the role of social equality and cooperation in schools and society. It has been found that although income is important for improving the subjective well-being of poor people, there is a threshold of income beyond which increased income does not improve that well-being. After analyzing international data on income and subjective well-being, Roberts Cummins of Deakin University in Melbourne, Australia asserts,

> In conclusion, it seems clear from this investigation that, in terms of SWB [subjective well-being], money does matter but more may not be better; … the empirical data suggest that there is a ceiling beyond which income can no longer influence levels of SWB. However, if people are not wealthy then, for them, more income is better, and this highlights the condition of poverty. … Level of income has a major influence on the SWB of people living in poverty.[6]

Using Ruut Veenhoven's 1996 data, Frances Heylighen and Jan Bernheim conclude that per capita income is strongly correlated with happiness until a threshold level is reached, which in 1996 was about the level of the per capita income in Mexico. They write: "It seems that once people have sufficient money, further earnings contribute little to their QOL [quality of life], implying that wealth, like nutrition, is an indicator for the satisfaction of a deficiency need."[7]

The threshold effect also is applicable to discussions of the second category Longevity and Health . As mentioned at the beginning of Chapter 1, economist Amartya Sen advocates using longevity rates as an important measure of the quality of human life.[8] His longevity studies demonstrate that economic development as measured by per capita income is not necessarily an indicator of longer life spans. For instance, Sen cites the example of African American men in the United States who have a lower life span than men in China or men in the state of Kerala in India despite the fact that African American men have average incomes many times higher than those in China or Kerala. According to Sen, the reason for the shorter life span of African Americans is not income but "medical coverage, public health care, school education, law and order, prevalence of violence and so on."[9] Sen also points out that Kerala, China, and Sri Lanka have higher rates of longevity than the richer countries of Namibia, Brazil, South Africa, and Gabon.

Sen provides other evidence that economic growth and increases in personal income do not necessarily increase life spans. In the 19th century, Great Britain was the leading capitalist market economy in the world, but had life expectancy rates many times lower than poorer countries. It was a national health program and government support of proper nutrition in the 20th century that finally raised life expectancy rates in Great Britain. Dismissing economic growth as a factor, Sen argues that "a much more plausible explanation of the rapid increase in British life expectancy is provided by the changes in the extent of social sharing during the war decades, and the sharp increases in public support for social services (including nutritional support and health care) that went with this."[10]

Heylighen and Bernheim's third category of research findings, namely, social equality, cooperation, trust, government corruption, economic exchanges, and social relationships, is important for the organization of schools, methods of instruction, and the curriculum. For instance, social equality, Heylighen and Bernheim assert, has a "clear correlation between average happiness in a country, ... which is measured by equality between sexes, and equality between classes"[11] Social equality is also related to longevity and health.[12] In addition, "efficient cooperation among people" promotes subjective well-being because there is trust among people and a low level of government graft. Heylighen and Bernheim assert that "a society in which no one trusts anyone, and everybody is constantly trying to cheat others, will have a low social capital."[13] They suggest that one possible measurement of efficient cooperation or social capital could be a country's level of corruption, which has a strong negative correlation with the happiness of its population.

Heylighen and Bernheim's fourth category, namely, security from war, crime, terrorism, accidents, and political upheaval, encompasses security variables such as peace, safety, and political stability. Obviously, security affects longevity rates, with war shortening many lives. Their fifth condition is access to information either through schooling or media. Heylighen and Bernheim conclude that the research findings for these five categories are strongly correlated with longevity and happiness across nations and cultures.

SOCIAL EQUALITY, TRUST, AND CAPABILITIES

Heylighen and Bernheim's third category of research findings on social equality, cooperation, and trust is important for the organization of schools and instructional methods. A significant number of research studies on longevity and subjective well-being support the proposition that schools and instructional methods should be organized around principles of social equality and cooperation to promote the health, longevity, and happiness of students. Also, this research suggests that the content of instruction should reflect the principles of social equality and cooperation.

Research on social equality can be separated into the two interrelated categories of income equality and what Amartya Sen calls "capabilities."[14] Research finds that the degree of income inequality in a nation is directly related to subjective well-being and longevity, with large inequalities contributing to greater unhappiness and shorter lives. In addition, trust and cooperation are affected by income inequality. Michael Marmot, Professor of Epidemiology and Public Health at the University College, London, and Director of the International Center for Health and Society, concludes, after reviewing the research on social factors affecting health and longevity: "To put it at its most simple: if hierarchies are bad for health and cooperation and trust good for health, the level of health that we as individuals experience may depend on the balance between hierarchy and cooperation and trust of a society."[15] His findings support school practices that emphasize cooperation and trust and the preparation of students for supporting social equality and a cooperative life after graduation. Also, the interrelationship between capabilities, subjective well-being, and health strongly support the idea that students should be given more control over their school work, and that they should be prepared to maximize control over their own lives.

Amartya Sen's concept of "capabilities" defines social equality or inequality according to "people's ability to lead the kind of lives they value and have reason to value."[16] This definition is similar in meaning to equality of opportunity to live a long and happy life. Capabilities, as I explain, have serious implications for longevity and happiness and are an important part of Sen's explanation why African American men have a shorter life span than Chinese men with lower incomes. Capabilities are what Sen means by freedom and, he argues, development policies should be directed at maximizing human capabilities or freedom of people to maximize human ability to control their own lives. Sen writes,

> Having greater freedom to do the things one has reason to value is … important in fostering the person's opportunity to have valuable outcomes. … Greater freedom enhances the ability of people to help themselves and also to influence the world, and these matters are central to the process of development. The concern here relates to … the "agency" aspect of the individual. … I am using the term "agent" … [to mean] someone who acts and brings about change, and whose achievements can be judged in terms of her own values and objectives.[17]

Of course, income and capabilities are closely related. Personal capability is dependent on a level of income that will provide adequate nutrition, medical care, and shelter. In a meta-analysis of happiness studies, Michael Argyle found that there is an income threshold beyond which additional income does not contribute to happiness. Argyle writes that this may occur simply "because money makes a greater difference to the quality of life when it is spent on food, housing, and other necessities than when it is spent on larger cars, works of art, antiques, or jewelry."18 Certainly, education, development, and human rights goals should be directed at providing all people with an income for the necessities required to exercise "capabilities" and "agency."

Societies with greater income inequality are more hostile, less social, and lacking in trust.[19] Income inequality also can undermine trust in a society. One study compared states in the United States according to income inequality and trust.[20] The study found that the greater the income inequality, the less trust there was between people. The state with the highest inequality of incomes in the study was Louisiana, which also had the lowest rating of trust between people. Also near the top in inequality and lack of trust were

Mississippi, Alabama, and New York. Those states with the highest levels of trust also had the least income inequality, such as New Hampshire, North Dakota, Utah, Idaho, and Washington.[21] The same thing is true between nations. Residents of nations with greater inequality of incomes are less trustful of each other than those with less income inequality.[22]

Income inequality also is correlated with murder and other crime rates. Studies show, and so would commonsense, that feelings of subjective well-being are higher in societies with low crime rates.[23] This is part of a previously mentioned research category used by Frances Heylighen and Jan Bernheim to determine quality of life, namely, the effect of war, crime, terrorism, accidents, and political upheaval. In the United States, provinces in Canada, and nations of the world, there was a strong correlation between the high income inequality and high murder rates.[24] Wilkinson asserts, "So firmly established is the relationship between inequality and homicide ... that many criminologists regard it as the most well-established relation between homicide and *any* environmental factor."[25] Comparing the homicide rates between industrialized nations, the five industrialized nations with the least income inequality between 1999 and 2001 had an average homicide rate of 1.546 per 100,000 of the population. The industrialized nations with the greatest income inequality had an average homicide rate for the same period of 2.298. The United States had both the greatest income inequality of any industrialized nation and the highest homicide rate (5.56 per 100,000).[26]

Income inequality contributes to the existence of social hierarchies, which play a role in subjective well-being. Relative income identifies one's place in the social ladder, which also affects a person's feelings of subjective well-being.[27] In a famous study, Harvard students were asked to imagine that they could choose between two imaginary worlds in which the prices were the same. In the first world, the student could earn $50,000 per year while others averaged $25,000 per year. In the other world, the student could earn $100,000 a year while others averaged $250,000 a year. A majority of students chose the first world, in which their relative position would be higher, but their actual income would be lower. Economist Richard Layard summarizes: "People care greatly about their relative income, and they would be willing to accept a significant fall in living standards if they could move up compared with other people."[28] In considering the psychological issues of income inequality, Layard concludes: "If money is transferred from a richer person to a poorer person, the poor person gains more happiness than the rich person loses. So average happiness increases. Thus a country will have a higher level of average happiness the more equally its income is distributed—all else being equal."[29]

In addition to economists, public health experts emphasize the importance of relative wealth, particularly when feelings about relative wealth are related to differences in social statuses. Richard Wilkinson, Professor of

Social Epidemiology at the University of Nottingham Medical School, identifies three "intensely social risk factors" contributing to poor public health: "First, is low social status, which in this context is less a matter of low material living standards themselves than of their social consequences, such as *feeling looked down on, having an inferior position in the social hierarchy, and subordination (and therefore reduced ability to control one's circumstances and work)* [my emphasis]."[30] Ichiro Kawachi, Director of the Harvard Center for Society and Health, and Bruce P. Kennedy of the Harvard School of Public Health assert that "low social status and the accompanying sense of relative deprivation have been shown to produce physiological responses in individuals that may damage their health in multiple ways ... relative deprivation— being lower on the social ladder—is harmful to health."[31]Michael Marmot concludes that "where you stand in the social hierarchy is intimately related to your chances of getting ill, and your length of life. And the difference between top and bottom are getting bigger, and have been for a generation."[32]

In summary, income inequality reduces happiness by undermining trust and contributing to increased crime rates. In addition, income inequality is directly related to social hierarchies, which have a direct effect on a person's capabilities. The lower in the social hierarchy people are, the less ability they have to control their own destiny, which results in decreased feelings of subjective well-being. In addition, social inequality (i.e., inequality of income and capabilities) results in poorer health and a shorter life span. These findings have important implications for education. But before we turn to these implications, it is important explore why one's place in a social hierarchy affects happiness, health, and longevity.

BICYCLING: SOCIAL INEQUALITY, HAPPINESS, AND LONGEVITY

How could social inequality—meaning inequality of capabilities—affect happiness and longevity? Public health studies show that social inequality causes stress for those at the bottom of a hierarchy, which in turn contributes to poor health, a reduced life span, and a low sense of subjective well-being.[33] Stress in humans produces identifiable physical reactions, resulting, among other things, in high blood pressure, heart disease, and diabetes. As stress occurs, there is a rise in catecholamines, which causes an increase in blood pressure and pulse rate, as well as a diversion of blood from the intestines. Also, stress increases levels of glucocorticoid, which increases blood sugar, causing a resistance to insulin and resulting in the possibility of adult-onset diabetes. There also is a change in fats in the blood, causing low levels of high-density lipoprotein (HDL) (the good cholesterol), increased plasma triglyceride, blood glucose, and high blood pressure and resulting in potential heart disease. Simply stated, stress reduces longevity.[34]

How does social inequality cause stress? The answer to this question takes us back to the notion of capabilities or, as previously quoted from Sen, "people's ability to lead the kind of lives they value—and have reason to value."[35] If you are at the bottom of most social hierarchies, you have less chance of leading the type of life you value and, consequently, you suffer the physical results of stress. Also, given the structure of most hierarchies, such as corporations and government civil services, the "bicycling reaction" occurs, producing more stress.

Bicycling is an important image for understanding the effect of social hierarchies. The bicycle image is that of a person bending forward with hands on the handlebars while kicking back on the pedals, in other words, bowing to authority while abusing those below. There is anger and stress caused by bowing to authority, and there is anger and stress caused in the subordinates being kicked. Public health authority Richard Wilkinson quotes Volker Sommer, a distinguished primatologist, about how bicycling takes place in the animal world of which humans are a part: "It is very common in nonhuman primates that they, after having received aggression from a higher ranking individual, will redirect aggression towards lower ranking ones. It can be a real chain reaction: Alpha slaps beta, beta slaps gamma, gamma slaps delta, delta slaps …."[36] Wilkinson summarizes the bicycle reaction among humans: "There is a widespread tendency for those who have been most humiliated, who have had their sense of selfhood most reduced by low social status, to try to regain it by asserting their superiority over any weaker or more vulnerable groups."[37]

Michael Marmot's famous longitudinal study of the British civil service demonstrates the negative effects of reduced capabilities and the bicycle syndrome. The British civil service has a well-defined social hierarchy, with clear lines of authority and job descriptions. Also, all members of the civil service are covered by the same national health plan, which removes the issue of availability of adequate health care. At the bottom of the British civil service hierarchy are messengers, guards, and carriers of supplies. Above them are the clerical grades, and above the clerical grades are the executive grades who implement policy such as scientists, statisticians, and economists. And at the top are the permanent secretaries who work with politicians and government ministers to develop and implement policies.

Capabilities increase as a person moves up in the civil service hierarchy. Upward movement also gives the civil service worker more decision-making opportunities. Contrary to the popular myth that decision makers suffer more stress then those taking orders, findings show that those at the bottom of hierarchy with less power actually suffer more stress. Consequently, Marmot found that there was a health gradient that paralleled a person's rank in the civil service. Taking into account all possible factors that might influence health and longevity, including education, genetics, and personal habits, Marmot found that those at the top of the civil service hierarchy were healthier and lived longer than those at each rank below. This was true of both women and men.

A surprising fact for Marmot was the existence of a health and longevity gradient from the top to the bottom of the hierarchy. Marmot summarizes his findings:

> The men at the bottom of the office hierarchy have, at ages forty to sixty-four, four times the risk of death of the administrators at the top of the hierarchy. More dramatic than the difference between top and bottom is the gradient. The group second from the top have higher mortality than those above them in the ranking. … Both the gradient and fourfold difference between top and bottom are dramatic.[38]

The previously mentioned finding by Sen that African American men have a shorter life span than Chinese and Kerala men with lower incomes can be explained by the effect of stress on longevity. Racism in American society reduces capabilities and increases the feelings of subservience in the bicycle syndrome. A very stressful aspect of the bicycle syndrome is not having anyone below you to kick. Sen's findings were supported also by a comparison of African American men's and women's incomes and longevity with those experienced by poorer residents of Bangladesh. Bangladeshi men have a better chance of living past the age of 40 years than African Americans living in the Harlem neighborhood of New York City. This results in what Sen refers to as different forms of deprivation: "So it is not only the case that American blacks suffer from *relative* deprivation in terms of income per head vis-à-vis American whites; they also are *absolutely* more deprived than the low-income residents in Kerala (for both women and men), and the Chinese (in the case of men), in terms of living to ripe old ages."[39]

The violence and stress of social inequality contributes both to a reduction in a society's feelings of subjective well-being and to its longevity and health. One of the most studied national groups is African Americans. For instance, in a comparison of 23 rich and poor areas in the United States, white women in rich districts could expect to live until their 86th year, whereas black women living in poor districts could expect to live only until their 70th, a startling difference of 16 years. The same disparity exists between white and black men living in rich and poor areas. The average longevity of white men in rich areas is between 74 and 75 years, as compared with only 59 years for black men in poor districts.[40]

Like income inequalities, inequalities in capabilities are correlated with crime and lack of trust. Marmot illustrates the health gradient and causes of violence by imagining a ride on the Washington, D.C. subway from downtown Washington to Montgomery County, Maryland. For each mile traveled, he claims, life expectancy rises about a year and a half.[41] Poor black men living in downtown Washington, D.C. are surrounded by the most powerful government officials in the United States. As the bicycle image suggests, these poor black men are at the bottom of the social hierarchy and have no one to kick as they bow to power. One option in releasing stress is violence to other black people or those higher up in social status and wealth. Another is protection of their "self-respect." A study of Washington, D.C.'s underclass youth found that "these youths are obsessed with issues of pride and dignity. Never lose your cool, even when you are fighting. All they have is this cool. Cool is like building a fortress around yourself."[42] The concern about respect and pride is evidenced in prison populations, in which prisoners are rendered powerless in terms of capabilities. Prisoners told one researcher that the reason they got into fights was because "he disrespected me." The researcher concluded that "the word 'disrespect' is so central in the vocabulary, moral value system, and psychodynamics of these chronically violent men that they have abbreviated it into the slang term, 'he dis'ed me'."[43]

There is a cultural dimension to social inequality. Researchers have focused on the differences between collectivist and individualist societies. In a collectivist society, a person wants to be capable of ensuring a positive relationship with others. For a person in a collectivist society, capabilities often have to do with fulfilling obligations to others, whereas for people in individualist societies, capabilities are related to personal achievement.

This difference between collectivist and individualist societies is sometimes used to explain differences in crime rates. Out of 22 industrialized nations, Japan is the fifth most unequal society in terms of income. The only industrialized nations with greater inequality of income are Ireland, Australia, United Kingdom, and the United States.[44] Despite this ranking on income inequality, the crime rate is very low in Japan, as compared with other industrialized nations. The reason given by most experts is the Confucian nature of Japanese society and the resulting sense of social responsibility.[45] The major differences in crime rates between the United States and Japan indicated in Table 2.4 could demonstrate that cultural factors between collectivist and individualist societies are more important than income inequalities. The findings suggest that if you want a heavy dose of crime, mix social inequality with individualism.

SOCIAL INEQUALITY AND SCHOOLS

What do findings about social inequality mean for education? First, a distinction must be made between capabilities within schools and preparation to be capable in society after graduation. As suggested by previously discussed

TABLE 2.4
Crime Rates per 100,000 for the Year 2000

	United States	*Japan*
Murder	7.5	1.0
Robbery	256	1.8
Rape	37	1.5
Aggravated Assault	440	5.4
Burglary	1,099	187

Source: T.R. Reid. (2000) *Confucius lives next door.* New York: Vintage, p. 23.

research, reducing social inequalities in school increases subjective well-being and contributes to a longer life span for teachers and students. Of course, all social inequality cannot be eliminated because some form of institutional organization is needed, with someone taking responsibility for ensuring a safe and purposeful educational environment. But, whenever possible, there should be an attempt to reduce social inequality.

Human capital education policies incites the bicycle syndrome by fostering a corporate model of schooling that relies on the control of teachers and students through assessment requirements. In its worst bureaucratic form, teachers bow forward to school administrative authority while kicking back at students. In addition, capabilities among teachers and students are severely limited. Administrators might order teachers to follow a lesson script that would require exacting conformity to a particular content and method of instruction. The worst scenario would be a scripted education that specified the methods, the day, and the time for teaching a particular topic, and the amount of time to be spent on a topic. Administrators would be constantly supervising teachers to ensure their conformity to the script. In turn, teacher pay would depend on ratings by administrators on how well the script was followed and the performance of students on standardized tests.

The preceding scenario eliminates the capability of teachers to pursue "the kind of lives they value—and have reason to value." In this case, teachers would be unable to make their own decisions about the best method of instruction and the content of instruction. The constant supervision by administrators to ensure that teachers do not act independently and the use of student standardized test scores to determine teacher pay would increase teachers' stress, shorten their lives, and reduce their subjective well-being.

School administrators also can fall victim to the bicycle syndrome either through a hierarchy of administrators or by subservience to politicians. In this scenario, the top administrator bows to the politician while kicking at the administrators below, who in turn kick at the teachers, who then kick at the students. At each level, the range of capabilities is reduced: the politician tells the top education administrator what to do, and she or he plans how these orders will be actualized. The next level of the bureaucracy plans a strategy for actual implementation, and the next level tells teachers what they should do. The actual limitation of capabilities is dependent on the leeway given to administrators and teachers to make decisions. The greatest limitation of capabilities could take place where a politician demands specific results such as increasing scores on standardized tests. In turn, administrators are forced to narrow their educational planning to raising student test scores and to order teachers to follow scripted lessons. A reduction in health, subject well-being, and longevity would follow a gradient leading from the top of the administrative hierarchy to the teachers at the bottom.

For students, a scripted curriculum would lessen their capabilities, which in this case would mean eliminating any control over how and what they learn. In the framework of the bicycle syndrome, stressed and angry teachers might kick back at their students through open displays of hostility. Because of their anger, teachers in this scenario might try to ensure that all joy is removed from learning, and that students suffer as much stress as the teachers are feeling. Therefore, students might find themselves being forced by angry and hostile teachers to conform to scripted teaching or to learn bits of information for standardized tests. With the lowest social status in this rigid educational hierarchy, students would suffer low levels of subjective well-being, poor health, and shortened life spans.

Who do the students kick back at? One possibility for them is just to conform, to accept being unhappy as students, and to endure the chemical damage caused by the stress. Another possibility is to act out against teachers and administrators. The concept of a culture of student resistance has been around for years. It is anti-school and plays out in the classroom through student disruptions, an unwillingness to complete school work, and a disrespect for school authorities, including teachers. Forming peer groups, members reinforce the anti-school attitudes of each other by bragging about not doing homework, about failing tests, and sometimes about acts of vandalism against school property. One of the earliest studies examining this phenomenon was conducted by British sociologist Paul Willis and reported in his 1979 book *Learning to Labour.*[46] Students from working-class families were the primary group to form anti-school cultures. Willis interpreted anti-school attitudes and actions as resulting from students feeling that schools were out of touch with the male working-class world from which they came and that they expected to enter as adults. Willis found that resistant students believed that school would not provide them with any opportunity for mobility out of working-class jobs. Some American scholars, such as Henry Giroux, tried to romanticize this resistance culture, and called upon educators to use it as a vehicle for educational change. In *Theory of Resistance: A Pedagogy for the Opposition,* Henry Giroux argues that student resistance can be the vehicle for developing an educational method that will empower students and teachers to transform society.[47]

Student resistance cultures also can be interpreted within the framework of social inequality and the bicycle syndrome. First, students forming these resistance cultures often come from families with low incomes and grow up in neighborhoods where social inequality contributes to increased crime and violence. Second, in schools, as shown by numerous sociological studies, students from low-income families often are the victims of discrimination by teachers, administrators, and other students.[48] Students from low-income homes often feel at the bottom of the social hierarchy, either because they attend a school that serves only low-income students or because they attend a school with a diverse student body in which they are placed at the bottom of the hierarchy by administrators, teachers, and fellow students.

In a highly bureaucratic school system with scripted learning and constant monitoring of teachers, students from low-income families could become the victims of the bicycle syndrome. Using the language of the previously quoted primatologist Volker Sommer, politicians slap administrators, administrators slap teachers, teachers slap students, and privileged students slap the underprivileged. At the bottom of the chain, the underprivileged student has no one to slap. The only option is to slap or kick back at the hierarchy above. Consequently, the culture of resistance among students comes to resemble the previously described reactions of low-income African Americans and prisoners who direct their anger at those above them in the social hierarchy and focus on the protection of their self-respect.

EQUALIZING CAPABILITIES BETWEEN NATIONAL POPULATIONS: EDUCATION FOR ALL AND THE WORLD BANK

Any consideration of equal educational opportunity must begin with educational inequalities between nations. To overcome social inequalities, it is important to equalize capabilities and reduce the bicycle syndrome between national populations. There exist vast disparities in educational conditions between rich and poor nations. The summary of the 2005 monitoring report for the United Nations' Education for All program states:

TABLE 2.5
Class Size: Mean Average for Grade 1 and All Primary Classes for Least Developed Nations

Nation	*Grade 1*	*All Primary Classes*
Bangladesh	56.9	44.3
Benin	71.3	51.9
Bhutan	26.1	31.5
Burkina Faso	72.1	61.5
Cape Verde	33.2	32.8
Equatorial Guinea	112.3	75.1
Madagascar	33.5	22.6
Maldives	24.5	22.6
Tanzania	40.2	36.6
Togo	67.2	42.9
Uganda	62.6	39.6
Zambia	35.9	34.9

Adapted from Table 2 in Neville Postlethwaite, "The Conditions in Primary Schools in Least Developed Nations," *International Review of Education* 44:1998, p. 298.

> Public expenditure on education represents a higher proportion of GDP [Gross Domestic Product] in rich countries, where the EFA [Education for All] goals are already achieved, than in poorer ones, where the coverage of under-resourced systems needs to be both expanded and improved. Spending has increased over the past decade in many developing countries, notably in East Asia and the Pacific and in Latin America and the Caribbean. Pupil/teacher ratios remain higher than is desirable in many countries of sub-Saharan Africa (regional median: 44:1) and South and West Asia (40:1). In many low-income countries, teachers do not meet even the minimum standards for entry into teaching and many have not fully mastered the curriculum. The HIV/AIDS pandemic is severely undermining the provision of good education and contributing significantly to teacher absenteeism.[49]

The disparities in educational conditions among the least developed nations are highlighted in Tables 2.5 and 2.6 based on data describing class size complied by Neville Postlethwaite.[50] In *Development as Freedom,* Amartya Sen stressed that capability is dependent on economic and social conditions. Individuals are not capable of living the life they want if they are experiencing famine. Likewise, one cannot talk about education enhancing capabilities if the people of a nation are without schools. Table 2.5 shows major differences between class size averages of 71.3 in Benin and 112.3 in Equatorial Guinea, as compared with 26.1 in Bhutan and 33.2 in Cape Verde. In addition, Table 2.6 shows major differences in the percentages of students with

TABLE 2.6
Percentage of Students With Full-Time Teachers and Annual Instruction Time for Least Developed Nations

Nation	*Students With Full-Time Teachers in the Primary Grades (%)*	*Official Annual Instructional Time for the Lowest Grade (hours)*
Bangladesh	0.4	447
Benin	0.0	920
Bhutan	14.1	868
Burkina Faso	0.7	994
Cape Verde	62.6	660
Equatorial Guinea	19.1	960
Madagascar	0.6	886
Maldives	46.3	646
Tanzania	63.5	628
Togo	17.5	1,011
Uganda	20.1	789
Zambia	1.0	608

Adapted from Tables 3 and 4 in Neville Postlethwaite. (1998). The conditions in primary schools in least developed nations. *International Review of Education,* 44, 300, 304.

full-time teachers (62.6% in Cape Verde vs 0.4% in Bangladesh) and in the total annual hours of schooling (660 in Cape Verde vs 447 in Bangladesh).

Providing equality of educational opportunity to live a happy and long life requires full-time teachers, reasonable class sizes, and support for a reasonable number of hours spent in school.[51] If a school day is considered to be 6 hours, then children in Zambia are receiving a little more than 100 days of instruction with mainly part-time teachers. At the same time, students in Burkina Faso have about 166 days of school in classes averaging 61 students taught mainly by part-time teachers. In addition, most of the schools in these countries lack adequate facilities and classroom materials.[52] The monitoring group for the United Nation's Education for All reported that between 1998 and 2001, the actual number of primary-aged students not in school declined from 106.9 million to 103.5 million, still a shockingly high level. In the same report, figures were given for 2005, which indicated that sub-Saharan Africa offered an average of 0.3 years of pre-primary education, whereas North American and Western Europe offered 2.3 years.[53] Obviously, educational equality is going to require some form of wealth redistribution between nations, particularly from richer to poorer nations, if these disparities are to be overcome.

The most important current effort to achieve social equality in education between nations is the Education for All [EFA] program. The World Declaration on Education for All was originally issued in 1990 in Jomtien, Thailand.[54] In 2000, the World Education Forum met in Dakar and adopted six action goals.[55] A 2002 Education for All report stated that at the 2000 World Forum, "focus was placed squarely at the national level and on the responsibility of national governments towards education. The Dakar Framework clearly asks for a commitment to create the right conditions for EFA in each country, recognizing that some countries will need help in doing so and recognizing, too, the responsibility of those with the means to make such help available."[56] The first action goal of the World Education Forum is to pressure countries into providing early childhood care and education. The second goal is Universal Primary Education. The remaining four goals are devoted to youth and adult learning, adult literacy, gender equality, and improved quality of education.[57]

The Dakar meeting established the following time line for action:

- 2005: eliminating gender disparities in primary and secondary education
- 2015: ensuring that all children, particularly girls, children in difficult circumstances, and those belonging to ethnic minorities, have access to and complete, free and compulsory primary education of good quality
- 2015 achieving a 50% improvement in levels of adult literacy, especially for women, and equitable access to basic and continuing education for all adults
- 2015 achieving gender equality in education, with a focus on ensuring girls' full and equal access to and achievement in basic education of good quality.[58]

The current strategy for meeting Education for All goals is to gain international financing and to apply sustained pressure on national governments. The 2002 *Education for All: An International Strategy to Put the Dakar Framework for Action on Education for All Into Operation* recognizes the need for international support to help poorer nations:

> Since increased external aid is the only way for some of the poorest countries to build capacity in basic education and other social domains, it is now urgent to ensure that these new commitments translate into significant new resources for EFA. Financing agencies and bilateral donors must not shy away from the long-term investment in education in favor of short-term results, but rather commit themselves to the six Dakar goals all the way to 2015.[59]

One part of the plan calls for national forums on achieving Education for All goals. In addition, national Education for All efforts are to be integrated into development plans. At a meeting of EFA partners in Amsterdam in 2002, the World Bank pledged that it would provide funding for the Education for All to finance primary education, with the goal of universal primary education by 2015.[60] The Education for All strategy calls for an integration of what is called the Monterrey consensus resulting from the United Nations' 2002 International Conference on Financing for Development.[61]

Education for All is tied to economic development goals including involvement with the World Bank and acceptance of the Monterrey consensus. Tied to economic goals, Education for All does not guarantee an overall reduction of social inequality within nations or between nations. However, it could result in economic growth that will provide all people with basic needs in medical care, nutrition, and shelter, improving their subjective well-being. Therefore, it would be unrealistic for me to dismiss this effort because of its goals. Universal primary education will improve the capabilities of people. The reality is that all people are now affected by the global economy and culture. The capabilities of people to live the life they want will be increased by a basic primary education. All people should have the basic educational tools to decide what of the world's knowledge they wish to incorporate into their cultures.

WILL SOCIAL INEQUALITIES BE OVERCOME BY EDUCATION FOR ALL AND THE WORLD BANK?

Ironically, Education for All and its support by the World Bank is based on human capital goals, which might have contributed to the major economic differences between rich and poor nations. Also, insistence on economic growth as a measure of progress may not increase human capabilities. Workers in developing nations might, as now in many cases, simply end up as low-level workers in global factories, corporations, and agricultural conglomerates. The World Bank's support of Education for All as part of human capital development is clearly stated in the World Bank publication *Achieving Universal Primary Education by 2015: A Chance for Every Child*:

> Combined with sound macroeconomic policies, education is fundamental for the construction of globally competitive economies and democratic societies. Education is key to creating, applying, and spreading new ideas and technologies, which in turn are critical for sustained growth; it augments cognitive and other skills, which in turn increase labor productivity."[62]

The World Bank document indicates that the Bank's support of education is to avoid any redistribution of wealth: "The expansion of educational opportunity is a 'win-win' strategy that in most societies is far easier to implement than the redistribution of other assets such as land or capital."[63] In other words, increased educational opportunities will supposedly create new wealth without any changes in inequalities of wealth between nations and between people in developing nations. This could be construed as a verbal ruse to avoid suggesting that inequalities between nations might have to be solved through the redistribution of wealth from rich nations to poor nations. I wonder if increased "educational opportunity" is a "win-win strategy" for the poor.

In addition, the World Bank's interest in education is tied to what it calls "Education for the Knowledge Economy," which, as the Bank explains, provides

> assistance aimed at helping developing countries equip themselves with the highly skilled and flexible human capital needed to compete effectively in today's dynamic global markets. Such assistance recognizes first and foremost that the ability to produce and use knowledge has become a major factor in development and critical to a nation's comparative advantage.[64]

The link to human capital education results in concerns about "measurable" progress in teaching literacy and arithmetic skills to prepare children to work in a global economy based on an industrial-consumer paradigm. The term "measurable" suggests that instruction would be dictated by assessment examinations such as those now common in countries driven by the human capital model of education. "Measurable outcomes" are a clearly stated goal of the Dakar World Education Forum Goals for Education For All:

> Improve all aspects of the quality of education and ensure excellence of all so that recognized and measurable learning outcomes are achieved by all, especially in literacy, numeracy, and life skills.[65]

Another hope for funding Education for All came from the United Nations' Monterrey consensus on financing economic development, which also stressed economic growth through international financing:

> We recognize the need to pursue sound macroeconomic policies aimed at high rates of economic growth, full employment, poverty eradication, price stability and sustainable fiscal and external balances to ensure that the benefits of growth reach all people, especially the poor.[66]

In summary, the work of the United Nations, particularly the work of Education for All and the World Bank, represents the major global effort to reduce educational inequalities among nations. This important effort is a first step in reducing social inequalities between nations. Poverty must be overcome before all people can maximize their capabilities to achieve a long and happy life. The United Nations' Millennium report painted this picture of the world's poor:

> While more of us enjoy better standards of living than ever before, many others remain desperately poor. Nearly half the world's population still has to make do on less than $2 per day. Approximately 1.2 billion people 500 million in South Asia and 300 million in Africa struggle on less than $1. People living in Africa south of the Sahara are almost as poor today as they were 20 years ago. With that kind of deprivation comes pain, powerlessness, despair and lack of fundamental freedom, all of which, in turn, perpetuate poverty. Of a total world labor force of some 3 billion, 140 million workers are out of work altogether, and a quarter to a third are underemployed.[67]

SOCIAL INEQUALITY, ECONOMIC GROWTH, AND ENVIRONMENTAL EDUCATION

It is hard to criticize the effort to provide universal primary schooling and to free people from the dire struggle against poverty, but economic development does have environmental consequences. I argue that any plan for universal primary education should contain a component of environmental education. Protecting the environment is a key element in living a long and happy life. A major source of social inequality among nations is the massive consumption of natural resources by rich nations and pollution in poorer nations. The United Nations' Millennium report provides the following description of environmental inequality:

> In the rich countries, the byproducts of industrial and agribusiness production poison soils and waterways. … Carbon dioxide emissions are widely believed to be a major source of global climate change, and the burning of fossil fuels is their main source. The one fifth of the world's population living in the industrialized countries accounts for nearly 60 per cent of the world's total consumption of energy, but the developing world's share is rising rapidly. … In the developing countries, massive deforestation, harmful farming practices and uncontrolled urbanization are major causes of environmental degradation."[68]

The World Bank and the Monterrey consensus stress sustainable development. However, none of the plans for Education for All mention any form of environmental education that would support sustainable development. Yet all the official documents on sustainable development stress the importance of environmental education.[69] The idea of sustainable development was presented in the 1980 *World Conservation Strategy* report and became a central theme of the World Commission on Environment and Development. The *World Conservation Strategy* was prepared by the United Nations Environment Program, the World Wildlife Fund, and the International Union for the

Conservation of Nature and Natural Resources. It contains a clear statement on the role of environmental education in creating a global ethic supporting sustainable development. The report states:

> Ultimately, the behavior of entire societies towards the biosphere must be transformed if the achievement of conservation objectives is to be assured; … the long term task of environmental education [is] *to foster or reinforce attitudes and behavior, compatible with a new ethic* [my emphasis].[70]

Other calls for sustainable development have argued for the integration of indigenous knowledge systems, something completely missing from Education for All proposals. For instance, at the 2002 Johannesburg summit on the environment, the Global People's Forum issued a Civil Society Declaration, which declared that "governments and civil society should (A) implement educational methods enhancing ethos and methods of *sustainable development, including the mainstreaming of indigenous knowledge systems.*[71]

World Bank documents related to Education for All often refer to sustainable development without any mention of environmental education. The World Bank publication *Achieving Universal Primary Education by 2015: A Chance for Every Child* mentions sustainable development in the context of human capabilities:

> Education provides people with what Nobel laureate Amartya Sen (1999) calls human "capabilities"—the essential and individual power to reflect, make better choices, seek a voice in society, and enjoy a better life. Education, and particularly primary education, also promotes achievement of all of the other Millennium Development Goals: poverty reduction, gender equity, child health, maternal health, lower HIV/AIDS and other communicable diseases, and environmental sustainability.[72]

The actual Millennium goals for sustainability, besides failing to mention environmental education, are quite limited and do not address the issue of the inequality in natural resource usage between nations. The Millennium goals have three targets: (a) integrate sustainability principles into national planning; (b) half the number of people without safe water by 2015; and (c) make significant improvement in the lives of 100 million slum dwellers by 2020.[73] Again, these are important and laudable goals. Yet, despite the passing mention of Amartya Sen, they do not specify how the school curriculum will be organized to achieve these goals and prepare people to grapple with the larger issue of social inequalities between nations.

Currently, with World Bank support, Education for All is the most noteworthy effort to equalize education between nations. However, discussions of sustainability in Education for All documents seem like a sop given to environmentalists. Education for All plans could include environmental education in the teaching of arithmetic and literacy skills. Literacy and arithmetic skills can be a means for teaching environmental issues, which, as I discuss later in this book, are important ingredients in helping people to achieve a long and healthy life. Also, given the social inequalities resulting from the unequal use of natural resources by already developed nations, it would enhance the capabilities of people in developing nations, and in all nations, to include environmental education in universal primary instruction. I discuss the inclusion of environmental education and its relationship to indigenous rights when I deal with the specifics of a global core curriculum in chapter 3.

MIDDLE-CLASS STRESS

The long-term limitations of the human capital approach to education are shown by research on the relationship between social inequality, longevity, and subjective well-being. Certainly, basic education, as represent by the efforts of Education for All and the World Bank, might improve human capabilities in the current globalized economy and culture. Moreover, as studies show, escape from poverty will increase longevity and improve feelings of subjective well-being. It is beyond the scope of this book to contest the argument that a global free market based on an industrial-consumer paradigm and supported by human capital economics will eliminate the overwhelming poverty in the poorest nations of the world. Even if the human capital model works, there is a threshold of wealth beyond which there will be little improvement in longevity and subjective well-being unless something is done about social inequalities between nations and within nations, including social inequalities related to the use of natural resources and environmental conditions.

There are findings that free markets and economic growth do not necessarily increase the happiness of the middle class in developing nations. In *Happiness & Hardship: Opportunity and Insecurity in New Market Economies*, Carol Graham and Stefano Pettinato, two supporters of free markets as a key to economic development, worry that the middle class in developing nations are "frustrated achievers." While the poor languish at the bottom of the income scale, the frustrated achievers of the middle class feel what the authors call "stress" at trying to achieve the income and lifestyles of those in the top income bracket. The degree of stress felt by middle-class achievers is directly correlated with the degree of income inequality: the greater the income inequality in a developing nation, the greater the stress felt by middle-class achievers. The middle class is trapped on an achievement treadmill. Although their real incomes might increase, they still are frustrated by the comparison of their incomes with those at the top of the income ladder. Graham and Pettinato conclude by saying, "Our results also suggest that relative income differences are more important for those in the middle of the distribution [income] than for either the very wealthy or the very poor. In the Peru sample, those in the middle, not the poor, were the most frustrated despite their absolute gains."[74]

It seems logical that free markets and competition do not necessarily increase happiness. Free markets and competition cause feelings of instability and uncertainty as the middle-class achievers measure their progress according to their position relative to the rich in their own developing country and already developed countries. Despite having reached the income threshold that provides adequate shelter, nutrition, and medical care, the middle-class achievers remain unhappy with their status. Graham and Pettinato argue that their study of developing nations supports "the literature on happiness in the developed economies, which emphasize the importance of variables other than absolute income gains in enhancing welfare: relative differences, changes in employment and other status (uncertainty)."[75] The authors emphasize the importance of "the effects of volatility and distributional shifts, which appear to have stronger effects on the attitudes of lower- and middle-income urban groups than on those of the very poor or the wealthy."[76]

Oddly, despite the fact that Graham and Pettinato's studies suggest the need for something other than free markets and competition as the method for promoting happiness in developing countries, they call for more human capital education as a means of ensuring public support of free-market reforms. They want more opportunity for mobility through expansion of social services to reduce the unhappiness of "frustrated achievers" and the "stress" of the middle class. Under the subtitle, Broadening Social Services, they begin with this statement: "The first and most obvious way of enhancing the mobility and opportunity of both poor and those in the middle-income strata is improving access to good-quality education beyond the secondary level."[77] In other words, they suggest more education for a better paying job. Graham and Pettinato provide no evidence that this will increase the happiness of middle-class achievers. In fact, it might lead to more frustration and anxiety as the middle class tries to climb the income and status ladder.

Graham and Pettinato and other economists seem unable to imagine an alternative to schooling based on human capital principles, which define the purpose of education as economic growth and preparing students for jobs. Also, human capital education is based on assessment-driven instruction, which contributes little to the subjective well-being of students unless the tests lead to a high-paying job. For both low-income nations and students from low-income families living in high-income nations, there is no reason not to organize schools that provide conditions supporting the subjective well-being of students and student capabilities.

CONCLUSION: GLOBAL GUIDELINES FOR A CORE CURRICULUM, METHODS OF INSTRUCTION, AND SCHOOL ORGANIZATION

The reviewed research can be used to create educational guidelines that contribute to the happiness and long life of students and school graduates beyond simply gaining a better job and a higher income. I am dividing these guidelines into three categories: core curriculum, methods of instruction, and school organization. The guidelines are aligned with my definitions for equality of opportunity and equality of educational opportunity. My definitions are as follows:

- Equality of opportunity: Everyone will have an equal chance to live in environmental, social, economic, and cultural conditions that will maximize the opportunities to a long and happy life.
- Equality of educational opportunity: Everyone will have an equal chance to receive an education that gives the knowledge and skills to ensure that environmental, social, economic, political, and cultural conditions will support a long and happy life for all people.

As I have suggested, these definitions could be used to change the mission of the global Education for All effort from its current emphasis on teaching the knowledge and skills needed to compete in the global economy.

The reviewed research suggests the following guidelines for a global core curriculum, with variations based on local cultures.

Guidelines for a Global Core Curriculum

1. The curriculum should contain the knowledge and skills, including knowledge about research on the causal factors, influencing longevity and subjective well-being, so that school graduates will be able actively to ensure that environmental, social, political, and economic conditions promote a long and happy life for themselves and all other people.
2. The curriculum should contain the knowledge and skills needed to maximize a person's capabilities to choose a life he or she values.
3. The curriculum should contain knowledge and skills that will create the emotional desire and ethical belief in school graduates that will cause them actively to help others live a long and happy life.

Research on longevity and subjective well-being suggest that instructional methods should be concerned about issues of social inequality and optimal learning experiences. The bicycling syndrome can appear among students when they are separated according to ability or achievement. Also, too much reliance on competition for grades can breed unhealthy stress and greater social inequality, which will enhance the effect of the bicycle syndrome. On the basis of the research cited in this chapter, it could be hypothesized that a student with failing grades who is ranked at the bottom of the class and placed in an ability group or classroom with low educational status will suffer negative effects on their potential longevity as compared with a student at the other end of the spectrum.

Guidelines for Global Methods of Instruction

1. Instructional methods should avoid increasing social inequalities between students.
2. Methods of instruction should enhance cooperation and trust between students and between students and teachers.
3. Methods of instruction should enhance optimal learning experiences or flow.

Finally, research suggests the following guidelines for organizing schools.

Guidelines for Global School Organization

1. Schools should be organized to reduce the stress caused by the "bicycle syndrome."
2. As part of reducing the effect of the bicycle syndrome, there should be a reduction—an elimination would not be possible or necessarily desirable—of social inequalities between administrators, teachers, and students.
3. Principles of trust and cooperation should permeate the school environment.
4. The environmental conditions of the school, including its architectural design, landscaping, and availability of clean air, safe water, and healthy food, should maximize the opportunity for administrators, teachers, and students to live a long and happy life.
5. Whenever possible schools should include physical and mental health facilities that maximize the health and subjective well-being of administrators, teachers, and students.

NOTES

1 Ruut Veenhoven, *Conditions of Happiness and Databook of Happiness* (Dordrecht, Netherlands: Kluwer Academic, 1984), pp. 386-387 and see National Center for Education Statistics, *Digest of Education Statistics, 2003, Chapter 2. Elementary and Secondary*

Education, Table 36 retrieved on September 12, 2005 from http://nces.ed.gov/programs/digest/d03/ tables/dt036.asp.

2 Ruut Veenhoven, *Trend Average Happiness in Nations 1946–2004: How Much People Like the Life They Live* (World Database of Happiness, Trend Report 2005-1d, http://www2.eur.nl/fsw/research/happiness).Retrieved on August 2, 2005.

3 Veenhoven, *Conditions of Happiness* . . ., pp. 386–387.

4 Ruut Veenhoven, Ed Diener, and Alex Michalos, "Editorial: What This Journal Is About," *Journal of Happiness Studies* 1: 2000, p. v.

5 Frances Heylighen and Jan Bernheim, "Global Progress I: Empirical Evidence for Ongoing Increase in Quality–Of–Life," *Journal of Happiness Studies* 1: 2000, pp. 323–346.

6 Robert A. Cummins, "Personal Income and Subjective Well-Being," *Journal of Happiness Studies* 1: 2000, p. 153.

7 Frances Heylighen and Jan Bernheim, "Global Progress I: Empirical Evidence for Ongoing Increase in Quality-of-Life," *Journal of Happiness Studies* 1: 2000, p. 333.

8 Amartya Sen, *Development as Freedom* (New York: Anchor Books, 2000).

9 Ibid., pp. 22–23.

10 Ibid., p. 51.

11 Heylighen and Bernheim, p. 334.

12 For instance, see Michael Marmot, *The Status Syndrome: How Social Standing Affects Our Health and Longevity* (New York: Henry Holt and Company, 2004) and Richard Wilkinson, *The Impact of Inequality: How to Make Sick Societies Healthier* (New York: The New Press, 2005).

13 Heylighen and Bernheim, p. 334.

14 Sen, pp. 18–21.

15 Marmot, p. 166.

16 Sen, p. 18.

17 Ibid., pp. 18–19.

18 Michael Argyle, "Causes and Correlates of Happiness" in *Well-Being: The Foundations of Hedonic Psychology* edited by Daniel Kahneman, Ed Diener, and Norbert Schwarz (New York: Russell Sage Foundation, 2003), p. 358.

19 See Richard Wilkinson, *The Impact of Inequality: How to Make Sick Societies Healthier* (New York: The New Press, 2005), pp. 33–100.

20 The study was conducted by I. Kawachi et al., "Social Capital, Income Inequality, and Morality," *American Journal of Public Health* 87: 1991, pp. 491–498. I am using the summary of this study as presented by Wilkinson, p. 41.

21 Wilkinson, p. 41.

22 For this comparison between countries, Wilkinson on page 42 uses statistics provided by E. Uslaner, *The Moral Foundations of Trust* (New York: Cambridge University Press, 2002).

23 Heylighen and Bernheim, p. 334.

24 Wilkinson, pp. 48–49.

25 Ibid, p. 50.

26 These figures were calculated by using the statistics on "Income Inequality in 22 Industrialized Nations" provided by Ichiro Kawachi and Bruce P. Kennedy in *The Health of Nations: Inequality Is Harmful to Your Health* (New York: The New Press, 2002), p. 27, and Gordon Barclay and Cynthia Tavares, *International Comparisons of Criminal Justice Statistics 2001* (London: Home Office: Research, Development and Statistics Directorate, 2001), p. 10.

27 See Richard Layard, *Happiness: Lessons from a New Science* (New York: The Penguin Press, 2005), pp. 41–55 and Marmot, pp. 82–103.

28 Ibid., pp. 41–42.

29 Ibid., p. 52.

30 Wilkinson, p. 25.
31 Kawachi and Kennedy, p. 51.
32 Marmot, p. 1.
33 See studies reported in previously cited works: Ichiro Kawachi and Bruce P. Kennedy, *The Health of Nations* ..., Richard Wilkinson, *The Impact of Inequality* ..., Michael Marmot, *The Status Syndrome* ... and Richard Wilkinson, *The Impact of Inequality* ...
34 Marmot, pp. 113–115.
35 Sen, p. 18.
36 See Wilkinson, p. 224.
37 Ibid., p. 225.
38 Marmot, p. 39.
39 Sen, p. 22.
40 Wilkinson, pp. 14–15.
41 Marmot, p. 2.
42 Quoted in Marmot, pp. 99–100.
43 Quoted by Wilkinson, p. 149.
44 Kawachi and Kennedy, p. 27.
45 See Marmot, p.173.
46 Paul Willis, *Learning to Labour.* (Lexington, MA: D.C. Heath, 1979).
47 Henry Giroux, *Theory of Resistance: A Pedagogy for the Opposition* (South Hadley, MA: Bergin and Garvey, 1983).
48 As an example of the many studies over the years exploring the treatment by school administrators and teachers of students from low-income families, see A. B. Hollingshead, *Elmtown's Youth* (New York: John Wiley, 1949); Melvin Kohn, *Class and Conformity: A Study of Values* (Homewood, IL: Dorsey, 1969); Jonathan Kozol, *Savage Inequalities: Children in America's Schools* (New York: Crown Publishers, 1991); and Jeannie Oakes, *Keeping Track: How Schools Structure Inequality* (New Haven: Yale University Press, 1985).
49 Global Monitoring Report 2005, *Education for All: The Quality Imperative,* p. 4. Retrieved from UNESCO Web site for Education for All, http://www.unesco.org/education/efa/index.shtml, on August 22, 2005.
50 Neville Postlethwaite, "The Conditions in Primary Schools in Least Developed Nations," *International Review of Education* 44: 1998, pp. 289-317.
51 I use the term "reasonable" to avoid entering the thicket of research on what is the best class size and length of school year for learning.
52 See Postlethwaite, pp. 307–314.
53 Global Monitoring Report 2005, *Education for All* ... , p. 1.
54 For a discussion of the origins of Education for All, see Joel Spring, *Education and the Rise of the Global Economy* (Mahwah, New Jersey: Lawrence Erlbaum Associates, 1998), pp. 190–220.
55 See *Education for All: An International Strategy to Put the Dakar Framework for Action on Education for All Into Operation* (Paris: UNESCO, 2002).
56 Ibid., p. 7.
57 Global Monitoring Report 2005, *Education for All* ... p. 1.
58 *Education for All: An International Strategy* ... p. 31.
59 *Education for All: An International Strategy* ... p. 8.
60 *Education for All: An International Strategy* ..., p. 15, and see World Bank, "Education For All," *http://web.worldbank.org/WBSITE/EXTERNAL/TOPICS/EXTEDUCATION/0,,contentMDK:20374062~menuPK:540090~pagePK:148956~piPK:216618~theSitePK:282386,00.html.* The World Bank document was retrieved on November 20, 2005.
61 *Education for All: An International Strategy* ..., pp. 8, 15, and 23.

62 Barbara Bruns, Alain Mingat, and Ramahatra Rakotomalala, *Achieving Universal Primary Education by 2015: A Chance for Every Child* (Washington, D.C.: The World Bank, 2003), p. 1.

63 Ibid., p. 1.

64 World Bank, "Education for the Knowledge Economy," *http://web.worldbank.org/WBSITE/EXTERNAL/TOPICS/EXTEDUCATION/0,,contentMDK:20161496~menuPK:540092~pagePK:148956~piPK:216618~theSitePK:282386,00.html.*

65 *Education for All: An International Strategy* ... p. 25.

66 United Nations, *Report of the International Conference on Financing for Development: Monterrey Mexico, 18–22 March 2002* (New York: United Nations, 2002), p. 4.

67 Koji A. Adnan, *"We the Peoples": The Role of the United Nations in the 21st Century* (New York: United Nations, 2000), p. 19.

68 Ibid., p. 55.

69 See Joel Spring, *How Educational Ideologies Are Shaping Global Society: Intergovernmental Organizations, NGOs, and the Decline of the Nation–State* (Mahwah, New Jersey: Lawrence Erlbaum Associates, 2004), pp. 100–163.

70 Joy A. Palmer, *Environmental Education in the 21st Century: Theory, Practice, and Progress* (London: Routledge, 1998), p. 15.

71 See Spring, *How Educational Ideologies* . . . , p. 106.

72 Bruns, Mingat, and Rakotomalala, p. 28.

73 Ibid., p. 24.

74 Carol Graham and Stefano Pettinato, *Happiness & Hardship: Opportunity and Insecurity in New Market Economies* (Washington, D.C.: Brookings Institution Press, 2002), p. 143

75 Ibid., p. 144.

76 Ibid., p. 77.

77 Ibid., p. 146.

Chapter 3

A New Paradigm for a Global Curriculum

In this chapter, I examine the existing global curriculum and propose guidelines for new global curriculum based on the goals of a long life and happiness. I realize that there are important cultural differences in ways of knowing, which I will explore in chapter 6. Currently, the common global curriculum is based on the historical policy goals of economic and military development, and preparation of citizens to serve the nation-state. In this model, students are treated as human capital. Based on a factory or bureaucratic model, this global curriculum divides knowledge into discrete and separate courses taught in age-based classrooms. Pleas for an integrated curriculum to counter this factory and bureaucratic model, whereby subjects are taught as interrelated components of knowledge, have been advocated in different forms by progressive educators such as John Dewey and Paulo Freire. In contrast to these progressive educators, human rights and environmental educators have adapted progressive methods to specific agendas that do not support the current direction of economic development. In both the current global curriculum and the work of Dewey and Freire, concerns about improving subjective well-being and increasing longevity either have been neglected or have taken a place secondary to economic and military goals. On the other hand, human rights and environmental curricula often touch on these goals without making them a central focus.

There are important dissenting traditions challenging the current human capital curriculum. These dissenting traditions provide important curricular and instructional methods that can be used in creating a curriculum supportive of a long life and happiness. However, this dissenting tradition has some problems. I believe the progressive tradition, as represented by Dewey and Freire, did not provide any specific social, political, and economic goals. In contrast, human rights and environmental education curricula do have specific social, political, and economic objectives. I will use the methods and examples of lessons from progressive, human rights, and environmental educators to create a new curriculum paradigm.

GLOBAL CURRICULA: HUMAN CAPITAL AND ECONOMIC GROWTH

As noted in chapter 1, global educational structures and organizations have forced local cultures to conform to a particular pattern of socialization in childrearing. In addition, there is a global curricula common to national school systems. This global curriculum originated in the 18th-century Western Enlightenment with a belief that schooling would be key to forming the nation-state, eliminating poverty, preparing more productive workers, and creating a just society. A key element in these Enlightenment educational goals was literacy instruction along with the teaching of math and science. It is this tradition that became the human capital global model that now dominates schooling. As David H. Kamens and Yun–Kyung Cha explain, "This enlightenment view today is enshrined in human capital theories of modernization. Its [enlightenment tradition] prominence helps account for the extraordinary importance placed on math and science test scores around the world."[1]

In my discussions of different education models, I make a distinction between the teaching of math and science and the teaching of "political math" and "politically oriented science." I use "politically-oriented" to avoid confusion with the discipline of political science. The term "political math" was used when arithmetic was introduced into U.S. schools in the 19th century to educate analytical citizens. Arithmetic was to be used to understand social problems such as the number of people afflicted with diseases and mental illness, crime rates, and economic growth. Numbers were considered to be politically objective, and it was believed that they would guide citizens to make objective decisions about social, political, and economic problems. "Proponents argued," write David Kamens and Aaron Benavot, "that 'political arithmetic' was objective and opinion free. Numbers could be used both to measure social progress and to demonstrate the need for community action in areas where progress was being impeded. … Numbers were thought capable of generating political consequences on crucial moral issues of the day."[2]

"Politically oriented science" refers to the use of science to solve problems of human living. There was a utopian dream of creating a better society through the introduction of science into the curriculum. Science, like numbers, could be used to highlight social problems and to provide solutions. In the 19th- and early 20th-century American curriculum, science was considered a means of preparing students for understanding and solving community and personal health problems by actively preventing the spread of disease, improving nutrition, and correcting problems in the handling of sewage, garbage, and street cleaning. Science was to be a powerful instrument for educating students to participate in municipal health problems. Science teaching was to result in improving home life by giving students knowledge of household chemistry, sanitation, and scientific menu planning. Knowledge of arithmetic was to ensure the ability to maintain a household budget so that a family did not slide into poverty.[3] Ironically, in later years, science instruction was intended to prepare students for some of the negative consequences of science. In the United States, as part of defense mobilization in the 1950s, students were instructed about the impact of nuclear weapons, and how to survive by proper treatment of radiation wounds and radiated food and water. In the 1960s, environmental education, which of course requires scientific instruction. became a hot topic as humans faced the environmental consequences of the fruits of scientific–technological developments.[4]

In contrast to political arithmetic and politically oriented science, the teaching of math and science in the human capital curriculum is primarily for learning job skills. Taught in this framework, students might not learn that math and science can be used to improve the quality of their lives and that of others.

In the Enlightenment model, "instruction" on how to perform a particular task, such as just teaching students how to read, write, and add, was replaced by the concept of "total education," in which the school takes responsibility for educating the whole child. This model of "total education" of the child became globalized in the 19th and 20th centuries. David H. Kamens and Yun–Kyung Cha summarize this trend: "'Education' won out over mere 'instruction' as the dominant ideology. That is, schooling was now defined as more diffuse in nature and purpose. It was to mold the character, values and loyalties of students as future participants in civil society."[5]

The Western curricular model spread as a result of Western colonialism in Asia, Africa, the Americas, and the Middle East; global trade and the flow of ideas; and Japanese imperialism in the late 19th and early 20th centuries.[6] The Western model replaced local forms of education, including Islamic, Confucian, indigenous, and Hindu approaches. In *Knowledge for the Masses: World Models and National Curricula, 1920–1986,* the writers conclude:

TABLE 3.1
Global Core Subjects and Percentage of Instructional Time 1970–1986

Subject	*Countries Offering Subject in Primary School Curriculum (%)*	*Total Instructional Time Allocated to Subject in Primary School Curriculum (%)*
Language (reading and writing)	100	33.9
Mathematics	100	18.2
Natural sciences	100	7.9
Social sciences (history, geography, civics, social studies)	100	8.1
Aesthetic education	98.7	10.2
Religious or moral education	74.7	5.2
Physical education	96.1	7.1
Hygiene/health education	42.1	1.2
Practical/vocational	68.0	5.1

Source: Adapted from Tables 1 and 2 in Aaron Benavot, Yun–Kyung Cha, David Kamens, John Meyer, and Suk–Ying Wong. (1991, February). "Knowledge for the masses: World models and national curricula, 1920–1986. *American Sociological Review* (February, 1999), 90–91.

> Modern models of society and education and their interrelation are similar around the world and generate educational systems and school curricula that are strikingly similar; ... increasingly similar world curriculum takes up most of the instructional time; ... for most of the twentieth century a standard world curriculum for primary education has been in operation.[7]

Packaged in discrete units for age-graded classrooms, this world curriculum contains the subjects and average instructional times devoted to a particular subject shown in Table 3.1.

Reading and writing occupies the largest part of the global school day, averaging 33.9% of the total instructional time. As part of the nationalizing effect of global education, language instruction is most often in national languages, with the trend being for national or official languages to supplant minority languages. After studying global language instruction, sociologist Yun–Kyung Cha concludes: "Local languages and nonofficial indigenous languages that are spoken by ethnic minorities (including various tribal languages in Africa, India, and Latin America) are taught as a regular school subject in some multilingual societies. But instruction in local languages is offered mainly during a transitional period before students are introduced to a major national/official language" [my emphasis].[8]

As nations emphasized economic development and military prowess, mathematics and science became standard parts of the global curriculum, occupying 26.1% of the average total instructional time in a global school day.[9] Arithmetic was included in early 19th-century Western curricula for both its practical applications and its supposed training of reason. By the late 19th and early 20th century, arithmetic was included in the curricula of Japan and China as these nations tried to resist Western imperialism. In the West, science often was resisted by religious leaders, who felt that it was a threat to their teachings. In fact, the battle between science in the form of evolutionary theory in schools and religion continued into the 21st century. Both the teaching of arithmetic and science were considered essential for industrial development.

Currently, countries compare national achievement scores in math and science as an indication of future strength in the global economy. For instance, in the United States, where federal control of the public school curriculum has been evolving for some time, a 2006 *New York Times* article about federal aid for college attendance reported: "Senator Bill Frist of Tennessee, the majority leader, responding to rising anxiety over America's economic competitiveness, sponsored legislation establishing new grants to college juniors and seniors majoring in math, science, or engineering."[10] These subjects, because of the work of international organizations, are becoming standardized at the global level. In their study on the global spread of mathematics and science curricula, David Kamens and Aaron Benavot conclude: "Overall, as a result of political and economic crises and growing international discourse, the link between the teaching of arithmetic and science and the construction of rational, productive citizen-subjects became a taken-for-granted component of international ideology."[11]

Currently, math and science instruction is displacing interest in teaching of the social sciences. After studying the spread of Western, particularly American, social science instruction, Suk–Ying Wong writes: "In the present period, the social science curriculum often commands less attention among national authorities than subjects like mathematics or science, and in the educational profession, this component of the curriculum may be of secondary importance."[12]

Social science instruction, 8.1% of the average total instructional time in a global school day, has changed over time. In the school systems that developed in the 19th century, the primary emphasis was on teaching separate subjects such as history, geography, and civics to build nationalism by emphasizing, according to Suk–Ying Wong, "the outstanding heroes or accomplishments of the nation's past or the particularities of the national identity."[13] Eventually, many nations merged these separate subjects into a social science or social studies course. There exist significant regional variations in the amount of time spent on social science in the primary school curriculum. By the late 20th century, Latin American schools spent the largest portion of the school day on social science (13.1% of instructional time) because, according to Suk–Ying Wong, "in Latin American countries ... the disestablishment of religion seems to have been replaced with an intensified teaching of social scientific knowledge"[14]

In contrast, less time is spent on the social sciences in the Middle East and North Africa (6.4% of instructional time), sub-Saharan Africa (7.8 % of instructional time), and Eastern Europe (6.3% of instructional time). The decline in time spent teaching social sciences in Eastern Europe has resulted from the demise of communist states, which emphasized the teaching of Marxist ideology in school. Between 1920 and 1940, Eastern European countries devoted 11.4% of instructional time to the social sciences, which was 5.1% more time than these schools provided in the late 20th century.[15]

Aesthetic education, occupying 10.2% of global instructional time, became increasingly important in the global curriculum after World War II. In Western schools, aesthetic education in the form of music, art, and dance played an important role in building nationalist feelings by imbuing students with a passion for a nation's cultural traditions. Also, art was considered important as training for jobs requiring drawing skills, such as in drafting and architecture. Aesthetic education spread to postcolonial nations after World War II because "art education [could] now be viewed as celebrating glorious national traditions that will be the source of future prosperity and civilization."[16]

Therefore, the core global curriculum–language, mathematics, science, social sciences, and aesthetic education–occupies, on the average, 78.3% of the total instructional time in global schools. What is missing or neglected? Given my concern about longevity, I would say that health and hygiene instruction is neglected, with only 42.1% of nations including the subject in their national curricula and allowing it, on the average, only 1.2% of instructional time. Not surprisingly, unless it is included in the social science curriculum, which I doubt, consideration of the social causes underlying subjective well-being find no place in the global curriculum. What about preparing children to participate actively in improving the social, political, and economic conditions of humans? This topic might find a place in social science instruction, but most likely that part of the curricula is devoted to educating for obedience to the law, patriotism, and acceptance of the national economic system. Also, this topic might find a place in religious and moral instruction, but my suspicion is that most of this instruction is devoted to teaching students to conform to moral and religious precepts.

In summary, there exists a standardized global core curriculum divided into discrete units that match the global structure of schools, which are divided into age-graded classrooms. The global curriculum is designed to build national identity through teaching a common language and local citizenship, and to prepare citizens for participation in the global economy. The decline of interest in social science instruction in favor of more math and science highlights the neglect of preparing students to participate in political, economic, and social change. The primary goal of the human capital curriculum model is preparation for work in the global economy. This human capital goal involves the integration of citizens into what I call the educational security state, which is devoted to maintaining an industrial-consumer economy for competition in the global economy.[17]

THE CONSEQUENCES OF A HUMAN CAPITAL CURRICULUM

The human capital curriculum, with its separate subjects, declining interest in the social sciences, and expansion of math and science, does not prepare humans to participate actively in charting their own futures (capabilities) and creating a world that promotes a long life and happiness. There is nothing inherently wrong with the expansion of math and science in the curriculum, except that it is separate from any study investigating the consequences of these subjects on human life. The very division of the curriculum into separate subjects limits the perspective of students. Isolated from the social sciences, math and science are abstracted from their social context to become merely, as intended by proponents of human capital education, preparation for work.

After studying math and science in isolation from other subjects, students may leave school completely unaware of the potential social and environmental consequences of their jobs, particularly if the occupations are related to industrial and technological development. These graduates might not have the skills or ethical desire to evaluate the potential impact of industrial development to human society. They might become mere pawns in the game of economic growth as they are manipulated by their bosses. Trapped by the mistaken belief that economic growth is the path to a long life and happiness, school graduates might be engaged in enterprises that actually destroy the quality of their lives.

There are several issues related to this criticism of the human capital curriculum. The first issue is the traditional role of the social sciences. Does it make any difference that interest in teaching the social sciences is waning when the subject has traditionally been concerned with educating patriotic and law-abiding citizens who feel integrated into a nation-state?

There is a progressive educational tradition that considers social studies a vehicle for preparing students to be active citizens. However, this progressive tradition, which I discuss in more detail later, has played a lesser role in shaping the social science curriculum than the needs of the nation-state for social control of its citizens. Despite the tendency of social science subjects to serve the interests of political power, the very teaching of laws, government, and history does give the student some fundamental political knowledge that can be used to change political conditions. Without this fundamental knowledge, the student leaves school with little sense of a starting point for political action.

The decline in the social sciences and the teaching of math and science as discrete subjects represent almost criminal neglect of world environmental and health problems. Knowledge can free individuals to act in their own best interests if they understand it as an integrated whole connected to all human activity within the biosphere. As currently organized, the curriculum contributes to schooling as a mechanism of social control to produce compliant workers and political pawns for multinational corporations and nation-states, citizens who do not question the ultimate consequences of the industrial-consumer economic model for the quality of human life. What we need is a corrective to the current global curriculum.

PROGRESSIVE CURRICULA: INCREASING CAPABILITIES WITHOUT AN IDEOLOGICAL DIRECTION

I believe that progressive education provides some important curriculum and instructional models that can be used in preparing students to strive for a society that promotes happiness and longevity. As I see it, the problem with progressive education is that it never had a clear economic and political agenda, but only provided methods for social change. As the major dissenting curricula challenging the human capital model, progressive curricula as a world model does focus on increasing student capabilities, as defined by Amartya Sen, but it has consistently lacked any clear social goals. Therefore, I examine the progressive education tradition for instructional methods that prepare students to actively change society. I argue that these progressive educational methods can be tied to a concrete social agenda promoting a long and happy life. I also provide specific examples of lessons that combine progressive methods with the goal of a long and happy life.

Usually considered as originating in the work of John Dewey, progressive curricula, as I have described in other volumes, spread around the world as a result Dewey's visits to China in the 1920s, the use of progressive methods in the Soviet Union, the influence of Leo Tolstoy on the educational work of Mohandas Ghandi in South Africa, the international recognition of the educational work at the Summerhill school in England, the educational ideas and influence of Mao Zedong, and most recently, the global influence of Brazilian educator Paulo Freire.[18]

For this discussion, I focus on only certain aspects of the progressive tradition—a complete analysis is beyond the scope of this book—that need to be considered in developing a curriculum that supports happiness and a long life. The lack of concrete social goals I consider to be a severe limitation to the progressive movement. Early in the progressive education movement, John Dewey urged that students be prepared so they could actively participate in the continual reconstruction of society without ever specifying what that society should look like except that it be should organized so as to allow everyone to participate in its continual reconstruction. Recently, Paulo Freire called for the liberation of consciousness without any concrete examples of a liberated society. In fairness to Dewey and Freire, it should be acknowledged that they did not want to provide a social blueprint for the future, but hoped that the "good" society would result from democratic participation in social change (Dewey) or the work of a liberated consciousness promoting the liberation of others (Freire).

In *My Pedagogic Creed,* Dewey's famous 1897 declaration, he devotes the last part, Article V, to The School and Social Progress. Consistent with his writings throughout his career, Dewey argues in the Creed that education can lead to a controlled form of social progress in which, during the process of reconstruction, social goals will be established. It is important to note that Dewey wanted to bring social progress under human control rather than leave it to the "haphazard" struggle for existence. In calling education the community's "paramount moral duty," Dewey contrast two forms of social change, one based on uncontrolled developments and the other on an education that prepared people to control social change. Dewey wrote: "By law and punishment, by social agitation and discussion, society can regulate and form itself in a more or less haphazard and chance way." In contrast, Dewey continued: "But through education society can formulate its own purposes, can organize its own means of resources, and thus shape itself with definiteness and economy in the direction in which it wishes to move."[19]

Similar to Dewey, Paulo Freire later thought of education as a method for giving people the tools to define their own goals for society. Freire's method attempts to raise people's consciousness about the factors that shape personal and human history. This consciousness raising is to result in people demanding liberation and the liberation of others to construct the "good" society. Freire defined two stages in his educational process leading from personal liberation to working for an undefined liberated society. "In the first [stage]," Freire asserted, "the oppressed unveil the world of oppression and through praxis commit themselves to its transformation."[20] His educational method, similar to Dewey's, would prepare the student: "In the second stage, in which the reality of oppression has already been transformed, this pedagogy ceases to belong to the oppressed and becomes a pedagogy of all men in the process of permanent liberation. In both stages, it is always through action in depth that the culture of domination is culturally confronted."[21] Whereas Dewey's students were to be guided by the principles of science, Freire's students were to be guided by the emotion of love to liberate people. Freire proclaimed: "I am more and more convinced that true revolutionaries must perceive the revolution, because of its creative and liberating nature, as an act of love"[22] Furthermore, he asserted: "Dialogue cannot exist, however, in the absence of a profound love for the world and for men. The naming of the world, which is an act of creation and recreation, is not possible if it is not infused in love."[23]

Freire never described this future world of love because, "in a dialectic ... the future evolves from the transformation of the present as it occurs. Thus, the future takes on a problematic and undetermined character. The future is not what it needs to be, but whatever we make of it in the present."[24]

On the one hand, the progressive tradition cannot be faulted for not specifying the details of the future society. Not defining the future seems sensible if it is assumed that humanity at this stage of development has not discovered the ideal social, political, or economic organization that would support a "just" society.

On the other hand, progressive education results in a vacuum of ideas for directing social change. It can legitimately be asked, "Social reconstruction for what?" and "Liberation for what?" Because of this lack of specific social goals, Deweyan forms of progressive education can simply drift from topic to topic according to student interest with the teacher acting as guide. Whereas the progressive teacher might guide students to attain deeper levels of social understanding as a topic is examined, progressive education principles do not give the teacher any specific social purpose other than to create a society that allows for this type of social analysis. Therefore, although progressive education provides important instructional models for helping students understand how they might change society, I believe that the goals of a long and happy life will provide students with a more concrete agenda for social change.

HAPPINESS AND LONGEVITY AS A CURRICULUM GOAL FOR PROGRESSIVE EDUCATION

I am interested in adapting progressive educational models to a curriculum designed to promote a long life and happiness. My example for how this might be done is taken from John Dewey's famous The School and Society lectures delivered in 1899 to explain the work of his laboratory school. Dewey's lectures described a lesson that exemplifies how students can learn that knowledge and institutions are products of social activity. The lesson explores the historic occupations of humans, which according to Dewey, provide "the point of departure from which the child can trace and follow the progress of mankind in history, getting an insight also into the materials used and principles involved. In connection with these occupations, the historic development of man is recapitulated."[25] In the lesson, children are given raw cotton and wool to spin and make into cloth. Students study the raw material, the agricultural conditions needed to produce the material, the historic development of machinery to make cloth, and the social consequences of these developments. These activities raise the children's awareness of how human actions can change living conditions. Dewey made a clear distinction between his lesson and schooling based on a human capital model:

> In educational terms, this means that these occupations in the school shall not be mere practical devices or modes of routine employment, the gaining of better technical skill as cooks, seamstresses, or carpenters, but active centers of scientific insight into natural materials and processes, points of departure whence *children shall be led out into a realization of the historic development of man* [my emphasis].[26]

Dewey declared geography to include the "unity of all sciences."[27] Dewey's conceptualization of geography was similar to what would later be called the biosphere, which represents the interrelationship of all environmental factors. In words that sounded similar to those of later environmental educators, Dewey asserted: "The significance of geography is that it presents the earth as the enduring home of the occupations of man… . The earth is the final source of all man's food. It is his continual shelter and protection, the raw material of all his activities, and the home to whose humanizing and idealizing all his achievement returns."[28] Unaware of the environmental damage that would be caused by the march of progress, Dewey lauded the earth for supplying the raw materials of industrial growth and declared:

> It is through occupations determined by this environment that mankind has made its historical and political progress. It is through these occupations that the intellectual and emotional interpretation of nature has been developed. It is through what we do in and with the world that we read its meaning and measure its value.[29]

The problem with Dewey's lesson and, as I suggested, with most progressive education is that no standards were used to measure the value of human occupations and progress. The student might leave the lesson with an understanding of how human occupations change, but would be without standards by which to judge those changes. For instance, military occupations play a major role in human history. Does a student simply study the evolution of military organization, methods, and technology for the purpose of improving them? Are there any standards by which the student can judge the value to humans of military jobs? Are there any standards for measuring the impact of military activities on the environment? Of course, Dewey, imbued with the industrial spirit of the 19th century and a faith in evolution, assumed that progress or the evolution of human species would inevitably be in a positive direction if brought under human control rather than left to haphazard circumstances. The goal for Dewey was simply to put humans in control of the evolutionary process.

Consider how Dewey's lesson in occupations could be adapted to the curriculum guidelines presented in chapter 2. These guidelines include "the knowledge and skills to maximize physical and mental health for living a long and happy life" and "the knowledge and skills needed to maximize a person's capabilities to choose a life he or she values." Importantly, because of Dewey's goal to prepare students to reconstruct society, the following guideline is given:

> The curriculum should contain the knowledge and skills, including knowledge about research on the causal factors influencing longevity and subjective well-being, so that school graduates will be able to actively ensure that environmental, social, political, and economic conditions promote a long and happy life for themselves and all other people.

Under these guidelines, the study of occupations used by Dewey in the Laboratory School takes on a different meaning without undermining Dewey's purpose of students gaining an understanding about how humans construct their social world. For instance, students would be asked to judge historical changes in occupations and the resulting changes in economic and social structures according to their contribution to human happiness and longevity. Using these standards, military occupations would be judged according to their potential destructiveness to subjective well-being and life. The transition from the production of cloth in the home to textile industries would be considered according to the same standards. Did this transition in methods of production increase the happiness and life span of workers and consumers? In response, students might think about the mixed blessings of industrial change in relationship to a person's position in society.

Judgments based on the standards of happiness and longevity also would affect Dewey's contention that geography represented "the unity of all sciences" with "the earth as the enduring home of the occupations of man."

How and why humans use the earth would be judged according to its enhancement of human life. Students might be asked to explore this question: As a result of industrial development, what changes in the biosphere improved or reduced the happiness and life spans of humans?

A similar approach could be taken with Paulo Freire's dialogical methods. As participants unpacked the causal determinants of their current circumstances, they could be called upon to think about the consequences of these causes to the quality of their lives. Rather than simply participating and aiding the effort to raise consciousness about students' lives, the instructor also would be asking questions about the value of the factors that determined their lives to their subjective well-being and life span. In this context, the teacher would be participating in a revolution of love and liberation with the goal of people living long and happy lives.

Guided by judgments about what contributes to subjective well-being and longevity, Dewey's declaration that geography represents "the unity of all sciences" and his proposal that human occupations be studied provides a means for increasing the capability of students to choose a life that they value. It also provides an escape from the factory-like curriculum of human capital schooling, in which subjects are divided into boxlike categories that fit neatly into age-graded classrooms. Breaking with this factory tradition, learning becomes integrated into a whole such that in the study of occupations, students learn reading, writing, political math, politically oriented science, history, economics, and literature as part of a single learning experience. From the standpoint of environmental education, students learn to think about the effect of human activity, in this case, occupations or work, on the biosphere. The study causes that human subjective well-being and longevity to be integrated into this unitary curriculum. Consider Dewey's use of the study of occupations as the possible center of a unitary curriculum. If students are to make judgments about the effect of changes in work on the quality of life, then part of their studies must be devoted to the causes of subjective well-being and a long life.

INCREASING CAPABILITIES AND THE PROGRESSIVE TRADITION

The progressive tradition as represented by Dewey and Freire has made an important contribution to increasing capabilities or the ability to choose a life that a person values. As previously discussed, increasing capabilities has a positive effect on longevity and subjective well-being. The progressive tradition increases capabilities by preparing students to understand that human social interactions create new knowledge and institutions, and that people have the power to bring about social change. From Dewey to Paulo

Freire, the heart of the progressive tradition is teaching students that they can be the subjects of history as opposed to mere objects of history. As subjects of history, they can change the course of human events by consciously making choices. As objects of history, they are merely pushed along by history without being aware that human history is determined by human interaction and that they have the inherent ability to participate consciously in making history.

Student capabilities are increased by making them aware of the social construction of knowledge and institutions and their ability to influence social change. In The Child and the Curriculum, another lecture given at the Laboratory School in 1902, Dewey argued that a major division in approaches to the curriculum was between those who focused on the subject matter of the curriculum and those who focused on the development of the child. Dewey offered a third approach whereby the subject matter is integrated into the experience and interests of the child. Whereas the scientist might treat subject matter as a given body of truth, the teacher, Dewey argued, "is concerned with the subject matter of the science *as representing a given stage and phase of the development of experience.* His [the teacher's] problem is that of inducing a vital and personal experiencing."[30] Paulo Freire provided a similar argument by using thematic representations of the participants' experiences, such as photos and audiotapes, to initiate a dialogue about the world of the participants. It was from these dialogues that participants were to move in their thinking from a passive acceptance of their immediate world to an understanding of how social, political, and economic forces determined their lives and how they could liberate themselves by acting to change their world.

By relating the subject matter to the experiences and interests of the child, Dewey hoped children would attain an understanding concerning the ability of humans to influence the course of history or, in other words, the social reconstruction of society. For instance, Dewey describes a lesson in which children imagine that the current world disappears and they are left dependent on subsistence hunting and fishing. The child then is asked to imagine the progress of human civilization. Reaching the iron age in this imaginative lesson, the children construct a smelter out of clay, which provides them with the opportunity to study mineralogy and the principles of combustion. Imagining changes in the earth's landscape and searching to find minerals for the smelter provides a geography lesson. In Dewey's words, the students make a greater "acquaintance with facts of science, geography, and anthropology than they get where information is the professed end and object."[31] Most importantly, Dewey stated about the lesson:

> Thus they gained ideas of the various forms of the configuration of the earth, and at the same time have seen them in their relation to human activity, so

> that they are not simply external facts, but are fused and welded with social conceptions regarding the life and progress of humanity.[32]

I would add to this lesson concerns about whether historic changes increased longevity and happiness or decreased it. To accomplish this goal, students could make a list of historic changes as people evolved from hunter and gatherers to the iron age. This would give another dimension to learning in the discovery that humans through interaction with the environment influenced the conditions under which they lived. Instead of a neutral study without judgments positively or negatively about changes in human circumstances, the student would be asked to think about these changes according to certain standards. These judgments would help the student to understand that he or she can influence changes in social and economic circumstances that benefit human happiness and longevity.

HUMAN RIGHTS AND SUBJECTIVE WELL-BEING: GLOBAL CORE CURRICULUM FOR YOUNG CHILDREN

Unlike the progressive tradition as represented by John Dewey and Paulo Freire, human rights and environmental educators use progressive methods to push their political agendas. They also, like Dewey and Freire, dissent from the dominant human capital curriculum. For instance, consider a human rights lesson on needs and wants for students about the age of 6 years. The purpose of the lesson is for students to begin thinking about human rights in providing the necessary conditions for survival.

The reader should be cautioned that using a lesson from human rights education does not necessarily mean support of the Universal Declaration of Human Rights or other human rights documents. The acceptance or rejection of these documents should be decided by the students. However, international agreements do proclaim the protection of life as the central purpose in protecting human rights. The 1948 United Nations' Universal Declaration of Human Rights declares in Article 3: "Everyone has the right to life, liberty and security of person."[33] Article 3 includes some of the basic goals for a global core curriculum. Protection of life supports the goal of increased longevity. I do not discuss the controversial issue of abortion or when life begins, which is frequently discussed regarding Article 3. The right to liberty can be interpreted as the right to the capability of choosing that life a person values. And, as discussed in the preceding chapter, security is an essential component for increasing longevity and supporting subjective well-being.

The wants and needs lesson is derived from an exercise outlined by Betty Reardon called Wishing a World Fit for Children—Understanding Human Needs.[34] The purpose of Reardon's exercise is to have children reflect on their needs as a preparation for thinking about the needs of all humans. In the lesson, the children plan a surprise party for a newly born baby and prepare gifts wrapped in a wish. For gifts, the students are asked to draw pictures, make something of clay, or choose a single word that represents something the baby might need such as food, a bed, a desk, clothing, or any other thing the students think the baby might need for a healthy infancy and childhood. Wishes for the new baby are written on paper used to wrap the gifts. The teacher is encouraged to help students think of wishes that provide a secure and happy childhood such as "other children to play with," "good schools to go to," "peace in her country," and "jobs for parents."[35]

The teacher then leads a discussion on the gifts and wishes, and with the class creates a list of the Needs of a Child. The teacher then points out that many children in the world, including possibly those in the class, do not have these needs fulfilled. The next part of the lesson fulfills the standard given in chapter 2 for Guidelines for a Global Core Curriculum, which is to "create the emotional desire and ethical belief in school graduates that will cause them to actively help others live a long and happy life." Reardon proposes that the teacher help students understand that for children lacking fulfillment of needs required for a healthy and happy life by stating: "part of what we need to learn is how to change the world so all children can have these things [items on list of Needs of Child]."[36] Reardon then explains the ethical imperative that should result from education: "Going to school is supposed to help to learn how to make our wishes for a better world come true. If they do their best to learn, they will be helping to make a better world for the baby and for themselves."[37]

The final step in Reardon's lesson is extremely important for guiding student learning and setting students on a path to think about how they can create a world that supports long and happy human lives. This step also reinforces the ethical imperative to act to improve world conditions. Reardon proposes that students "look at the list of wishes for a better world and think about what we need to learn to make a better world."[38]

Besides helping students to think about human needs, instilling an ethical desire to improve world conditions, and sparking creative thought about how to improve human conditions, the lesson also provides a vehicle for imparting academic knowledge and skills. First, the children must practice writing, including spelling and sentence structure, in preparing their gifts and wishes. Second, they must learn about physiology, nutrition, and disease in considering the needs of the newborn baby; this would be a lesson in human biology. Third, the students must learn geography including economic and environmental conditions affecting human life. Teachers must play an active role in supplying and helping students find information. Reardon poses a series of questions that students must answer to create a list of Needs of a Child and to consider situations in which children are deprived of their basic needs. The answers to these questions touch upon a variety of academic subjects and add a multicultural dimension to the lesson.

How does a baby grow? Ask the students to tell stories of how the baby is cared for and grows up to be seven years old.

- In what part of the world does the child live? Point it out on the globe.
- What food does the child eat?
- In what kind of home does the child live?
- What games do children play in that part of the world?
- How is the life of the child the same or different from their own lives?[39]

A variation of Reardon's lesson is to ask students to prepare a list of things that they believe they need to live. The students may list items not directly related to survival, but what they believe are necessary for living, such as sports, games, friends, parents, and the like. The students then are asked to divide their lists into two lists, with one list containing items they believe are absolutely needed for survival and the other list containing things that might aid in survival. The list of necessities for survival might include food, water, shelter, and air, which students could examine for the role they play in maintaining the human body. As in the lesson on newborn infants, the teacher points out places on a world map where people might be struggling to obtain the aforementioned life necessities including clean air and water. An examination of the list of necessities for survival opens the door to lessons on biology, geography, and environmentalism. It also causes students at an early age to think about social, political, and economic conditions that might cause famine and deny people access to shelter, clean air, and water. As in the lesson on children's needs, the students are asked to look at the list of necessities for survival and to think about what they need to learn to change the world so that all humans have the things needed to survive.

The second list of items, which includes the things students believe they need, introduces the idea that psychological and social factors play an important part in maintaining life. For instance, sports provide recreation needed to maintain the body and make people feel better; friends provide a support group and they are a source of recreation; and parents provide love and guidance. This discussion would prepare students when they are older to examine research on the social, economic, political, and mental conditions that support longevity.

A similar lesson might ask students to make lists of what makes them happy and what makes them sad. Besides listing emotional situations that make them happy or unhappy, such as parental love or scolding and friendship or loss of friendships, the children likely would list the acquisition or loss of consumer items such as games, dolls, or other toys. The children might also list items related to survival such as a good meal or hunger. The class should discuss their lists and create for the whole class two master lists of the top five things that make class members happy or sad. The students then should be asked what they need to learn to change the world so that all humans might be happy.

An obvious goal of the preceding three lessons is to cause children to think about the conditions for a long and happy life, and how the world might be changed to maximize the opportunity for all people to experience these conditions. This exploration provides an opportunity for students to learn about health, biology, environmental science, reading, arithmetic, writing, and geography. As a culminating experience to these lessons, the students could be asked to combine the class lists of necessities for survival, items that help people survive, and conditions that make people happy. This combined list could serve as the class's goals for working to create a better world.

ENVIRONMENTAL EDUCATION AND CAPABILITIES

Protection of the biosphere is an important aspect of promoting longevity and subjective well-being. Dewey's lesson on the evolution of humans from hunters and gatherers to the iron age and the building and use of a smelter exemplifies how issues regarding the environment can be integrated into school lessons. Dewey was primarily concerned about the social and economic development of humans. However, one could add to his lesson a study investigating the impact of humans on the environment. This integrating theme and holistic approach would place human development in the context of the biosphere. For instance, the development of smelters changed not only human activity, but also the surrounding environment through the mining of minerals and the creation of better weapons for hunting. To enhance capabilities and prepare children for active participation in creating a society that maximizes human life and happiness, children need to be taught about the unity of biosphere and the interconnecting effect of all elements of the biosphere, including living organisms, earth, air, and water. In this way, children can understand how their actions can effect the interrelated pieces of the environment.

The environmental education program at the Beancross Primary School in Grangemouth, Scotland, provides a very concrete approach to helping students understand the place of humans in the biosphere. I use the term "concrete" because Dewey's historical lesson depended on students imagining the evolution of humans. Teachers at Beancross use the school and surrounding community as the focus of their lessons. Working cooperatively, students, staff, and community members planned a series of play areas and gardens as part of the school's landscape. The students participated in and experienced actual changes in the school's environment. A time line was created to catalogue these changes. Also, the students participated in the maintenance of the gardens and play areas. Moira Laing, a lecturer in primary education at Scotland's University of Strathclyde, writes about the school's landscaping program: "Such networking of the school and its community has paid dividends in creating an outdoor classroom where the pupils can learn about the living environment and enjoy experiences that develop their sensitivity to the environment, the first essential step toward developing a custodial concern for the environment."[40] Importantly, the Beancross school relates its environmental education program to issues of human health, which is an important part of preparing students to protect human life. The school staff considers health education to be an extension of its environmental program.

By having students actively participate in the planning and maintenance of the playgrounds and gardens, staff members believe they are preparing them to continue protecting the environment after graduation. Central to the discussion of environmental issues, the students are asked:

- What could I do to change things for the better?
- What are the difficulties/barriers to changing things?
- What is the workable range of possibilities?

Finally, students are asked to complete this statement: "I have decided to take this action, ..."[41]

Dewey's lesson and the Beancross Primary School landscaping project exemplify a holistic approach to environmental education—holistic in this case meaning the integration of traditional subject matter into single lessons on the environment. These approaches can stimulate students to think about how they might improve the environment and how they can act to create a world in which they want to live. Other examples can be found in educational programs associated with the Earth Charter.

THE EARTH CHARTER

The Earth Charter sparked educational activities that also can be considered for a curriculum promoting subjective well-being. Since its 2000 promulgation from the Peace Palace in The Hague, the Earth Charter has influenced many environmental educators. Moacir Gadotti, the Director of Brazil's Paulo Freire Institute, advocates planetary citizenship, with the Earth

Charter serving as an ethical guide. He asserts: "The Earth Charter ... [provides] a universal code of ethics and it should lend an important contribution, not only by its proclamation through Member states, but especially through the impact that its principles may have on the daily life of a planetary citizen."[42] Although the Earth Charter does not specifically focus on human life span and happiness, it does deal directly with related issues. The Earth Charter contains the following plea for a global responsibility and ethic to maintain the biosphere similar to my call for an ethic that leads to active protection of the lives and happiness of humans.

Ethical Statement from the Earth Charter

Universal Responsibility
To realize these aspirations, we must decide to live with a sense of universal responsibility, identifying ourselves with the whole Earth community as well as our local communities. We are at once citizens of different nations and of one world in which the local and global are linked. Everyone shares responsibility for the present and future well-being of the human family and the larger living world. The spirit of human solidarity and kinship with all life is strengthened when we live with reverence for the mystery of being, gratitude for the gift of life, and humility regarding the human place in nature.[43]

The following list describes other principles from the Earth Charter that are important for a global core curriculum. Earth Charter principles are necessary for a long and happy life because they are concerned with the possible death of the biosphere and the resulting extinction of human life. The Charter's Preamble warns: "We stand at a critical moment in Earth's history, a time when humanity must choose its future. As the world becomes increasingly interdependent and fragile, the future at once holds great peril and great promise."[44]

While recognizing the overall importance of the Earth Charter to human survival, I have extracted these pertinent principles for my global curriculum:

Curriculum Principles from the Earth Charter

1. Ensure universal access to health care that fosters reproductive health and responsible reproduction.
2. Adopt lifestyles that emphasize quality of life and material sufficiency in a finite world.
3. Promote the equitable distribution of wealth within and among nations.
4. Uphold the right of everyone to receive clear and timely information on environmental matters and all development plans and activities that are likely to affect them or in which they have an interest.

5. Provide all, especially children and youth, with educational opportunities that empower them to contribute actively to sustainable development.
6. Promote the contribution of the arts and humanities as well as the sciences to sustainability education.
7. Demilitarize national security systems to the level of a nonprovocative defense posture, and convert military resources to peaceful purposes, including ecological restoration.[45]

There likely will be some religious reaction to the first principle concerning "responsible reproduction" because of implications for the use birth control methods. However, the effect of human reproduction, particularly the spiraling increase in the world's population, does have an impact on environmental issues ranging from the availability of natural resources to the handling of human waste. Students should be encouraged to think about the environmental impact from the size of the human population and what, if necessary, should be done to control population growth. Also, students should consider what lifestyles are protective of the biosphere and contribute to human happiness and longevity. The third principle in the list is important because of the previously discussed impact of inequality on longevity and subjective well-being. The fourth principle also is important because it is essential for any citizen, student, or educational worker to have timely access to information on environment matters. The fifth principle listed supports the teaching of an ethical responsibility to protect human life and happiness, and the sixth principle reflects the holistic approach to knowledge discussed throughout this chapter. And, of course, war, the subject of the last principle, is the most destructive human activity to affect life spans and happiness.

LESSONS FROM THE EARTH CHARTER

Since the issuance of the Earth Charter, there have been a number of educational proposals for achieving its goals. These proposals provide another set of lessons to be considered in organizing a global curriculum. Similar to other environmental and human rights lessons, these proposals support the idea of a holistic approach to learning. For instance, the sixth principle in the preceding list is embodied in a lesson by Brendan Mackey of the Earth Charter International Secretariat. Mackey's lesson is important because it uses aesthetic education, which is one of the subjects in the current global human capital curriculum. After restating the Earth Charter's call to use the arts and humanities in education for sustainability, Mackey asserts at the beginning of his lesson:

> The creative arts, like all other areas of learning, have a contribution to make in addressing our global environmental and social problems.
>
> With the creative arts you can express your interest in, and concern for, the environment in ways that engage the heart as well as the head, emotion as well as intellect. Many of the things we value about a place cannot be measured by science but can find expression in art—for example, the spiritual inspiration and renewal many people experience in a wild landscape or in a sacred site like a Mosque or a Cathedral.[46]

Using an approach similar to that for most progressive education, Mackey proposes that the lesson begin with a place familiar to the learner that "may currently, or in the future, be under threat—from local council development plans, pollution or even deforestation."[47] The students are asked to find a place that is special to them, and to consider any possible current or future environmental threats to that place. The student is asked to create an artwork, in the form of music, painting, dance, or sculpture, that expresses the personal value of the place and any possible environmental threats. Then the student is asked to think of earth as a special place, and to create an artwork that expresses positive feelings about earth. This lesson does force the student to think about environmental problems while heightening emotional attachments to nature.

Regarding ethical development, Mackey suggests teaching students to write so that the behavior of others is changed. In Mackey's lesson, students are asked to study documents that have inspired and motivated people to action, including the Earth Charter. The student is asked to write a persuasive essay, poem, short story, play, or speech supporting the Earth Charter. For my purposes, I would modify the lesson so that the goal is for the student to produce a written document that would persuade people that they had an ethical responsibility to protect the life and happiness of others. I think this is an important political approach to the teaching of writing that forces students to examine their own values and produce a document designed to change society. This could be called politically oriented rhetoric.

Mackey proposes a combined politically oriented science, economics, and arithmetic lessons that, similar to Dewey's lesson, requires students to think about the evolution of human life, changes in human occupations, and changes in the environment. The important thing about Mackey's lesson is that it integrates the learning of science and math with social issues, and it provides a good example of political arithmetic and politically oriented science. In an excellent example of political arithmetic, Macky's lesson has students comparing national rates of per capita consumption of energy and natural resources, pollution levels, and percentage of land cleared for development. Then students are asked to determine the amount of energy consumed by their class, school, and families, and to calculate the cost in national monetary units such as in pesos, euros, or dollars. The student also is directed as follows: "Think about all the things that a forest ecosystem is valued for. Which of these values cannot be measured in dollar terms?"[48] The student might also be asked a similar question about a human life. A final example of Mackey's work is a lesson entitled Technology/Social Studies. He directs the student as follows: "Imagine a world where the atmosphere no longer existed, and all humans lived under domed cities—a world where there were no wild populations of plants and animals. Is this kind of world for humans technologically possible? Is this kind of world one we would want to live in?"[49]

Some of the lessons associated with the Earth Charter involve students in planning social change. For instance, Brazil's Instituto Pedra Grande de Preservaçao's Implementing a Program for Environmental Education provides an example of an activist student project. This type of student involvement in social change may foster a lifetime of working for the improvement of human life:

> In 2001, for example, a school produced a big document with designs, texts, and many signatures, demanding more care for the river that bathes the city of Atibaia and the building of a station for the treatment of sewers. They denounced the existence of dead fish with black spots in their bodies. A school committee was formed with a representative of each grade (1–8), which delivered a copy of this document to the Secretary of Environment and to the Superintendent of Environmental Sanitation. This action had great repercussion [sic] and was seen by the media as "a legitimate action pressure to the public power executed by a school community in search of a solution for collective problems."[50]

Student activism regarding the city of Atibaia's river, dead fish, and needed sewage plant highlights the importance of environmental education for human health. Health issues are central to concerns about a long life and happiness. At the Modern Educational Institute, a preschool and primary education institution in Costa Rica, the Earth Charter is made part of the health education program. The school is devoted to a "vision of building a more participatory and just world, as strategy to obtain peace and human sustainable development."[51] The principles of the Earth Charter are incorporated into the school's science program, making it politically oriented science: "The Science Program ... focuses its analysis in the scientific study of the energy sources and promotes the analysis of the rational use of those sources. In this way, we have generated a program called Let's Be Converted Into the Guardians of the Universe."[52]

One might call the Modern Educational Institute's health program "political" health education. The school directly relates the Earth Charter to health education to instill a responsibility for the health of all other humans, particularly as related to environmental issues. School leaders state: "As part of the Health Education Program, the IEM [Modern Educational Institute] promotes activities related to the theme of Natural Disasters with the slogan 'the disasters are not natural', showing the participation of the human being in what causes them; for this particular item the Earth Charter offers excellent opportunity of analysis."[53]

The goal of happiness along with environmental health can be made part of a human rights and environmental education. Exemplifying an approach that combines human rights, environmentalism, and the teaching of a social activist ethic, Spain's Collegi Públic [Public School] Santa Maria del Mar involves 11-year-olds in Suggested Activities for Working With the Earth Charter. Under the theme Respect and Care of Living Things, students engage in activities with the aim of developing love and respect for people, plants, and animals. Two of the six weeks of activities under this theme encompass the idea of human happiness. The discussion in this part of the theme is focused on building an ethic that requires students to work for the happiness of others:

> You can act so that many people enjoy good and beautiful things

- Because you respect everything that lives
- Because you want happiness
- Because you are preparing a place for the children yet to be born.[54]

The associated activities for the first theme are limited to discussion and the display of objects related to human happiness. Also, relationships between cultures are made part of the conversation:

- Talk about the good things we can do for others and the bad things that we should not do.
- What things can we do to improve relations with people from other cultures, beginning with those we have closest to the school.
- We can maintain communication with people from other places.
- *Exhibit of objects that serve around the world for good, for happiness* [my emphasis].[55]

The school's second theme, In Life Everything Is Connected, teaches students about the interrelationships within the biosphere. The range of second theme activities includes field trips, student actions to protect the biosphere, exploring human rights, and making posters on protecting plants, animals, and cultures. In concluding the theme, the study guide emphasizes the importance of what I call "political' health": "At the end it is important to come to conclusions about what we, human beings, need, wherever we are, to live healthily."[56]

The next week is devoted to the theme Everybody Should Have What They Need, which is similar to the previously discussed human rights exercise devoted to needs and wants. The theme stresses the importance of children understanding the difference between needs and wants: "Promote work to change the attitudes of the children through dialogue: How many times do we ask our parents for things we don't need, what are our true needs and what others are superfluous and we can do without."[57] The lessons on this theme are directly related to my approach to a global core curriculum. For instance, the ethical imperative to help others be happy is specified as an item to be discussed:

> You must help so that everybody makes an effort to live better.

- The rich must help the poor.
- You should have only what you need.
- There will be peace and happiness and everybody will be happier.[58]

In summary, progressive, human rights, and environmental education provide important examples of lessons and curricula that can be used to develop a global core curriculum. These educational traditions represent the major countermovement to the continuing global domination of the human capital curriculum. Common to these educational approaches are lessons that integrate traditional subjects, a conception of the human as part of a biosphere, the development of an ethical responsibility to protect other humans, a belief in the right of humans to the necessary conditions to sustain life, increasing human capabilities, and the teaching of political arithmetic and politically oriented science. All these can be incorporated into a global core curriculum supporting longevity and subjective well-being.

A NEW PARADIGM FOR A GLOBAL CORE CURRICULUM

In the chapter 2, I developed guidelines for a new global curriculum. I conclude this discussion by providing a paradigm for a new global core curriculum based on the examples analyzed in this chapter. In this new paradigm, I integrate learning subjects serving the global human capital curriculum, namely, language, arithmetic, science, social sciences, aesthetic education, and physical education. In the human capital model, each of these are taught as separate subjects rather than as part of what we could call the classic progressive integrated or holistic curriculum. Similar to progressive, human rights, and environmental education, the proposed global core curriculum would emphasize an integrated curriculum designed to give students the tools to change the world.

The overarching framework for integration of the curriculum is the biosphere. I use the concept of the biosphere because it links human actions and knowledge to all aspects earthly living; the biosphere encompasses all global human activity. The concept of the biosphere was first articulated in Vladimir Vernadsky's 1926 book *The Biosphere*.[59] Vernadsky argued that traditional biologists studied living organisms as isolated creatures. He claimed:

> In most of their works studying living organisms, the biologists disregard the indissoluble connection between the surrounding milieu and the living organism. In studying the organism as something quite distinct from the environment, the cosmic milieu … they study not a natural body but a pure product of their thinking.[60]

In Vernadsky's concept of the biosphere, the conditions necessary for sustaining life include the interrelationships between solar radiation, the atmosphere, oceans, and the earth's surface. Important to his formulation of the biosphere is the effect of life on geology as part of the biosphere's interdependence. In the forward to the Russian edition of his book, he wrote, "Let us consider all empirical facts from the point of view of a *holistic mechanism* that combines all parts of the planet in an indivisible whole. Only then will we be able to perceive the perfect correspondence between this idea and the geological effects of life… . Included in the [holistic] mechanism is the biosphere, the domain of manifestation of life."[61]

I am placing humans and my concern for human longevity and subjective well-being at the center of the biosphere. In other words, I am focusing on the role of the human in the biosphere. My conceptualization might be termed a "human-centered" biosphere. I realize that in using the concept of a human-centered biosphere, I might be charged by animal rights activists with speciesism or discrimination against other species. Speciesism is a form of discrimination comparable with racial and gender discrimination among humans in which humans, to maximize their survival and power, discriminate against other species. In the Preface to the 1975 edition of *Animal Liberation*, Singer writes:

> This book is about the tyranny of human over nonhuman animals. This tyranny has caused and today is still causing an amount of pain and suffering that can only be compared with that which resulted from the centuries of tyranny by white humans over black humans. The struggle against this tyranny is a struggle as important as any of the moral and social issues that have been fought over in recent years.[62]

In rejecting Singer's concept of speciesism, I am openly committing myself to the protection of humans within the framework of the biosphere.

However, I do accept the commitment of animal rights activists to reducing the pain and suffering of other living species.

In a human-centered biosphere, students would think about the interconnectedness of humans, the reciprocal effect of human actions on the biosphere, and the effect of the biosphere on human actions, particularly with regard to human longevity and happiness. Consequently, traditional environmental education is an important source for developing individual lessons within the proposed curriculum paradigm. However, the approach of environmental educators has certain limitations.

Although environmental education pioneered the idea of teaching about the consequences of human actions and knowledge to the biosphere, it has emphasized sustainability of resources for economic development. In the context of sustainability, environmental education simply provides another approach to human capital education, which ensures that there are enough natural resources to feed the industrial machine.[63] The 1992 United Nations Conference defined sustainable development as "development that meets the needs of the present without compromising the ability of future generations to meet their own needs."[64] Environmentalism taught in the framework of human capital economics is focused on the management and protection of natural resources for economic growth rather than on how the environment contributes to the long life and happiness of humans.

I am proposing that environmental education shift its focus from sustainability of the earth's resources to how the biosphere can protect human life and happiness. Of course, sustainability of natural resources remains a concern, but not for reasons of economic growth. In my framework, protection of the environment is conceived as a means for protecting human longevity and subjective well-being. This definition of environmental education provides a justification for an important aspect of what environmentalists call "deep ecology." Deep ecology emphasizes the important psychological and aesthetic relationship of humans to the biosphere, such as human appreciation and joy gained from hearing birdsongs or viewing mountains, waves, clouds, sunsets, flowers, animals, and waterfalls. Humans have always gained a great deal of happiness, inspiration, and fulfillment through contact with their environment.[65]

The problem with environmental education that focuses on sustainability is that it might neglect the happiness gained by humans from interacting with nature. From the standpoint of sustainable development, the destruction of a mountain for its resources or the damming of a river would be evaluated according to how these actions affect the sustainability of resources for the future. From the perspective of deep ecology, these actions would also be evaluated according to how they might enhance or reduce human pleasure. An advocate of ecopedagogy and an active supporter of the Earth Charter, Moacir Gadotti, the head of Instituto Paulo Freire, states, "We don't learn to love Earth by reading books on this subject, nor books on integral ecology. Our own experience is what counts."[66]

Whereas Freire celebrated the liberation of consciousness, Gadotti rhapsodizes about human connections with the environment. "To plant and live through the growth of a tree or a plant," he states in reference to the importance of experience for learning, "walking the city streets, or venturing into a forest, feeling the birds' chirping on sunny mornings, or … watching how the wind sways the plants, feeling the warm sands of our beaches gazing at the stars on a dark night … pollution and environmental defacement … should remind us that we are able to destroy this wonder, and also to create our ecological awareness and move us to take action."[67]

Therefore, the overarching framework for the paradigm I am proposing would be a human-centered biosphere in which the concern centers on promoting human happiness and longevity. This new global educational paradigm would have as a goal to teach students to think about human actions and knowledge as part of the biosphere. Within the framework of the biosphere, student concerns, thinking, and actions would be directed to the improvement of human longevity and happiness. Traditional global subjects would be taught not as discrete subjects, but as interrelated forms of knowledge that are part of the interplay between humans and the biosphere. An important goal of this holistic instruction would be to provide students with the tools to fulfill their ethical responsibilities to protect the quality of human life.

Also, the proposed paradigm would be concerned with student happiness. In other words, the goal of providing students with the tools to fulfill their ethical responsibilities would have to include educational practices that promoted student subjective well-being. In addition, I do not want to teach students that knowledge is instrumental only for solving human problems. I believe that study and thinking is a source of human joy. In chapter 1, I discuss the importance of flow or optimal experience as a source of human pleasure in learning and creating. Currently, the global human capital curriculum emphasizes knowledge as instrumental for economic growth. Besides the instrumental nature of knowledge, scholarship and creativity, as we know from optimal experience studies, can be a source of personal happiness.

Therefore, both the instrumental and personal happiness aspects of learning should be emphasized. Language (reading and writing), the major subject in the existing global curriculum, would be an important tool for understanding the human-centered biosphere and a direct source of student pleasure. As discussed in chapter 1, reading is the major source of flow for humans, and therefore should be taught in a manner that optimizes the flow experience. Children should gain pleasure from reading. Within the proposed paradigm, reading also would be taught as a tool for understanding existing human knowledge. Writing should be taught as both political writing and writing for pleasure or flow. By political writing,

I mean that students should be taught to write to persuade others to act to protect the happiness and lives of others.

The teaching of other parts of the existing global curriculum in an integrated manner involves the same combination of concerns about students having an optimal learning experience, learning in the framework of a human-centered biosphere, and gaining the tools for promoting long life and happiness. For instance, arithmetic would be taught as political arithmetic and with a desire to provide optimal learning experiences. The teaching of political arithmetic would combine the use of arithmetic to understand social, political, and economic issues, to persuade others that action is needed to solve human problems, and to experience flow. Politically oriented science would be a means for understanding the biosphere, identifying and solving problems affecting human longevity and happiness, and providing students with optimal learning experiences. Taught as part of a holistic curriculum, the social sciences would focus on the problems and solutions related to conditions that hurt or harm human progress to happiness and a long life, and would use problem solving to help students experience optimal learning experiences. Aesthetic education is a major source of flow. Aesthetic education, as discussed in this chapter, also can be a means for students to use in describing and deconstructing conditions affecting the quality of human life. The use of imagination in aesthetic education can help students to envision a better world. Finally, as part of the current global curriculum, physical education provides flow through recreational activities and through health instruction knowledge for increasing the human life span.

In summary, I am proposing a new global curriculum paradigm based on my analysis of the existing global human capital curriculum and alternative proposals by progressive, human rights, and environmental educators. This following list describes this paradigm.

Paradigm for a Global Core Curriculum

1. The overarching framework for learning would be a human-centered biosphere.
2. The focus of learning would be on how the biosphere can promote human happiness and longevity.
3. As part of the concern with human happiness, learning would be organized to achieve optimal experiences or flow for students.
4. The traditional subjects of the human capital curriculum along with environmental and human rights education would be integrated in holistic lessons that would
    a. Teach students the political, social, and economic conditions that have decreased and increased human life spans and subjective well-being

b. Require the use of problem-solving methods, including the use of imagination, to create conditions that promote a long life and happiness
c. Give students the tools to change the world
d. Develop the ethical responsibility needed to protect the happiness and lives of others.

CONCLUSION: EXPANDING ON THE GLOBAL CORE CURRICULUM

In the next chapter, I discuss cultural differences in ways of knowing that will have an important impact on how my paradigm for a global core curriculum is interpreted at the local level. In chapters 5 and 6, I give substance to the paradigm by providing prototypes for a global school and textbook. In chapter 5, I use subjective well-being and longevity research to suggest a prototype of a global school that will promote the well-being of the school staff, the students, the community, and, of course, the environment. The prototype for a global textbook described in chapter 6 expands on the paradigm for a global curriculum by providing an organizational structure for its goals and model lessons.

NOTES

1 David H. Kamens and Yun–Kyung, "The Formation of New Subjects in Mass Schooling: Nineteenth Century Origins and Twentieth Century Diffusion of Art and Physical Education," in *School Knowledge for the Masses: World Models and National Primary Curricular Categories in the Twentieth Century* edited by John W. Meyer, David H. Kamens, and Aaron Benavot (Washington, D.C.: The Falmer Press, 1992), p. 153.

2 David Kamens and Aaron Benavot ..., p. 109.

3 For a study of these social goals for science, see Joel Spring, *Educating the Consumer– Citizen: A History of the Marriage of Schools, Advertising, and Media* (Mahwah, New Jersey: Lawrence Erlbaum Associates, 2003), pp. 28–62.

4 For a history of this nuclear and environmentally concerned education, see Joel Spring, *The American School: 1642–2004 Sixth Edition* (New York: McGraw–Hill, 2005), pp. 375-402, 441–472.

5 Ibid., p. 156.

6 See Joel Spring, *Pedagogies of Globalization: The Rise of the Educational Security State* (Mahwah: Lawrence Erlbaum Associates, 2006) for a study of the global spread of human capital and progressive models of schooling.

7 Aaron Benavot, Yun–Kyung Cha, David Kamens, John Meyer, and Suk–Ying Wong, "Knowledge for the Masses: World Models and National Curricula, 1920–1986," *American Sociological Review* (February, 1991), pp. 86, 92.

8 Yun–Kyung Cha, "Effect of the Global system on Language Instruction, 1850–1986," Sociology of Education, (January, 1991), p. 20. Also see Un–Kyung Cha, "Language Instruction in National Curricula, 1850–1986: The Effect of the Global System," in School Knowledge for the Masses ... pp. 84–100.

9 See Spring, *Pedagogies of Globalization* …
10 Sam Dillon, "College Aid Plan Widens U.S. Role in High Schools (January 22, 2006)," *New York Times on the Web*. Retrieved from http://www.nytimes.com/on January 22, 2006.
11 David H. Kamens and Aaron Benavot, "A Comparative and Historical Analysis of Mathematics and Science Curricula, 1800–1986," in *School Knowledge for the Masses* … p. 116.
12 Suk–Ying Wong, "The Evolution and Organization of the Social Science Curriculum," in *School Knowledge for the Masses* … p. 125.
13 Ibid., p. 124.
14 Ibid., pp. 133.
15 Ibid., see Table 9.2 on p. 131.
16 Yun-Kyung, Suk-Ying and Meyer … p. 163.
17 I develop this argument in Spring, *Pedagogies of Globalization* ….
18 For a study on the global spread of the progressive educational ideas, see Joel Spring, *Pedagogies of Globalization: The Rise of the Educational Security State* (Mahwah, New Jersey: Lawrence Erlbaum Associates, 2006), and for a broader discussion of progressive traditions, see Joel Spring, *Wheels in the Head: Educational Philosophies of Authority, Freedom, and Culture From Socrates to Human Rights* (New York: McGraw-Hill, 1999).
19 John Dewey, "My Pedagogic Creed" in *Dewey on Education Selections* edited by Martin S. Dworkin (New York: Teachers College Press, 1959), p. 31.
20 Paulo Freire, *Pedagogy of the Oppressed* (New York: Herder and Herder, 1970), p. 40.
21 Ibid., p. 40.
22 Freire, *Pedagogy of the Oppressed* … p. 77.
23 This quote is taken from footnote #4 of *Pedagogy of the Oppressed*, p. 77.
24 Paulo Freire, *Letters to Cristina: Reflections on My Life and Work* (New York: Routledge, 1996), p. 111.
25 John Dewey, "The School and Society," in *Dewey on Education Selections* … , p. 43.
26 Ibid., pp. 42–43.
27 Ibid., p. 42.
28 Ibid., p. 42.
29 Ibid., p. 42.
30 John Dewey, "The Child and the Curriculum," in *Dewey on Education Selections* … , p. 105.
31 Dewey, *The School and Society* …, p. 65.
32 Ibid., p. 65.
33 "Universal Declaration of Human Rights, 1948," in *Basic Documents on Human Rights, Third Edition* edited by Ian Brownlie (Oxford: Oxford University Press, 1992), p. 23
34 Betty A. Reardon, *Educating for Human Dignity: Learning About Rights and Responsibilities* (Philadelphia: University of Pennsylvania Press, 1995), pp. 33–35.
35 Ibid., p. 34.
36 Ibid., p. 35.
37 Ibid., p. 35.
38 Ibid., p. 35.
39 Ibid., pp. 34–35.
40 Moria Laing, "Taking Action for the Environment in Scotland," in *Environmental Education in the 21st Century: Theory, Practice, Progress and Promise* edited by Joy A. Palmer (New York: Falmer Press, 1998), p. 155.
41 Ibid., p. 157.
42 Moacir Gadotti, "Pedagogy of the Earth and Culture of Sustainability" (Sao Paulo, Brazil: Instituto Paulo Freire, Undated), p. 8.
43 "Earth Charter," http://www.earthcharter.org/. Retrieved on January 25, 2006.
44 Ibid.
45 Ibid.

46 Brendan Mackey, "Earth Charter Curriculum Stimulus Material: The Creative Arts," *http://www.earthcharter.org/files/resources/curriculum_stimulus_material.doc.* Retrieved on January 25, 2005.
47 Ibid.
48 Ibid.
49 Ibid.
50 Instituto Pedra Grande de Preservaçao, "Implementing a Program for Environmental Education" http://www.earthcharter.org/files/resources/Ciancas%20de%20Paz%-%20 English.doc. Retrieved on January 25, 2006.
51 Modern Educational Institute, "An Environmental Education Experience, Focused in Earth Charter Initiative," *http://www.earthcharter.org/files/resources/IEM%20english.doc.* Retrieved on January 26, 2006.
52 Ibid.
53 Ibid.
54 Spain's Collegi Públic [Public School] Santa Maria del Mar, "Suggested Activities for Working With the Earth Charter." http://www.earthcharter.org/files/resources/vivim%20plegats%20themes%20and%20suggestions.doc. Retrieved on January 28, 2006.
55 Ibid.
56 Ibid.
57 Ibid.
58 Ibid.
59 Lynton Keith Caldwell, *International Environmental Policy From the Twentieth to the Twenty-First Century: Third Edition* (Durham, North Carolina: Duke University Press, 1996), pp. 24–25.
60 Vladimir I. Vernadsky's *The Biosphere* (New York: Copernicus, Springer-Verlag, 1997), p. 30.
61 Vernadsky, p. 40.
62 Peter Singer, *Animal Liberation* (New York: HarperCollins Publisher, 2002), p. xx.
63 The idea of sustainable development was presented in the 1980 *World Conservation Strategy* report and became a central theme of the World Commission on Environment and Development. See Joy A. Palmer, *Environmental Education in the 21st Century: Theory, Practice, and Progress* (London: Routledge, 1998), p. 15.
64 National Council for Science and the Environment, "Education for a Sustainable and Secure Future," http://www.ncseonline.org/NCSEconference/2003conference/page.cfm? fid=2344. Retrieved on January 3, 2004.
65 For a good summary of Deep Ecology ideas, see Christopher Manes, *Green Rage: Radical Environmentalism and the Unmaking of Civilization* (Boston: Little, Brown and Company, 1990), pp. 139–151.
66 Moacir Gadotti, "Pedagogy of the Earth and Culture of Sustainability" (Sao Paulo, Brazil: Instituto Paulo Freire, Undated), p. 5.
67 Ibid., p. 5.

Chapter 4

Ways of Seeing and a Global Core Curriculum

School staff need to be sensitive to cultural differences in adapting the global core curriculum to local communities. People have different ways of seeing and understanding the world. In chapter 1, I discussed the differences between collectivist and individualist societies regarding subjective well-being. The intention of this chapter is to provide insight into holistic world views and views that divide the world into discrete parts. These views are respectively associated with collectivist and individualist cultures. How people see the world is one form of knowing, which, as I explain, varies between cultures. I cannot discuss all cultural differences. Therefore, my limited goal is to provide school staff with differing cultural frameworks to think about and use in adjusting school material to local conditions. Sometimes teachers may be educated in methods and intellectual constructs that are foreign to the communities in which they teach. School staff may assume that everyone sees the world in the same way. Therefore, teachers should understand their own cultural bias and how their education may have made their worldview different from that of the local community.

Most cultural comparisons are made with the West, which I am defining as the countries of North America and the European Union. I recognize that the term "the West" is problematic because not all people of these countries share the same worldview. This distinction is carefully made by Russell Means, early leader of the American Indian Movement, when he uses the term "European" in the same way that I am using the term "the West." "When I use the term *European*," he writes, "I'm not referring to a skin color or a particular genetic structure. What I'm referring to is a mind-set, a worldview that is a product of the development of European culture."[1] What this Western worldview is I discuss as a topic of cultural comparisons in this chapter.

One reason for the available resources on cultural comparisons between the West and other parts of the world is the West's imperialistic ventures over the past 500 years. Often, these imperialistic actions involved attempts at cultural domination. One major set of comparative research findings involves Indigenous cultures in the Americas, Africa, Australia, New Zealand, South Pacific islands, and parts of Asia. Western imperialist forces sometimes attempted to destroy Indigenous cultures. Many Indigenous groups are now engaged in cultural restoration, which is resulting in a growing body of research between Western and Indigenous cultures.

Another major area of comparative studies is between the West and Confucian-based societies such as those of China, Korea, Taiwan, and Japan. This research focus is mainly a result of economic competition and the growth of multinational corporations, which stimulated a desire to understand the cultural differences between these two parts of the world. From the Western perspective, particularly that of the United States and the European Union, Confucian-based societies are economic rivals that seem better able to manage their human resources in the workplace and in schools. In addition, multinational corporations dominated by either Western or Eastern corporate leaders operate in a multicultural world requiring cross-cultural contacts between international business people and an understanding of how to market goods in different cultural settings.

There is a danger in attributing common ways of seeing the world to all Indigenous peoples and all people in Confucian-based societies. As I discuss, there are many books and articles claiming to define ways of knowing for all Indigenous peoples of Africa and North America. To prove or disprove these claims would be difficult given the large number of Indigenous nations on both continents. The attributing of common cultural characteristics to all Indigenous peoples results, in part, from a fear that economic development, particularly in Africa, is continuing to destroy local cultures by imposing economic structures that are unsuitable to local conditions and cultures. As a result, some people are trying to define common characteristics among Indigenous peoples. Given the difficulty of claiming pan-Africanism or pan-Americanism for Indigenous tribes, I am not contending that my discussion of Indigenous ways of seeing in this chapter reflects the cultures of all Indigenous peoples of the world. All I can describe is what particular people report as the culture of some Indigenous peoples.

Feelings of cultural unity among Indigenous peoples may also be a result of facing common imperialist forces, which results in sharing a common enemy or "other." The problem of modern Indigenous identity is expressed in the following dialogue between two Nigerian university people in a short story by Nigerian writer Chimamanda Ngozi Adichie. The narrator is a newly hired houseboy fresh from a remote Nigerian village who calls his boss "Master."

> "Of course we are all alike; we all have white oppression in common," Miss Adelbayo said dryly. "Pan-Africanism is simply the most sensible response to this."
>
> "Of course, of course, but my point is that the only authentic identity for the African is the tribe," the Master said … . "I am Nigerian because a White man created Nigeria and gave me that identity. I am Black because the White man constructed Black to be as different as possible from his White. But I was Igbo before the White man came."
>
> Professor Ezeka snorted … . "But you became aware that you were Igbo because of the White man. The pan-Igbo idea itself came only in the face of White domination. You must see that tribe as it is today is as colonial a product as nation and race."[2]

Complicating the dilemmas embodied in the preceding dialogue are issues involving cultural stereotypes and cultural hybridity. A danger in studying cultural differences is the tendency to create cultural stereotypes. The cultural characteristics I identify are generalizations that could take on different meanings for different individuals. Also, in our global society cultures are not isolated from each other. Media, information technologies, and transportation systems are speeding up the rate of cultural contact. The result is a melding of cultures. A central issue for Indigenous cultures is the ability of local cultures to retain power over the influence of global cultural influences. Indigenous cultures were forced to change by imperialistic powers. Currently, the issue is how to retain control over outside cultural influences.

Biculturalism is another result of globalization. Studies show that people can be bicultural in their ways of knowing. These studies suggest that as cultures are brought into closer contact, humans may be developing multicultural ways of knowing or there may be a melding of different approaches to knowing. In researching the differences between Western and Confucian ways of knowing, social psychologist Richard Nisbett reports that Hong Kong Chinese, who have been influenced by British schools and traditions as well as Chinese culture, could be prompted to think within either Confucian or Western epistemology. They are bicultural in their ways of seeing the world.[3] I talk more about biculturalism and Nisbett's pioneering studies throughout this chapter.

This chapter is organized around the two aforementioned prominent areas of cultural research, namely, Indigenous as compared with Western and Confucius-based societies. The intention is to help teachers understand differences in ways of knowing so they can adapt to local contexts the proposed global core curriculum and discussions in chapters 5 and 6 about prototypes for a global school structure and global textbook. Also, this discussion is designed to help teachers think how they can provide multicultural perspectives for their students. I begin by discussing Indigenous ways of knowing and then turn to the research on differences between the Western and Confucian-based cultures.

INDIGENOUS PEOPLES AND KNOWLEDGE: ECONOMIC DEVELOPMENT AND BIOPIRACY

Who are the Indigenous peoples of the world? What is Indigenous knowledge? What are the uses of Indigenous knowledges? One answer is provided by the editors of *Indigenous Knowledges in Global Contexts:* "We conceptualize an 'Indigenous knowledge' as a body of knowledge associated with the long-term occupancy of a certain place. This knowledge refers to traditional norms and social values, as well as to mental constructs that guide, organize, and regulate the people's way of living and making sense of their world."[4]

Of course, the preceding definition still is not precise because of the possible meanings that might be given to "long-term occupancy." The Indigenous nations of Canada emphasize "long-term occupancy" by choosing the self-identifier "First Nations." Also, some groups that currently identify themselves as Indigenous were previously imperialistic powers with empires that dominated other peoples and lands, such as the Aztecs, Mayans, and Incas of the Americas. Are these nations or the peoples they dominated the long-term occupiers? To resolve the issue of who is Indigenous I simply rely on self-identification.

Global political forces, such as the World Bank, use a more elaborate definition that includes "subsistence-oriented production" along with "self-identification." The World Bank defines "Indigenous Peoples" as follows:

> The term "Indigenous Peoples" (also often referred to as "Indigenous ethnic minorities", "tribal groups", and "scheduled tribes") describes social groups with a social and cultural identity distinct from the dominant society which makes them vulnerable to being disadvantaged in the development process. Key characteristics identifying Indigenous Peoples:
>
> 1. Close attachment to ancestral territories and their natural resources
> 2. Self-identification and identification by others as members of a distinct cultural group
> 3. An Indigenous language, often different from the national language
> 4. Presence of customary social and political institutions
> 5. Primarily subsistence-oriented production.[5]

However, "subsistence-oriented production" does not realistically describe the work of some self-identified Indigenous peoples who hold jobs in modern factories, corporate agriculture, or urban service industries.

How is Indigenous knowledge used? As one example, the World Bank uses the term "ethnodevelopment" when incorporating Indigenous knowledge in plans for economic development. In this context, Indigenous knowledge becomes instrumental for developing industrial-consumer economies. World Bank officially acknowledges the instrumental use of Indigenous knowledge in its official publication, *Defining Ethnodevelopment in Operational Terms: Lessons From the Ecuador Indigenous and Afro-Ecuadoran Peoples Development Project*: "Ethnodevelopment builds on the positive qualities of Indigenous cultures and societies to promote local employment and [economic] growth."[6] As stated, World Bank officials focus on the so-called "positive qualities", which is another way of saying those qualities that can be used for economic development. In other words, Indigenous cultures are recognized or used only to fulfill the goal of economic development. This World Bank project identified the Indigenous characteristics that it wanted to include in its planning: "these peoples' strong sense of ethnic identity, close attachments to ancestral land, and capacity to mobilize labor, capital, and other resources to achieve shared goals."[7] Even traditional Inca administrative structures are to be used in economic development, which World Bank organizers acknowledge were used by Spanish imperialists for exploitive purposes.

> The Indigenous population of Ecuador is highly organized. Organizations along ethnic lines were recognized during the Inca Empire. The Conquistadors tried to dismantle and destroy these organizations, and during colonial times community-based organizations were used by the Spaniards to wring taxes and labor from the Indigenous population. However, the organizations persisted, and in the period following Ecuador's independence they were known *asparcialidades indigenas*.[8]

In recent years, the World Bank has become sensitive to the potential impact of its plans on Indigenous peoples. In its Operational Directive 4.20 on Indigenous Peoples, the World Bank requires an assessment of the impact of its loans in what it calls An Indigenous Peoples Development Plan (IPDP). Using the acronym IP for Indigenous peoples, the language of Operational Directive 4.20 reflects the World Bank's attitude that Indigenous peoples and knowledge are just another factor in its economic development plans. The World Bank reduces Indigenous cultures to the language of bureaucracy. I quote its evaluation of Operational Directive 4.20 because it exemplifies the reduction of Indigenous peoples to a bureaucratic component in fostering development along the lines of an industrial-consumer society:

> An Indigenous Peoples Development (IPDP) is the main instrument through which the Bank addresses IP-related issues at the project level. For an investment project that affects IP, the Borrower should prepare an IPDP by appraisal. The IPDP aims to mitigate the potential adverse project effects on IP and to ensure that beneficiaries "receive culturally compatible social and economic benefit." When the bulk of the beneficiaries are IP, "the Bank's concerns would be addressed by the project itself, and the provisions of the OD apply to the project in its entirety." The IPDP needs to be based on a comprehensive diagnosis of the socioeconomic context within which the IP operate and on their informed participation.[9]

This approach ignores knowledge that is not useful for economic growth. Critical of this approach, Political scientist Arun Agrawal writes: "Only forms of such [Indigenous] knowledge that are potentially relevant to development, then, need attention and protection. Other forms of such knowledge … can be allowed to pass away."[10] Development planners are creating Indigenous knowledge databases that will remove that knowledge from ritualistic and traditional practices and environmental contexts that give meaning to that knowledge. Agrawal warns:

> It is easy to see how the process of creating databases of Indigenous knowledge is in error precisely in stripping away all the detailed, contextual, applied aspects of knowledge [such as rituals, traditions, and environmental factors] that might be crucial in producing positive effects claimed for that particular piece of Indigenous knowledge… . But … contextual factors … might be responsible for the effects being claimed for a particular Indigenous practice.[11]

Indigenous knowledge is the target of biopiracy in which individuals and corporations patent traditional knowledge to make pharmaceuticals and agricultural chemicals. There have been a number of well-publicized cases, including the patenting of turmeric, long used in India to heal wounds and rashes; neem, a traditional medicine, insect repellant, and fertilizer; and hoodia, used by the San of the Kalahari to stave off hunger and thirst, which was patented and sold to the pharmaceutical company Pfizer as an appetite suppressant.[12] The 2002 Commission on Intellectual Property Rights defines *biopiracy* as "the appropriation of the knowledge and genetic resources of Indigenous communities by individuals or institutions seeking exclusive monopoly control (usually patents or plant breeders' rights) over these resources and knowledge."[13]

There are many attempts to protect Indigenous knowledge from biopiracy, including the First International Conference on the Cultural & Intellectual Property Rights of Indigenous Peoples held in Aotearoa, New Zealand in 1993, attended by 150 Indigenous representatives from 14 countries including Ainu (Japan), Australia, Cook Islands, Fiji, India, Panama, Peru, Philippines, Surinam, USA, and New Zealand. The meeting issued *The Mataatua Declaration on Cultural and Intellectual Property Rights of Indigenous Peoples,* which asserted that the world should

> Acknowledge that Indigenous Peoples have a commonality of experiences relating to the exploitation of their cultural and intellectual property
> Affirm that the knowledge of the Indigenous Peoples of the world are of benefit to all humanity
> Recognize that Indigenous Peoples are capable of managing their traditional knowledge themselves, but are willing to offer it to all humanity provided their fundamental rights to define and control this knowledge are protected by the international community
> Insist that the first beneficiaries of Indigenous knowledge (cultural and intellectual property rights) must be the direct indigenous descendants of such knowledge.[14]

In summary, Indigenous knowledge is used for economic development and exploited through biopiracy. One result is a global recognition of something call Indigenous knowledge, which includes knowledge of the biosphere and ways of living based on centuries of experience. However, Indigenous knowledge should not be romanticized. There are things that can be criticized regarding Indigenous knowledge when the standard of contribution to long life and happiness is used. Certainly, the historical practices of some Indigenous tribes can be questioned, particularly cannibalism and human sacrifices among some peoples of the Americas, Africa, Sumatra, Polynesia, Australia, and New Zealand. Most of these practices have faded into the past as Indigenous groups have struggled with cultural identity after years of colonialism and the seductive power of a global industrial-consumer culture.

INDIGENOUS AND GLOBAL KNOWLEDGE

Many Indigenous cultures were in disarray by the time colonialism lost its grip. For some, it was hard to disentangle the imposed culture of colonialism from Indigenous traditions. Many realized that with globalization, it was impossible to return to a cultural past. An important early contribution to this discussion was the essay of Australian anthropologist A. P. Elkin on Indigenous rights, which he contributed to the 1947 United Nations Educational, Scientific, and Cultural Organization (UNESCO) symposium designed to find a common basis for what would be called the Universal Declaration of Human Rights (1948). Another important early contributor to the discussion was Julius K. Nyerere, the first president (1964–1985) of the newly liberated Tanzania (1964–1985). As president of a country recently freed from the power of British colonialism, Nyerere needed to deal in a very practical way with the relationship between Indigenous knowledge, colonialism, and globalization.

A. P. Elkin's essay for the UNESCO symposium recognized that Indigenous cultures were fundamentally changed by the colonial experience, and that these cultures would continue to be part of a world culture. Elkin wrote, "'Civilized' power and peoples have disturbed and confused native peoples' ways of life, upset their adjustment to their environments, and, indeed, changed the very environments."[15] Unfortunately, Elkin's essay contained the demeaning language used by Westerners of the time in referring to Indigenous peoples, such as "civilized" and "primitive man." In proposing educational rights for Indigenous cultures, he stressed the importance of Indigenous peoples controlling their use of world knowledge in contrast to it being imposed.[16] Elkin warned, "The instruments and methods of education introduced and used amongst primitive people must not be instruments of imposed propaganda."[17] Instead, he wanted to turn control over to Indigenous peoples as exemplified by the following statement:

Elkin's Educational Rights for Indigenous Cultures

1. The development of an appreciation by a people of its own cultural background and of … an awareness of the cultural changes resulting from contact with [so-called] civilization.
2. The opening of the door, on approved educational principles, to world thought, science, technical achievement, literature and religion, to be used and built into their own changing culture as they find possible.
3. Primitive peoples have a right to benefit from the [so-called] civilized world's advances in both the method and content of education, conceived of in the widest sense. This right derives from, and must be subservient to … [the right to his own pattern of civilization and personality].[18]

Therefore, Elkin's educational rights includes a restoration of Indigenous cultures based on knowledge of how colonialism destroyed or distorted them.

Julius Nyerere, 17 years after Elkin's presentation to UNESCO on the rights of Indigenous cultures, was faced with the concrete issue of educating Indigenous peoples after British withdrawal from Tanzania in 1961. At the time of British withdrawal, Tanzania's peoples were primarily rural and living in somewhat traditional villages. Nyerere described the colonial school system: "It was motivated by a desire to inculcate the values of the colonial society and to train individuals for the service of the colonial state... [it attempted] to replace traditional knowledge by the knowledge from a different society"[19] The issues for Nyerere were how to rid the country of colonial education forms, how to recognize Indigenous cultures, and how to ensure economic growth. An important educational goal, he maintained, was to ensure that the population could read and write in Swahili, which was now the national language.[20] Nyerere rejected the educational goal of creating an industrial-consumer society for one in which "progress is measured by human well-being, not prestige buildings, cars, or other such things."[21]

Nyerere reflected on the fact that the peoples of Tanzania had provided education to their children before the imposition of colonial schools. The children's informal education consisted of learning about farming, nature, and tribal traditions from other villagers and elders. One effect of colonialism was that people began to confuse schooling with being educated, and tended to think that only schooled people were wise. As a result, "the knowledge and wisdom of older people is despised, and they themselves regarded as being ignorant and of no account."[22]

Nyerere proposed that rural schools (the overwhelming majority of the population at the time was rural) become a combination of schools and farms. One reason for this proposal was that working school farms would help alleviate the financial strain of educational costs on the new government. Also, they would be a means of passing on traditional knowledge in a setting that combined a colonial model of school with traditional education. His vision was "that every school should also be a farm; that the school community should consist of people who are both teachers and farmers, and pupils and farmers."[23] Nyerere's ultimate educational goal was to increase the capabilities (as defined by Sen) and happiness of students: "We should determine the types of things taught, ... the skills he ought to acquire and the values he ought to cherish if he, or she, is to live happily and well in a socialist and predominantly rural society, and contribute to the improvement of life there."[24]

Like Elkin, Nyerere felt Indigenous people could not slip back into some romantic past, but could exercise the power to choose from the available fund of world knowledge. He recognized that people had gained many years of experience from a "struggle with nature; even rules and taboos they honor have a basis in reason." This knowledge, he argued, needed to be combined with knowledge about newer forms of farming technology: "Our young people have to learn both a practical respect for the knowledge of the old 'uneducated' farmer and an understanding of new methods and the reason for them."[25]

Therefore, both Elkin and Nyerere offer one solution to balancing the restoration of Indigenous cultural after the brutal effects of colonialism with the reality of globalization. The key is giving Indigenous peoples the knowledge and power to choose how the world's knowledge is to be integrated into their cultures. This goal is congruent with Amartya Sen's concept of "capabilities," which defines equality for Indigenous peoples as a "people's ability to lead the kind of lives they value—and have reason to value."[26]

INDIGENOUS WAYS OF KNOWING

Learning to live with nature and fellow humans explains the origins of most Indigenous cultures, and indeed, most cultures. It also explains the diversity and similarities between cultures. Imagine groups of humans trying to survive when faced with differing environments ranging from the arctic to deserts to rain forests. To survive, each group develops its own social organization and food sources. The continued survival of a social organization might depend on religious rites, customs, folklore, and other methods of passing on and retaining social traditions. In the same manner, knowledge gained through interaction with nature might be passed on from generation to generation through stories, dances, rituals and, most often for Indigenous peoples, the wisdom of elders. These practices provide the context for Indigenous ways of knowing. Reliance on traditions and the wisdom of elders is characteristic of most Indigenous groups. Elders are the repositories of knowledge about social organization and environmental survival. In most cases, Indigenous groups do not separate in their thinking social life from the rest of the biosphere. This leads to a holistic worldview in which humans are one part of the biosphere.

In *The Geography of Thought,* social psychologist Richard Nisbett suggests that differing ways of thinking have evolved as a result of particular social adaptations to environmental circumstances.[27] Nisbett's work focuses on the differences in ways of thinking between Western and Confucian-based societies that originated, he argues, in differences in agricultural organization. As I discuss in more detail later, Nisbett's work uses the results of psychological testing to show differences in ways of seeing the world. His psychological work explains why cultures can have different ways of viewing the world and solving problems. Later in this chapter I discuss Nisbett's work in more detail, particularly how it is related to the holistic modes of seeing characteristic of many Indigenous peoples.

Justin Chisenga, a scholar at the South African Rand Afrikaans University, provides these broad characteristics of Indigenous knowledge:

- based on experience
- often tested over centuries of use
- adapted to the local culture and environment
- dynamic and changing.[28]

Similarly, Marlene Castellano asserts that there is a scholarly consensus about the First Nations of Canada: "Aboriginal knowledge is said to be personal, oral, experiential, holistic, and conveyed in narrative or metaphorical language."[29]

"For America to Live, Europe Must Die" is one of many speeches given by Russell Means, the previously mentioned leader of the American Indian Movement, about his perception of the differences between Western and Indigenous ways of seeing. This particular speech was given in 1980 at the Black Hills, North Dakota International Survival Meeting. In the speech, Means argues that beginning with Newton, Westerners despiritualized the universe by trying to reduce its meaning to a linear mathematical equation. This led Westerners, he asserts, to think of the mechanical as a source of perfection, and to seek efficiency in gaining material wealth. Making a distinction between a Native American concept of "being" as a spiritual proposition and a Western emphasis on "gaining" as a material act, Means claims that "part of the spiritual process [for Native Americans] was and is to give away wealth, to discard wealth in order *not* to gain ... while it is 'proof that the system works' to Europeans."[30] I do not know if Means is correct about the tradition of giving in all Native American nations, but it is true of many of the nations with which I have been in contact.

In distinguishing between Western and Native American ways of seeing the world, Means offers the powerful example of the difference between a European and Native American viewing a lake. The European thinks in terms of material gain, whereas the Native American feels the spiritual and observes the wonder of the lake. From the European perspective, Means contends, "the mountain becomes gravel, and lake becomes coolant for a factory, and the peoples are rounded up for processing through the indoctrination mills Europeans like to call schools."[31]

Means claims that there is an "indigenous worldview" and a "spiritual commonality" among Indigenous peoples. His list includes American Indians, Samme of Lapland, Ainu of Japan, Inuit, Maori, aboriginals of Australia, Miao, Rhade, Hmong, the San of the Kalahari desert, and many African tribes. The "vast majority of us," he contends, "maintain matrilineal societies that preserve harmony with all the life that surrounds us."[32] The problem with the spread of Christianity, he states, is that it placed humans at the center of the universe: "The Eurocentric male sees himself in the image of his god, and has gone about conquering the world to make everybody believe as he does, killing millions to save their souls."[33] Included in Indigenous worldviews is a deep distrust of Western-style schooling. Means states that Western schools isolate the child from the community and place them in the enclosed interior of a stifling age-graded classroom. He claims that most Indigenous peoples want children to learn from participation in the life of the community, with a minimum amount of time spent in Western-style schools.

It is understandable how holistic thinking might be common among groups living close to nature. I spent many summer months on an island off the coast of Alaska near the Tlingit nation. I had to learn how to read the weather by looking at cloud formations and paying attention to winds. After awhile I could predict the coming weather on the basis of the signs given to me by nature. I also learned the effect of weather on my food supply, which depended on salmon. Rainfall affected the size of the streams flowing into the ocean, which in turn affected salmon runs. I learned that tides determined the best times to fish. I found myself talking to ravens and eagles, which appeared at the best fishing times. Talking to animals has continued in modern urban settings, with people talking to their pets and understanding their pets' replies. I have a friend in Alaska who uses the same language and style when speaking to her dogs and cats as she uses in talking to sea lions, seals, and ravens.

Therefore, it seems reasonable that people living close to nature would have a holistic view of the interrelationship between humans, human organizations, and the rest of the biosphere. Within this holistic thinking, humans often are equal or inferior to other animal species. For instance, the Indigenous peoples of America's Northwest, such as the Tlingit and Haida nations, have an oral tradition in which raven stories help to explain the unpredictability of life. In these stories, the raven sometimes has more power than humans and acts as a trickster to change human life. The creation story involves a raven wandering down a beach and encountering a huge clam shell with creatures struggling to get out. The raven pries the clam shell apart to free human males. Following the men down the beach, the raven decides that there cannot be any fun unless there are females. The raven causes a storm to sweep chitons (a marine mollusk) off the tidal rocks onto the men's crotches. After allowing the men to roll in the sand in ecstasy, the raven causes another storm to blow the chitons back to their rocks. Nine months later human females emerge from the chitons. After that, humans are constantly interacting with the raven playing tricks on humans and humans fighting back. In this contest, humans are simply one among many other animals trying to survive.

In this pattern of holistic thought, emotions are inseparable from reason or, in other words, thought is not broken up into different parts—it is holistic. Consequently, for some Indigenous peoples, dreams, forethought, afterthought, and insight all are considered part of normal thinking. This holistic thinking is highlighted in the following table adapted from Maenette Benham and Ronald Heck's *Culture and Educational Policy in Hawaii: The Silencing of Native Voices.*[34]

As represented in Table 4.1, Benham and Heck argue that the Western view of thinking or the intellect is characterized by the possibility of separating emotion from intellectual activity, in contrast to traditional Hawaiian thought, in which thinking is viewed as holistic, with emotion, knowing,

TABLE 4.1
Comparison of Native Hawaiian Ways and Western Rational View

Concept	*Native Hawaiian Ways*	*Western Rational View*
Intellect	Na'au: Thinking comes from the intestines; the "gut" links the heart and mind. Thus, feelings and emotions are not separate from knowing, wisdom, and intelligence.	Separation of intellectual activity (cognitive domain) and emotion (affective domain). Thinking comes from the head and brain.
Relationship	When love is given, love should be returned. Because one is spiritually and physically connected to others, good relationships and reciprocity are highly valued. The connections between people must remain unbroken, harmonious, and correct.	Individuals are disconnected from each other. Because knowledge is seen more as a concrete set of ideas and skills that can be quantified, an individual grasp of knowledge is highlighted. This creates a commodity quality to knowledge that leads to individual-focused learning and being.
Knowledge	All learning must have aesthetic or practical use. Knowledge must link the spirit and the physical, and maintain relationships.	Knowledge for knowledge's sake has problematized Western education because the bridge between theory and practice has not been resolved.

Source: Excerpts from Maenette Benham and Ronald Heck. (1998) *Culture and educational policy in hawaii: The silencing of native voices.* Mahwah, NJ: Lawrence Erlbaum Associates, p. 33.

wisdom, and intelligence being inseparable. A holistic approach also characterizes differences in thinking about social relationships. According to Benham and Heck, traditional Hawaiians did not think of people as separate individuals that existed outside a group. They saw humans as interrelated to others humans and with the whole of nature. In contrast, Benham and Heck argue that Westerners see individuals as disconnected from each other. Knowledge also is holistic in traditional Hawaiian thought. The Hawaiians see knowledge as having an instrumental use in relationship to the spirit as well as physical and social relationships, whereas Westerners think of knowledge as existing outside human experience, or as Benham and Heck phrase it, "knowledge for knowledge's sake."

Richard Nisbett demonstrates that a holistic worldview results in different ways of knowing. Similar to Benham and Heck, Nisbett asserts that Westerners developed a belief that knowledge could exist separate from human experience. He traced this back to the ancient Greeks, who distrusted knowledge gained through the senses and favored abstract thought. "Plato," Nisbett writes, "thought that ideas—the forms—had a genuine reality, and that the world could be understood through logical approaches to their meaning, without reference to the world of senses. If the senses seemed to contradict conclusions reached from first principles and logic, it was the senses that had to be ignored."[35] Also, he argues, the Greeks believed that they could study an object in isolation from its total environment. With the object isolated, the Greeks tried to discern its disparate parts. This approach to seeing the world, he argues, set the stage for the later Western development of the scientific method and the use of science to search for the basic matter of the universe, such as the atom, in contrast to focusing on how the whole universe worked. The logic-chopping of the Greeks, according to communications theorist Robert Logan, led them to become "slaves to the linear, either–or orientation of their logic."[36]

Holistic seeing is characteristic of the Confucian-based societies Nisbett compared with the West. In an experiment conducted at the Kyoto University and the University of Michigan, students were shown eight colored animated scenes of underwater life in which one or more "focal" fish were brighter and larger than the others. The fish were shown swimming around plants, rocks, and bubbles. The results of the experiment are similar to the results of many other experiments conducted by Nisbett: after 20 seconds of viewing the scene, the Japanese students remembered many details of the whole scene, whereas the American students remembered primarily the focal fish. In other words, the Japanese students looked at the whole scene, whereas the Americans looked at the parts, particularly the most noticeable parts. In responding to questions, Japanese students began by describing the total environment ("It looked like a pond ...), whereas the Americans began by describing the focal fish.[37]

Nisbett cites many other experiments to support his conclusion that holistic thinking versus Western thinking does result in differing perceptions and understandings of the world. He traces these differences back to the ancient Chinese and Greeks. He asserts that because of differences in social organization for acquiring food, the ancient Chinese tended to see the world as a whole, whereas the Greeks tried to control the world by breaking it down into discrete parts. In a passage that could be used to compare Indigenous and Western thought, Nisbett writes: "People who live in a world in which external forces are the important ones could be expected to pay close attention to the environment. People who live in a world in which personal agency produces results might focus primarily on objects that they can manipulate to serve their own goals."[38]

Paul Wangoola, the Director of the Mpambo, the Afrikan Multiversity in Uganda, also attributes holistic thinking to African Indigenous peoples. Although the purpose of Mpambo is to advance Indigenous Afrikan scholarship, it also is a place to study all the world's knowledges. This is the reason for the term "multiversity," as contrasted with the word "university." Writing in a Report on the First International Cross-Cultural School held at Mpambo in March 2001, course coordinator David Wandira reports Wangoola's comments on the purpose of a multiversity: "He [Wangoola] referred to Mpambo Multiversity as a space to affirm, promote, advocate, and advance the multiplicity of thought and knowledges as a necessity to vitalize the world knowledges as well as human knowledge as a whole." Wangoola went on to tell the students:

> Hence the concept of the Uni–versity (i.e., single knowledge everywhere). That necessarily means western knowledge everywhere. He informed the students that contrary to the single knowledge concept (uni–versity), there are as many knowledges as there are ecosystems. And that just as it is important to recognize the diversity in life forms (i.e., biodiversity), so it is equally important to recognize the diversity in world knowledges.[39]

Writing about African Indigenous knowledge, Wangoola asserts, "Humans are part of rather than apart from nature and are the most vulnerable link in the vast chain of nature. The Earth is not for them to conquer and subdue, but their mother to live with in harmony and reverence."[40] This holistic vision of humans as part of the biosphere is accompanied by spirituality, something common to many Indigenous peoples. This form of spirituality rejects the idea of a single god for many gods with spirits existing in all animals and plants. It is sometimes spirits, among some Indigenous peoples, that visit the dream world of a person and act as a source of knowledge. Solomon Islanders David Welchman Gegeo and Karen Ann Watson-Gegeo report on the different ways of knowing among Kawara'ae villagers, which includes visitations by ancestors during dreams. In this context, holistic would include the spirit world.[41]

In sharp contrast to the Western emphasis on the possibility of knowledge existing apart from a person's senses, the Gegeos report on the holistic ways of knowing experienced by their fellow Solomon Islanders. Like Nisbett, the Gegeos characterize Western thought as linear and objective. They write, "All knowledge is subjective knowledge in Kwara'ae: there can be no detachment of the knower from the known as in mainstream Anglo-European epistemology, as exemplified in logical positivism with its focus on 'objective knowledge', especially Karl Popper's concept of 'knowledge without a knower'."[42] For the Kwara'ae, knowledge is gained through sensory experiences including five kinds of seeing. These five ways of seeing include the spirit world:

- physical seeing with the eyes
- seeing with the mind (insight, foresight)
- seeing the unseen or spirits
- seeing beyond temporal boundaries such as seeing something that indicates a future event
- seeing through a medium (often a traditional healer) things such as the nature of an illness or outcome of an event
- seeing a dream.[43]

As one means of seeing, the Kwara'ae identify two types of dreams:

- regular dreaming that may or may not be understandable
- psychic dreams occurring in a half-awake state accompanied by sweating and rapid heartbeat.[44]

There also are two ways of hearing:

- ordinary hearing
- hearing sounds that no one else hears, particularly in the early morning, which might be predictive of someone's death.[45]

Also, knowledge can be gained through communication with ancestors and through signs. Signs, such as a school of fish swimming where they are not ordinarily seen, are important indicators of a possible troubling event.

Oral tradition as a source of knowledge accompanies these sensory forms of knowing. This is where the wisdom of the elders plays an important role. Oral tradition is considered received knowledge based on past trial-and-error experimentation. Consequently, oral tradition is considered open to improvement or change based on changing conditions. The environmental devastation of the Solomon Islands resulted in additions and changes to oral traditions to cope with these changes. Village meetings allow for a discussion of events that leads to a form of justified truth. These discussions often work their way through a tangle of evidence, with the descriptive metaphor being gardening: "Inch with the fingers along it," as in following a tangle of roots and vines.[46]

It is claimed that the Indigenous tribes in North America share a similar worldview with the Indigenous peoples of Africa and the Solomon Islands.

Marlene Castellano reports the following sources of knowledge for First Nations peoples of Canada. Like many other Indigenous groups, elders are respected as sources of traditional knowledge and experience. Besides accumulated experience, traditional knowledge includes creation tales of earth and clans, the spirit world, life among animals, human relationships with animals and earth, and relationships of humans with each other. In addition, according Castellano, "through heroic and cautionary tales, it [oral traditions] reinforces values and beliefs; these in turn provide the substructure for civil society. In some of its forms, it passes on technologies refined over generations."[47]

An important part of traditional knowledge is the accumulated experience with relationships between humans and between humans and nature. Passed on through the words of elders, this accumulated experiential knowledge is constantly changing with social and environmental changes. Castellano calls this accumulated experiential knowledge "empirical knowledge" because it is gained through careful observation. In *Traditional Knowledge Systems: The Recognition of Indigenous History and Science,* Canadian scholar James Waldram writes about the accumulated observations of many people over a period of time: "This information processing forms a constant loop in which new information is interpreted in the context of existing information, and revisions to the state of knowledge concerning a particular phenomenon are made when necessary."[48]

Similar to Hawaiians and Solomon Islanders, Castellano reports that dreams and visions are important sources of "revealed knowledge" for First Nations peoples. Many Indigenous peoples consider dreams and/or visions another way of seeing. For instance, the Beaver people of Northeastern British Columbia believe that successful hunters depend on dreams for finding animal trails and prey.

Western psychoanalytic theory also focuses on the interpretation of dreams as revealed knowledge about individuals. The pioneer work is Sigmund Freud's *The Interpretation of Dreams* (1900). Among some Indigenous groups, elders or healers are sought out to interpret dreams. In the West, it is therapists. Freud used the language of Western science to explain the importance of dreams:

> I shall demonstrate that there is a psychological technique which makes it possible to interpret dreams, and that on the application of this technique every dream will reveal itself as a psychological structure full of significance, and one which may be assigned a specific place in the psychic activities of the waking state.[49]

Compare Freud's statement on dreams with that of Donald Fixico, who was raised in a Creek–Seminole tradition. Similar to Freud, Fixico accepts the importance of dreams, but places them in a holistic framework as revealed truth:

> "Seeing" involves mentally experiencing the relationships between tangible and nontangible things in the world and in the universe. It is like living one's dream that seems so real while you are sleeping. It is acceptance of fact that a relationship exists between a tangible idea like a mountain and a dream. In his visionary experience, Black Elk spoke of "seeing." As he stood on a high mountain, he recalled ... "I saw that the sacred hoop of my people was one of many hoops that made one circle, wide as daylight and as starlight, and in the center grew one mighty flowering tree to shelter all the children of one mother and one father. And I saw that it was holy."[50]

Western thought and science, as I previously discussed, believes in universal truth or "knowledge without a knower." For First Nations peoples, according to Castellano, because knowledge is rooted in personal experience, there is no claim that this knowledge is universal. The validity of the experience is based on judgments about the person reporting the experience, which can be a reflection of a person's integrity. On the other hand, there is an acceptance of conflicting perceptions from different people, with no judgment of whose perception is the "truth." Elders and councils might discuss different perceptions without arguing about the truth of one perception versus another. In these situations, a distinction is made between personal perceptions and "wisdom." "Wisdom" is traditional knowledge based on the accumulated experiences of generations.

These Indigenous tribes of North America dismiss as absurd that decisions should be based on a majority rule form of democracy. How can right decisions be made when the power of decision can be given to only 51% of voters while 49% disapprove? In talking circles or council meetings, decisions are arrived at by consensus. Speeches will touch on an issue being considered. Oral presentations may last for days. Castellano describes the final stage in decision making about issues affecting the well-being of the community:

> Gradually comments or experiences with a particular bent were heard reinforcing one another; and at a certain point, everyone would get up and leave. A perceptive observer might be able to see the exchange of looks or nods between certain elders, signaling the emergence of consensus; but such consensus would not normally be confirmed in a vote. Collective wisdom is arrived at by a process of "putting our minds together".[51]

HOLISTIC SEEING: INDIGENOUS AND CONFUCIAN

The acceptance of multiple perceptions and the process of consensus building is another aspect of a holistic perspective. Certainly, it is tempting to ascribe holistic viewpoints to all Indigenous peoples. However, the limited illustrations in this chapter do not allow me to claim that I am describing the ways of seeing for all of the world's Indigenous groups. I cannot even prove that all the native people of the Americas are holistic in their worldviews. Still, I can say that many observers, who themselves may be guilty of overgeneralization, attribute holistic ways of perceiving to the First Nations of the Americas. Commentators on the Hawaiian and Solomon islands, as discussed previously, also discern holistic thinking embedded in traditional ways. The pan-African assertions of Paul Wangoola at the African Multiversity point to holistic knowing among African groups. Writing about Peru, Mahia Maurial states, "One important basis of an Indigenous worldview expressed through Indigenous knowledge is *holisticity*. . . . The holistic basis of Indigenous knowledge is produced and reproduced within human relationships as well as their relationships with nature."[52]

What are the holistic perspectives that appear to exist among many of the world's Indigenous peoples? First, it is seeing, as Maurial states earlier, people and nature in relationship to other things rather than as separate and discrete. This is why North American Indigenous peoples are characterized—again I am trying to avoid saying this is true of all nations—as being willing to accept multiple perceptions of the same event because the meaning of the event is in its relationship to the observer while the observer is in relationship to others and nature. The tendency of Western thinking is to classify objects according attributes or taxonomic categories such as size, shape, weight, color, function, and the like.

In *The Geography of Thought*, Richard Nisbett provides the best illustration of the difference between seeing holistically and seeing in terms of taxonomic categories. He reports that a Chinese developmental psychologist, Lianghwang Chiu, presented a series of illustrations depicting three objects to American and Chinese children. The children were asked to place two of the objects together. One illustration showed a chicken, a cow, and grass. The American children grouped the chicken and the cow together because they were both animals. The Chinese children grouped the cow and the grass together because the cow eats grass. In fact the cow and the chicken ordinarily have no experiential relationship. Cows and chickens are not generally living together, and they do not live off each other. If a human were introduced into the illustration and children were asked to group three objects together, then it might be hypothesized that both American and Chinese children would group the cow, the chicken, and the human together, but for different reasons. The American children would put the three together because they are animals, whereas the Chinese children would put the three together because the human eats chickens and drinks cow's milk.[53]

Nisbett and two Chinese colleagues conducted a similar experiment yielding similar results using college students in the United States, Taiwan, and the Peoples Republic of China. They gave the participants three words and asked which two of the words were related. One set of words included panda, monkey, and banana. As the reader can guess from the previous discussion, the American college students tended to see the closest relationship between the panda and the monkey because they were animals, whereas the Chinese students grouped the monkey and the banana together because monkeys eat bananas.

These are significant differences in seeing the world. In experiment after experiment, Nisbett found that Westerners tended to see the world as made up of discrete categories of objects that could be defined by a set of rules. In Confucian-based societies, people tended to see the world as made up of relationships based on some form of contact or interaction between objects. Among many Indigenous peoples, these relationships include dreams and spirits (this also may be true of Confucian-based societies). Donald Fixico uses the following words to describe a holistic vision based on relationships: "To see properly, one must be aware of all surrounding things, including those that might not be in a physical sense, but choose to exist in the metaphysical sense.... Many native people see visions, ghosts, and spirits."[54]

Differences in "seeing" a forest is one way of illustrating the use of taxonomic categories and holistic relationships. Those seeing a forest through the lense of taxonomic categories, which is what many people call Western "seeing," would observe groups of trees, bushes, animals, birds, insects, moss, flowers, and so forth. Those seeing a forest through a holistic lens of relationships, which is what many people might call Indigenous and Asian ways of seeing, would view an interrelated world of birds eating berries and insects, moss growing on trees and the earth, animals eating the moss and leaves, bees pollinating flowers, bushes sheltering animals, and so on. Of course a Westerner could understand the interdependence of the forest, but according to the preceding discussion, the Westerner would initially focus on separate objects having common characteristics.

CONFUCIANISM AND HOLISTIC SEEING

I think a good example of holistic thinking regarding human virtue is Confucius's statement in *The Great Learning* (ca. 500 B.C.E.), which places personal virtue in the context of all social relationships. This famous passage demonstrates a reliance on knowledge gained from experience rather than, as in Plato, eternal and abstract truths:

> The ancients who wished to illustrate illustrious virtue throughout the kingdom, first ordered well their own states. Wishing to order well their states, they first regulated their families. Wishing to regulate their families, they first

> cultivated their persons. Wishing to cultivate their persons, they first rectified their hearts. Wishing to rectify their hearts, they first sought to be sincere in their thoughts. Wishing to be sincere in their thoughts, they first extended to the utmost their knowledge. Such extension of knowledge lay in the investigation of things.
>
> Things being investigated, knowledge became complete. Their knowledge being complete, their thoughts were sincere. Their thoughts being sincere, their hearts were then rectified. Their hearts being rectified, their persons were cultivated. Their persons being cultivated, their families were regulated. Their families being regulated, their states were rightly governed. Their states being rightly governed, the whole kingdom was made tranquil and happy.[55]

Holistic thinking is represented in the circular quality of this statement, which begins with the question of how to create virtue throughout a state, which then leads to the role of the family and person and then back to the family and to the nation. Essentially, Confucius's answer is that everything is connected, and that you cannot improve the quality of social life by trying to ameliorate a discrete part of the whole. You must think of improving all the interconnected parts.

An example can be seen in my experience with a textbook, *American Education,* which I have authored since the 1970s. In all its 13 editions, I have crammed an annual list of proposals for school improvement made by educational reformers, politicians, and private foundations. None of these proposals seem to have helped with the basic educational problems of inequality of educational opportunity in a society divided by race, culture, and social class. Imagine Confucius responding to the ongoing American school crisis of inequality of educational opportunity. Confucius might say:

> Citizens who want to eliminate inequality of educational opportunity must first eliminate economic and social inequalities in society. Wishing to eliminate economic and social inequalities, they must eliminate social and economic inequalities between families. Wishing to reduce social and economic inequalities between families, they must reduce inequalities between persons. Wishing to reduce social and economic inequalities between people, they investigated the causes of inequality.
>
> Inequality being investigated, knowledge made it possible to reduce social and economic inequalities between people. With greater equality between people, families were more equal. Families being more equal, economic and social inequalities were reduced in society. With economic and social inequalities being reduced, inequalities in educational opportunities were reduced.

The tendency in Western thought is to focus on a specific problem in an attempt to correct it without considering the world in which the problem is nested. When Western science is applied to social and institutional problems, it often focuses on a discrete issue instead of analyzing the whole system. Why are children from low-income families not performing as well in school as children from high-income families? Western researchers tend analyze individual parts of the problem such as instructional methods, teacher performance, children's cultural capital, school funding, family involvement, and the like. Looking at the results of these studies might cause someone to suggest that simply changing methods of instruction or family involvement is the solution for the poor performance of low-income students instead of placing the problem in the whole web of social conditions. Nisbett summarizes this difference—remember that he uses "Asian" to indicate the Confucius-based societies such as those of China, Taiwan, Japan and Korea—with Asians seeing "the world in holistic terms. They see a great deal of the field, especially background events; they are skilled in observing relationships between events… . Modern Westerners … see the world in analytic, atomistic terms; they see objects as discrete and separate from their environments."[56]

With a holistic vision, Confucian scholars recognized the importance of protecting the environment as one means of ensuring the welfare of people. What may be the first statement about sustainability is the response of Confucius's disciple Mencius's (372–289 B.C.E.) to King Hui's question asking why the number of people in his kingdom did not increase. Besides chiding the King for being too fond of war, Mencius replied, "If close nets are not allowed to enter the pools and ponds, the fishes and turtles will be more than can be consumed. If the axes and bills enter the hills and forests *only* at the proper time, the wood will be more than can be used. When the grain and fish and turtles are more than can be eaten, and there is more wood than can be used, this enables the people to nourish their living"[57] The reference to "close nets" and "proper time" to cut trees is to ancient Chinese environmental practices. Traditionally, the meshes in nets were kept larger than about four inches so that no fish smaller than about a foot would be caught. Traditional forestry practices limited harvest to the fall, after the growth of trees had stopped.[58]

Before Asian societies were introduced to Western scientific methods, there existed a concern with learning through investigation and practical experience. Consider the statement in the earlier quote from Confucius: "Wishing to be sincere in their thoughts, they first extended to the utmost their knowledge. Such extension of knowledge lay in the investigation of things." The continued practice of traditional Chinese medicine illustrates the fruits of a holistic approach and investigation based on experience. It involves an accumulation over time of experiential evidence. That the body is treated as an interconnecting whole becomes obvious in an examination of a traditional Chinese acupuncture or massage chart. Roxanna Ng, a

Professor at the Ontario Institute for Studies in Education, writes that traditional Chinese medicine refers to what Westerners call organs, but "these are not conceptualized as discrete physical structures and entities located in specific areas within the body. Rather, the term 'organs' is used to identify the function associated with them; … [traditional medicine] does not distinguish between physical functions and the emotional and spiritual dimensions governed by the 'organ' in question."[59] The body is conceptualized in terms of 'Qi'. There is no Western word for 'Qi', but it has been referred to as an energy flow that makes life possible and as a quality shared by all living things. One possible way of translating 'Qi' is that organs are viewed in relationship to what is required to keep the body living. The emphasis on relationships is supported by the previous discussion of Nisbett's experiments in which Chinese students tended to classify things according to relationships, in contrast to American classification by attributes.

Cyclical change is another aspect of the Confucian holistic perspective. Westerners create a sense of timelessness in their categorization of objects by attributes: trees will always be trees and flowers will always be flowers. However, when one sees the world as a set of relationships, then there is the possibility that these relationships will change in the future. This change has no particular direction. Nisbett confirms this perspective of Confucian-based societies in another set of experiments, from which he concludes that Westerners tend to view change as linear, whereas those in Confucian-based society see it as circular. In other words, Westerners believe fortunes will move up or down in a straight line, whereas Confucian-based societies see the possibility of constantly changing fortunes from up to down to up.[60]

A holistic view based on unpredictable and ever-changing relationships contributes to a feeling that one must accommodate to change rather than try to control or manipulate it. Students from American and Confucian-based societies were given a series of psychological tests designed to elicit views on future changes in the world. Nisbett concludes: "They [students in modern Confucian-based societies] see a great deal of the field, especially background events; they regard the world as complex and highly changeable … they see events as moving in cycles … and they feel that control over events requires coordination with others."[61]

HIERARCHY AND HOLISTIC PERSPECTIVES

As previously discussed, some Indigenous groups in North America combine a holistic worldview with a group consensus approach to decision making, in which elders have a major influence. In many Indigenous cultures, elders are influential as holders of accumulated knowledge. In Confucian-based societies, there also is an emphasis on the importance of elder scholars, but in the context of a much more hierarchically controlled society. Nothing better exemplifies the authoritarian vision of scholarly power than a statement by Confucius's disciple Mencius: "Some labor with their minds and some labor with their strength. Those who labor with their minds govern others; those who labor with their strength are governed by others. Those who are governed by others support them; those who govern others are supported by them."[62]

As consorts to rulers, Confucian scholars were to ensure harmony among the complex and interrelated parts of society and the environment. They were to guide the actions of governments and ensure the morality of the people. To ensure harmony, social order was to be maintained through the teaching of virtue and rites, in contrast to Western reliance on laws. Confucius warned:

> If the people be led by laws, and uniformity sought to be given them by punishments, they will try to avoid the punishment, but have no sense of shame. If they be led by virtue, and uniformity sought to be given them by the rules of propriety [rites], they will have the sense of shame, and moreover will become good.[63]

Therefore, harmony in social relations was to be maintained by 'rites'. In one sense, rites can be considered norms for social interactions. Social harmony includes *li* which is related to traditional patterns of social conduct and *jen*, which refers to a person who pursues proper social conduct and human relationships.[64] The neo-Confucian scholar, William DeBary, states: "Confucius saw … ritual decorum as an essential form of civility, fundamental to human governance and preferable to the attempted enforcement of laws."[65]

As governors of harmony, scholars assumed a lofty role in their holistic view of society. This is why Mencius could argue that those who did physical labor should support the wise. For instance, after Mencius describes how rulers can improve the land to ensure abundance for the people, he warns: "Men possess a moral nature; and if they are well fed, warmly clad and comfortably lodged, without being taught at the same time, they become almost like beasts."[66] Therefore, Mencius argues, the ruler should appoint a minister of instruction to ensure the virtue of the people after achieving a life of plenty. Aided by scholarly advice, Mencius portrays the virtuous ruler as instructing the minister of education: "Encourage them; lead them on; rectify them; straighten them; help them; give them wings—causing them to become possessors of themselves. Then follow this up by stimulating them, and conferring benefits on them."[67] After this portraiture, Mencius rhetorically asks, "When the sages were exercising their solicitude for the people in this way, had they leisure to cultivate the ground?"[68]

Therefore, this holistic view of society can be imagined as a complex interrelationship of people and the environment in which the scholar or wise elder and the political ruler ensure that whole system works harmoniously to provide material needs and ensure moral order. Confucius's advice to rulers is this: "Let him preside over them with gravity—then they will reverence him. Let him be filial and kind to all—then they will be faithful to him. Let him advance the good and teach the incompetent—then they will eagerly seek to be virtuous."[69]

As protector of virtue and harmony in the complex interrelationships of society and the environment, the wise scholars must be willing to sacrifice their own lives. The Emperor Taizu (1513–1587) ordered Qian Tang to remove material written by Mencius from the civil service examination used to select members of what had become a scholarly bureaucracy. Emperor Taizu claimed Mencius had insulted his imperial position. Taizu ordered the death of any scholars who refused to obey. Qian Tang brought a coffin to court and announced, "It would be an honor to die for Mencius."[70] Quian's actions reflected Mencius's insistence on the duty of scholar-ministers to criticize the ruler: "If the prince made serious mistakes, they [scholar-ministers] would remonstrate him."[71] Confucius warned, "If what he [the ruler] says is good and no one goes against him, good. But if what he says is not good and no one goes against him, then is this not almost a case of leading the state to ruin?"[72]

Compared with those Indigenous societies in which the elder becomes the influential adviser because of accumulated knowledge of age, Confucian scholars must study and reflect until, ideally, they become sages. Confucius said, "By nature, men are nearly alike; by practice, they get to be wide apart."[73] Through the study of things and reflection, the scholar eventually becomes a sage. A sage, according to Confucius is one "who, without an effort hits what is right, and apprehends, without the exercise of thought, ... who naturally and easily embodies the right way"[74] Confucius claimed to have become a sage at the age of 70 years. He provided this chronology of his life:

> At fifteen, I had my mind bent on learning.
> At thirty, I stood firm [interpreted, as he no longer needed to bend his will].
> At forty, I had no doubts [he knew what was proper in all circumstances].
> At fifty, I knew the decrees of Heaven [he understood the constitution of things].
> At sixty, my ear was obedient for the reception of truth.
> At seventy, I could follow what my heart desired without transgressing what was right.[75]

In summary, Confucian traditions support a holistic view of a hierarchical world defined by relationships between individuals and the environment. Social problems and personal virtue are nested in this complex set of relationships. Guided by elder scholars, the goal is to achieve harmony between the parts. Life is considered unpredictable because of the complexity and

TABLE 4.2
Summary of Nisbett's Comparative Research Findings on Confucian–based and Western Societies

Confucian–based	*Western*
Sees the self as part of a larger interdependent whole	Sees the self as a unitary free agent
Sees the world as complex, interrelated, constantly changing	Sees the world as divided into discrete and separate environments
Prefers blending harmoniously with the group	Desires individual distinctiveness
Remains attuned to feelings of others and strives for interpersonal harmony	Has more concern with knowing oneself and willing to sacrifice harmony for fairness
Preference for collective action	Insists on freedom of individual action
Accepts of hierarchy and ascribed status	Prefers for egalitarianism and achieved status
Prefers behavior adapted to the situation	Believes that behavioral rules should be universal
Attributes behavior to the situation	Attributes behavior to the person
Values success and achievement because they reflect well on the group	Values success and achievement because they make the individual look good

Source: John Nisbett. (2003). *The geography of thought: How Asians and Westerners think differently … and why.* New York: Free Press, pp. 61–62, 76–77,108–109, 114.

ever-changing relationships between humans, between parts of the environment, and between humans and the environment. Humans are expected to accept and accommodate to change rather than try to control it. Collective action to deal with change is preferred over individual effort. These differing worldviews are supported by Nisbett's comparative psychological research. Nesbett's findings are summarized in Table 4.2.

CONCLUSION: HOLISTIC TEACHING AND SEEING

An important finding of Nisbett is that people can be bicultural in their worldviews. There are advantages to both the Western view of the world broken into discrete parts and the holistic views of some Indigenous and

Confucian-based societies. Western science developed from a perspective that categorized according to attributes and searched for universal laws to describe and control the organic and physical elements that composed the cosmos. Sometimes a consideration of the whole is lost when Western science narrows its vision to finding the basic components of substances. Applying science to human behavior and social institutions tends to disconnect the individual from its environment as it tries to describe behavior as a product of the individual psyche. The unpredictability of human behavior and the work of social institutions remains the norm because of the complexity of the interrelationships between humans and between humans and the biosphere.

Although Western views might be faulted for missing the importance of a holistic perspective, Western science is providing a means for helping humans to prevent, control, and ameliorate disease, parasites, and other factors that can seriously limit human life. However, because a holistic vision is lacking, many of the results of Western science and technology are seriously damaging the biosphere and creating the possibility of eliminating human life. The emergence of the social sciences, which try to predict human behavior, has sometimes led to a loss of traditional knowledge based on accumulated experience about how humans can live together. Ironically, the Western urge to find universal laws may result in self-destruction through war or environmental catastrophes.

Ideally, I would argue, the school should help students to have a bicultural vision that combines Western interest in looking at the discrete parts of the universe with a holistic view. But what holistic view of the world should be taught in school? The problem with Confucian-based societies, I would argue, is a holistic view that requires political and moral authority. The whole is seen as chaotic, requiring the authority of rulers and scholars to achieve harmony among its parts. However, once given power, rulers and scholars can neglect their mission of ensuring harmony and use their authority for self-aggrandizement and corruption. Instead of achieving harmony, the rule of political and moral leaders can sometimes create reigns of terror, deprivation, and suffering.

Also, human capabilities can be seriously limited when a wholistic worldview sees the necessity of authority and control to produce harmony among the parts. An important goal of the proposed global core curriculum and of prototypes for a global school organization and textbook presented in Chapters 5 and 6 are to increase the capabilities of the school staff and students to choose the life they want. Within the school, this means maximizing the ability of teachers and students to plan and execute lessons. As discussed in previous chapters, the degree of a person's capabilities is correlated with his or her life expectancy and subjective wellbeing.

I consider the consensus-building process of some Northern American Indigenous peoples to be a model for guiding human actions to ensure subjective well-being and longevity. First, the participatory model heightens the exercise of capabilities. Second, it allows for consideration of a full range of possible consequences for human actions. The assumption is that any human problem is complex and must be considered from a variety of viewpoints. In this model, multiple perspectives on an issue are considered legitimate. Instead of debating, these differing perspectives are presented. As people listen to others, they modify their perspectives on the basis of others' comments. As the discussion progresses, with everyone having consensus as an objective, the circle of talk begins to narrow to a consensus. The wise elders, as contrasted with Confucian scholars, guide the discussion by sharing their knowledge of accumulated experience. They are participants in the discussion who are more influential than others because of the group's respect for their wisdom and integrity. In this scenario, the participants weigh the words of elders in reaching a consensus. One can imagine this process in a school where the students all voice their perspectives about planning a lesson, with the teacher playing the role of the wise elder guiding the discussion. The students and teacher know the goal is a consensus and consciously work to achieve that end.

"Holistic" has two interrelated meanings in the prototype of a global school presented in chapter 5 with Humanity Flag certification. First, it refers to holistic learning in which learning is not divided into discrete subjects such as math, science, social studies, and so on. Second, it refers to teaching students a holistic view of life in which everything is interrelated. Holistic learning is supportive of a holistic worldview. However, Western science also is used to understand the workings of particular parts of the whole. Western science can be used to understand the internal functioning of a tree, whereas a holistic view relates a tree to the insects and birds it protects and feeds, the tree's relationship to the atmosphere and watershed, and the tree's contribution to animal and human life. The holistic approach elicits questions about the impact of cutting down a tree on human life and the whole biosphere. The approach of traditional Western science might consider cutting down a tree to investigate its internal structure. Both approaches are needed and can complement each other.

We should not forget that the overall goal of this book is to replace the current educational paradigm, which focuses on economic development, with a paradigm that focuses on long life and subjective well-being. The triumph of an industrial-consumer society might be the greatest threat to holistic worldviews. Consider the case of the Dayak people of Indonesia and the agreement made by the Indonesian government to level their forest lands. These forests are so vital to the surrounding environment that they are called the "lungs of Southeast Asia." They also are home to a wide variety of animal, plant, and insect species. The rare first-growth timber will be used to build furniture and other products for China's expanding middle class, a consumer class that is a result of China's leaders replacing Mao Zedong's vision of an equalitarian society with an economy devoted to consumerism. The forest will be replaced by palm oil plantations, which will provide palm oil to the world's largest consumer-products company, Procter & Gamble, to be used in the manufacture of lipstick, detergents, and soaps.[76]

What do the Dayak people think of this change in their environment? The Dayak's elder, Anyie Apoui, says that they have tried for years to maintain a traditional way of life, which as late as the 1960s included headhunting. His own children moved to cities, and his villagers are now employed by palm oil plantations in Malaysia, which they can reach only by a three-day trek on foot. It is now time for a change according Anyie Apoui: "People have told me, 'Wood is gold, you're still too honest'."[77] In about 30 years, the forest will be gone. Although protecting the "lungs of Southeast Asia" is talked about and conservationists warn about the loss of species, the industrial-consumer paradigm reigns triumphant. Will the subjective well-being and longevity of the Dayak and Southeast Asian people be improved? Is anyone asking this question? Doesn't the question need to change from "how can we achieve economic growth?" to "how can we achieve a long life and happiness?" The desire to produce and consume more products leads to a narrow focus on how to exploit natural resources. Answers to the larger question of improving happiness and longevity requires a nonhierarchical holistic perspective. In summary, underlying my proposals for a global core curriculum and prototypes for a global school and textbook is a holistic worldview that rejects the authoritarian qualities of Confucianism and accepts the idea that the capabilities of people should be enhanced through participatory control.

NOTES

1 Russell Means, "For America to Live, Europe Must Die," in Russell Means with Marvin J. Wolf's *Where White Men Fear to Tread* (New York: St. Martin's Press, 1995), p. 552.

2 Chimamanda Ngozi Adichie, "The Master," *Granta 92: The View From Africa* (Winter 2005), p. 37.

3 Richard E. Nisbett, *The Geography of Thought: How Asians and Westerners Think Differently … and Why* (New York: Free Press, 2003), pp. 118–119.

4 George J. Sefa Dei, Budd L. Hall, and Dorothy Goldin Rosenberg, "Introduction," *Indigenous Knowledges in Global Contexts: Multiple Readings of Our World* edited by George J. Sefa Dei, Budd L. Hall, and Dorothy Goldin Rosenberg (Toronto: University of Toronto Press, 2000), p. 6.

5 The World Bank–Indigenous Peoples, "Key concepts," http://web.worldbank.org/WEBSITE/EXTERNAL/TOPICS/EXTSOCIALDEVELOPMENT/EXTINDPEOPLE/0,,contentMDK:20436173~menuPK:906311~pagePK:148956~piPK:216618~theSitePK:407802,00.html. Retrieved on April 18, 2006.

6 Martien van Nieuwkoop and Jorge E. Uquillas, *Defining Ethnodevelopment in Operational Terms: Lessons from the Ecuador Indigenous and Afro-Ecuadoran Peoples Development Project. Latin America and Caribbean Region Sustainable Development Working Paper No. 6* (Washington, D.C.: The World Bank, Latin America and Caribbean Region Environmentally and Socially Sustainable Development SMU, 2000), p. 1.

7 Ibid., p. 1.

8 Ibid., p. 6.

9 The World Bank, *Report No. 25752—Implementation of Operational Directive 4.20 on Indigenous Peoples: An Evaluation of Results* (Washington, D.C.: The World Bank, April 10, 2003), p. 11.

10 Arun Agrawal, "Indigenous Knowledge and the Politics of Classification" (Oxford: Blackwell Publishers, 2002), p. 290. This article was copyrighted by UNESCO, and it is available online from http://www-personal.umich.edu/~arunagra/papers/Indigenous%20 Knowledges.pdf . Retrieved on March 22, 2006.

11 Ibid., p. 292.

12 Report of the Commission on Intellectual Property Rights, *Integrating Intellectual Property Rights and Development Policy* (London: Commission on Intellectual Property Rights, 2002), pp. 76–78.

13 Ibid., p. 74.

14 Commission on Human Rights: Sub–Commission of Prevention of Discrimination and Protection of Minorities Working Group on Indigenous Populations, (19–30 July 1993): First International Conference on the Cultural & Intellectual Property Rights of Indigenous Peoples, *The Mataatua Declaration on Cultural and Intellectual Property rights of Indigenous People.* http://aotearoa.wellington.net.nz/imp/mata.htm Retrieved on April 19, 2006.

15 A. P. Elkin, "The Rights of Man in Primitive Society," *Human Rights: Comments and Interpretations: A Symposium edited by UNESCO* (Westport, Connecticut: Greenwood Press, 1973), p. 228.

16 These educational rights are derived from Elkin's manifesto in Ibid., pp. 228–237:
Elkin's 1947 Rights of Primitive Man
A basic right of primitive man today is the right to be considered a human being in the same manner and degree as civilized man
The Right to his own Pattern of Civilization and Personality
The Right to Education in Civilization
The Right to Community Land
The Right to Economic Development
The Right to the Disposal of One's Own Labour
Primitive Woman's Right to a Secure Sexual and Related Social and Economic Position
The Mixed-Blood Minority Group's Right to the Rights of the Society of Which It Forms Part
The Right of Justice
The Right to Political Self-Determination
The Community's Right to Freedom of Religious Beliefs and Practices
The Right to Health of Body, Mind, and Spirit

17 Ibid., p. 228.

18 Ibid., pp. 228–229.

19 Julius K. Nyerere, "Education for Self-Reliance" in *Freedom and Socialism: A Selection From Writings and Speeches 1965–1967* (London: Oxford University Press, 1968), p. 269–270.

20 Ibid., p. 289. Swahili was originally written in Arabic script and then began to appear in Latin script in the 19th century. There is a literary tradition in Swahili dating from the 17th century.

21 Ibid., p. 373.

22 Ibid., p. 277.

23 Ibid., p. 283.

24 Ibid., p. 282.
25 Ibid., p. 278.
26 Sen, p. 18.
27 Nisbett, *The Geography of Thought* ...
28 Justin Chisenga, "Indigenous Knowledge: Africa's Opportunity to Contribute to Global Information Content" *South African Journal of Library & Information Sciences*, 68 (1): 2002, p. 3.
29 Marlene Brant Castellano, "Updating Aboriginal Traditions of Knowledge," in *Indigenous Knowledges in Global Contexts* ... , p. 25.
30 Means, "For America to Live, Europe Must Die ... , p. 547.
31 Ibid., p. 548.
32 Russell Means, "Epilogue," in Russell Means with Marvin J. Wolf ... , p. 537.
33 Ibid., p. 537.
34 Maenette Benham and Ronald Heck, *Culture and Educational Policy in Hawaii: The Silencing of Native Voices* (Mahwah, New Jersey: Lawrence Erlbaum Associates, Inc., 1998).
35 Nisbett, pp. 8–9.
36 As quoted by Nisbett, p. 11.
37 Ibid., p. 89–92.
38 Ibid., p. 79.
39 David Wandira, Mpambo, "The Afrikan Multiversity: Report on the First International Cross-Cultural School, Isegero Campus, March 2001," www.osterlen.fhsk.se/afrika/***mpambo***%*20report.august.doc*, p. 5. Retrieved on April 20, 2006.
40 Paul Wangoola, "Mpambo, the African Multiversity: A Philosophy to Rekindle the African Spirit, in *Indigenous Knowledges* ... p. 265.
41 David Welchman Gegeo and Karen Ann Watson–Gegeo, "'How We Know': Kwara'ae Rural Villagers Doing Indigenous Epistemology (The Kwara'ae Genealogy Project, Solomon Islands)," *The Contemporary Pacific* 13(1): Spring 2001, pp. 55-88.
42 Ibid, p. 62.
43 Ibid., p. 62–63.
44 Ibid., p. 63.
45 Ibid., p. 63.
46 Ibid., p. 72.
47 Castellano, p. 23.
48 Quoted in Castellano, p. 23. The original article is James B. Waldram, "Traditional Knowledge Systems: The Recognition of Indigenous History and Science," *Saskatchewan Indian Federated College Journal* (1997), pp. 115-24.
49 Sigmund Freud's *The Interpretation of Dreams* (Whitefish, Montana: Kessinger Publishing, 2004), p. 4.
50 Donald L. Fixico, *The American Indian Mind in a Linear World: American Indian Studies and Traditional Knowledge* (New York: Routledge, 2003), pp. 3–4.
51 Castellano, p. 26.
52 Mahia Maurial, "Indigenous Knowledge and Schooling: A Continuum Between Conflict and Dialogue," in *What is Indigenous Knowledge? Voices from the Academy* edited by Ladislaus M. Semali and Joe L. Kincheloe (New York: Falmer Press, 1999), p. 63.
53 Nesbitt, pp. 139–140.
54 Fixico, p. 7.
55 Confucius, *The Great Learning* in *Confucius: Confucian Analects, The Great Learning, & The Doctrine of the Mean* translation with exegetical notes and dictionary of all characters by James Legge (New York: Dover Publication, Inc., 1971), pp. 357–358.
56 Nisbett, p. 109.
57 Mencius, *The Works of Mencius* translated, with critical and exegetical notes, prolegomena, and copious indexes by James Legge (New York: Dover Publication, Inc., 1970), pp. 130–131.
58 Legge's notes in Ibid., pp. 130–131.

59 Roxanna Ng, "Toward an Embodied Pedagogy: Exploring Health and the Body Through Chinese Medicine," in *Indigenous Knowledges in Global Contexts* ... p. 174.
60 See Nisbett, pp. 102–109.
61 Ibid., p. 109.
62 Mencius, pp. 249–250.
63 Confucius, *Analects* ... , p. 146.
64 Herbert Fingarette, *Confucius: The Secular as Sacred* (Prospect Heights, IL: Waveland Press, 1972), pp. 42–44.
65 William Theodore DeBary, "Confucian Education in Premodern East Asia," in *Confucian Traditions in East Asian Modernity: Moral Education and Economic Culture in Japan and the Four Mini-Dragons* edited by Tu Wei-Ming (Cambridge: Harvard University Press, 1996), p. 30.
66 Mencius, p. 251.
67 Ibid., p. 252.
68 Ibid., p. 252.
69 Confucius, *Analects* ..., p. 152.
70 William Theodore De Bary, *Asian Values and Human Rights: A Confucian Communitarian Perspective* (Cambridge: Harvard University press, 1998), p. 20.
71 Joseph Chan, "A Confucian Perspective on Human Rights for Contemporary China," in *The East Asian Challenge for Human Rights* edited by Joanne R Bauer and Daniel A. Bell (Cambridge: Cambridge University Press, 1999), p. 228.
72 Confucius, *Analects,* p. 121.
73 Ibid, p. 318.
74 Confucius, *The Doctrine of the Mean* in *Confucius: Confucian Analects, The Great Learning & The Doctrine of the Mean* ... p. 413.
75 Confucius, *Analects* ... , pp. 146–147.
76 Jane Perlez, "Southeast Asian Forests Fall to Prosperity's Ax as Chinese Boom Takes Heavy Toll," *The New York Times* (April 26, 2006), A1, A5.
77 Ibid., A5.

Chapter 5

A Prototype for a Global School and Humanity Flag Certification

This chapter presents a prototype for global schools and a method for achieving global Humanity Flag certification. The prototype for a global school gives more substance to the paradigm for a global core curriculum proposed in chapter 3. This global school prototype considers the relationships between school personnel, the physical plant, the grouping of students, global certification and resources, and school activities. The goal is to promote the longevity and happiness of school administrators, teachers, and students, while preparing students to assume the responsibility to ensure their own long life and happiness and that of others. Of course, the central focus of schools is the education of students. Therefore, the interests of schools staffs must be balanced with student educational needs.

In planning this global school structure, I use research data from longevity and happiness studies. With regard to school bureaucracy, I am interested in reducing the effect of the bicycle syndrome, promoting social equality, maximizing the capabilities of school staff, increasing supportive social networks, and providing optimal experiences for the school staff. Small schools, in contrast to large ones, may allow for a less hierarchical bureaucracy and may be more supportive social networks. The school's physical structure should be environmentally sound, should contribute to students' educations, and should promote long life and happiness. Global nongovernment organizations can be a source for resources and school certification. Maximizing the long life and happiness of students requires reducing inequalities caused by institutional practices such as ability grouping and high-stakes testing, increasing the capabilities of students in planning lessons, providing optimal learning experiences, allowing students to follow their interests, and helping students find their life's vocation to achieve personal fulfillment.

BUREAUCRATIC ORGANIZATION OF THE GLOBAL SCHOOL

In chapter 2, I discuss the importance of reducing the stress caused by the bicycle syndrome and social inequality. Social inequality also is correlated with feelings of trust, which is important for establishing supportive social networks. The lack of trust resulting from social inequalities, as noted in chapter 2, breeds crime and corruption. For instance, in U.S. schools, the frequent use of tests scores to measure the performance of teachers and adminstrators results in inequality of rewards and social standing for school staff. Consequently, there are numerous cases of teachers and administrators finding ways of cheating to make student test scores appear higher.[1] Happiness and longevity also depends, as discussed in chapter 2, on what Amartya Sen calls capabilities or the ability of people to lead the kind of lives they value. Linked to the concept of capabilities is flow or optimal experience. A school organization should allow school staff the maximum opportunity to exercise their capabilities and have optimal experiences.

Realistically, the best that can be done is to identify a type of school organization that fulfills the preceding objectives. Local cultural variations, community pressures, and the personalities of the school staff will always be factors in determining what actually happens in schools. Therefore, I am proposing simply a set of organizational factors based on research that would be supportive of the school staff's quality of life. Elimination of all social inequality in the school organization is not possible. Some member or members of the staff must assume responsibility for relations between the school and the outside world and manage internal school matters. In addition, there are problematic teachers and students. However, plans can be put into place to reduce the consequences of social inequality such as those found in previously cited studies of the British civil service. An obvious method would be to give teachers the power to hire and fire school administrators. Giving teachers this power would reduce social inequalities and increase teacher capabilities through participation in deciding the number of administrators and who should be hired. Although school administrators would still exercise power over teachers, this power would be limited by teacher control.

Small schools will help to decrease social inequalities. The larger the institution, the more bureaucracy is required for its operation. Research demonstrates that small schools are conducive to the creation of supportive social networks among school staff. A 2000 investigation of small schools by the British government's Office for Standards in Education concludes that "they [small schools] have a positive ethos with a family atmosphere, close links between staff and parents, an important place in the local community, and good standards of behavior."[2] A meta-analysis of research on school size conducted by Kathleen Cotton for the United States' Northwest Regional Educational Laboratory in 1996 concluded that "large schools appear to promote negative teacher perceptions of school administration and low staff morale.... There is less research on school size in relation to teacher or administrator variables, but what there is favors smaller schools."[3] A report by the British organization, Human Scale Education, comments that Cotton's updated meta-analysis in 2001 found the following: "Interpersonal relationships between and among students, teachers and administrators are more positive in small schools. Teachers' attitudes towards their work are more positive in small schools."[4] Cotton's work stresses the importance of small schools for building social networks for the school staff and students. Cotton summarizes:

Attributes associated with small school size that researchers have identified as accounting for their superiority include the following:

1. Everyone's participation is needed to populate the school's offices, teams, clubs, etc., so a far smaller percentage of students is overlooked or alienated.
2. Adults and students in the school know and care about one another to a greater degree than is possible in large schools.
3. Small schools have a higher rate of parent involvement.[5]

Important for the promotion of "capabilities," Cotton also concludes, is the fact that "students and staff generally have a stronger sense of personal efficacy in small schools."[6] Writing for the Northwest Regional Educational Laboratory, which specializes in research on school size, Suzie Boss asserts: "What's more, teachers in smaller schools tend to feel better about their work.... Small school size encourages teachers to innovate and students to participate, resulting in greater commitment for both groups."[7]

Previously discussed research on longevity and happiness shows that the type of social networking supported by small schools promotes both happiness and longevity. So ideally, global school structures would be small and operated by teachers' councils, which would have the power to determine the staffing needs of the school. Besides deciding on the school administration, teachers councils also would have the power to make final decisions about the hiring and firing of teachers.

To promote the capabilities and optimal experiences of teachers, the curriculum cannot be prescriptive. The proposed global core curriculum is a guide that allows teachers to plan lessons creatively. The planning of lessons increases teacher capabilities. In addition, the creative act of preparing lessons provides opportunities for teachers to have optimal experiences. Of course, teachers can use and vary the lesson plans of others. For instance, chapter 3 contains many examples of progressive, environmental, and human rights lessons. In the age of the Internet, there are many Web sites that teachers can explore for examples of lessons. These include the Human Rights Education Network, the United Nations' Cyberschoolbus, the World Wildlife Fund's education programs, the Earth Charter Initiative, and regional groups such as the North American Association for Environmental Education and the Globe Program, which is available in six languages.[8]

Teachers should decide how students will be grouped. Rather than thinking only in terms of an age-graded self-contained classroom, teachers should be given the opportunity to vary the number of students participating in an assignment and the number of teachers involved in any particular assignment. Small groups might meet for extra help from teachers, whereas large groups of students may be involved in other projects. For instance, the number of students might vary for lessons examining the quality of life in a local community and working to improve conditions in activities similar to Brazil's Instituto Pedra Grande de Preservaçao's project discussed in chapter 3 involving the improvement river sanitation in the city of Atibaia.

Teacher control of lesson planning will help adapt to the global core curriculum to local cultures. Assuming that teachers are drawn from the local population, increasing teacher capabilities for planning lessons will provide organizational conditions that will allow the adaptation of the curriculum to the local culture.

I also propose that teacher training focus on the paradigm for a global core curriculum, and that teacher candidates discuss model lessons and learn to apply their imaginations to lesson planning. Those training to be teachers should be given opportunities to have optimal learning experiences through imaginative lesson planning and practice teaching. They should be asked to think about how they might plan lessons to provide students with optimal learning experiences.

In summary, schools can be organized to maximize the opportunities for staff to experience subjective well-being and working conditions that contribute to a long life. The key is reducing social inequalities, increasing staff capabilities, and providing opportunities for optimal experiences. A small school appears to be most supportive of teachers' capabilities, or efficacy, and the creation of social networks. Of course, the school staff must receive an education that gives them the tools to work within this institutional context. In addition, the school structure, including buildings and grounds, must be supportive of this organization.

A MODEL FOR THE GLOBAL SCHOOL PLANT

Invited to speak at the 1999 Taipei International Conference on Education, I had a chance to inspect newly established schools for Taiwan's indigenous tribes and visit elementary schools in Taipei. I was immediately struck by how the school buildings both in the city and at indigenous tribal sites were similar to those in the United States and other parts of the world. The one major difference was the massive size of some elementary schools, with enrollments of about 6,000 students. Increasingly aware of the global nature of schooling practices, I began to pay more attention to school structures while visiting other countries. Except for impoverished areas, such as school sites in sub-Saharan African, where structures can be without walls or classes conducted in the open, or at madrasas in Pakistan, most school plants are constructed around self-contained age-graded classrooms.

Small schools have a positive effect on students while fostering social equality and networking among school staff. Kathleen Cotton's meta-analysis of school size studies concludes that research overwhelmingly supports the positive effect of small schools on students. The large number of supporting studies is impressive. For example, 19 studies show that small schools create positive attitudes among students toward school and particular subjects; 14 studies conclude that small schools improve social behavior problems; 6 studies find that small schools create a sense of belongingness among students; 9 studies show a relationship between small schools and positive student self-concepts; and 14 studies find that small schools improve interpersonal relations between students and between students and staff.[9]

Small schools can provide an environment that nurtures student social networking, positive self-concepts, and attitudes that support the long life and happiness of students. Regarding feelings of alienation, an indicator of an individual's sense of belonging to a social network, Cotton summarizes,

> Concerned about the emotional effects of different kinds of school environments, some researchers have studied the degree to which students feel a sense of belonging in their schools. Given the foregoing findings about other student variables, it is not surprising that these investigators have found a much greater sense of belonging (sometimes expressed as a lower level of alienation) among students in small schools than in large ones.[10]

Importantly, alienation is linked to student capabilities or, as Cotton refers to it, self-direction: "Unfortunately, alienation affects confidence, self-esteem, and *responsibility for self-direction* [my emphasis]."[11]

Small schools minimize the effect of social inequalities on students. Massive school buildings often lead to classes differentiated according to student abilities. According to research on social inequalities, separation of students by ability may cause students to be labeled as having low abilities and to suffer the health strains and reduction in subjective well-being similar to that experienced in the lower rungs of government and corporate bureaucracies. Also, separation by abilities may reduce the sense of self-worth among those labeled as slow learners.

Therefore, small schools support conditions that contribute to the long life and happiness of students and teachers by fostering close relations between all members of the school community and by providing the opportunity for students and school staff to maximize their capabilities. Of course, small schools are not a panacea because they only foster these positive factors, but do not guarantee them.

Small schools are part of the movement to build environmentally responsible schools or "green schools." In England, the Human Scale Education organization was founded in 1985 to"foster positive relationships that enable teachers to know their students well and make possible a more holistic approach to learning that engages the whole person."[12] The organization relates small schools to environmentalism: "The learning community [small schools] is underpinned by environmentally sustainable values and practices."[13] Similar to research findings in the United States, the organization stresses the importance of social values in small schools: "Small scale learning communities enable children and young people to be known and valued as individuals."[14]

According to our overall goals, the school building should promote personnel health and the health of the biosphere. Whether the school is already built or is being built, school staff and students should engage in discussions and planning about improving the school environment. Similar to the Beancross Primary School program discussed in chapter 3, lessons and opportunities should allow for students to participate in planning and maintaining school grounds as part of an environmental lesson. There should be an opportunity to maintain a school garden. School gardens are frequently mentioned in progressive and environmental literature as a means of teaching children biology, agriculture, and the requirements of the biosphere.

The actual school plant affects the biosphere and can have a positive or negative effect on the students, the staff, and the surrounding community. The environmental impact of school buildings is emphasized in the American School Board Journal's special publication, *Learning By Design,* which is described as "the school leader's guide to architectural services." An important article in this publication, Schools that Sustain, coauthored by Katherine N. Peele, chair of the American Institute of Architects' Committee on Architecture for Education and Sara Malone, editor/writer for the Professional Practice Group at the American Institute of Architects, warns:

> The construction of a new school facility affects our environment in a multitude of ways. The production of the building materials can deplete natural resources and consume fossil fuels. Waste of building materials during

> construction adds to our landfills. And, the grading operations necessary for construction of a school project can erode the topsoil and pollute streams with sediment and chemical runoff. But, if you look beyond the actual construction process itself, you see that some of the biggest impacts to the environment come with the long-term operation and location of the school.[15]

Architects Peele and Malone worry about the environmental impact of school buildings on the surrounding community as well as the environmental soundness of the construction. Peele and Malone believe that Walker Elementary School in McKinney, Texas, is a good example of an environmentally sound building. To reduce oil consumption caused by the transportation of children to school, the school was built near community biking and walking trails, which allow students to bike or walk to school. The school's roof was designed as a cistern to collect rainwater for flushing toilets and other nondrinking purposes. A windmill moves water between cisterns. Built with recycled and energy-efficient materials, the school also maximizes the use of winter sunlight and uses solar water heating.[16]

Just as important as the school's environmental design and community location is the use of the building and grounds as an object of study. Peele and Malone stress the use of a "green school" for student learning: "All of these elements [in reference to the Walker Elementary School] are used to instruct students in science, math, and environmental problems and issues."[17] The school becomes a source for integrated learning about the biosphere. Peele and Malone provide the following lists of consideration in making a school green:

Considerations for Making a School Green

1. *Landscaping:* A Los Angeles-based organization called Tree People discovered that a 12% to 18% energy savings can result from carefully considered planting of trees.
2. *Daylighting:* Windows that let in natural light create a better learning environment and result in lower utility bills and emissions. (The region's climate must be considered to avoid glare and heat buildup, however.)
3. *Energy-efficient building shell.*
4. *Solar power.*
5. *Energy-efficient light and electrical systems.*
6. *Mechanical/ventilation systems.*
7. *Environmentally sensitive building products and recycling systems.*
8. *Indoor air quality.*
9. *Water conservation:* Rainwater can be collected in reservoirs and cisterns to irrigate the landscape and fill toilets.
10. *Transportation:* Kids should be encouraged to walk or bike to school, cutting the use of single cars and buses and reducing emissions.[18]

As suggested by Peele and Malone, school buildings can serve to educate students about the biosphere through what they call "eco-education." Peele and Malone urge teachers to "make students aware of the connectivity of our world and the responsibility we all share to act as good stewards of our environment. Hopefully, they will take this message home to their parents and carry it with them the rest of their lives."[19] This approach is exemplified by the work of the California Green Schools Program by the Alliance to Save Energy based in Washington, D.C. A unique aspect of the program is the funding by a private corporation to support integrated school lessons on protection of the biosphere. The program started in California in 2000 with the sponsorship of a private utility, Southern California Edison. In 2002, funding shifted from private to government sources including the California Public Utilities Commission, the California Energy Commission, and the California State and Consumer Services Agency.

The Alliance to Save Energy program is an example of private and public support for integrated environmental education lessons and the building of green schools. The program recognizes that school plants can be environmentally damaging and can waste energy. Similar to the ethical responsibility emphasized in my proposed global core curriculum, the Alliance proposes to educate citizens to assume responsibility to act to protect the environment:

> While young people undoubtedly are the leaders of tomorrow, they also can play a leadership role in today's world. For example, children were the driving force behind the recycling movement, often prodding their parents to "do the right thing" for the environment by sorting bottles and bundling newspapers. The success of that effort and the resulting benefits to the planet are a testament to the power of the young people in our country. We believe it is within the power of students to achieve similar success in saving energy by stimulating their schools, families, and communities to incorporate energy efficiency into their daily habits and purchasing decisions.[20]

As part of the California green schools effort, the Alliance to Save Energy distributes a 72-page booklet of model integrated lessons, many of them based on student investigation of the school plant. The lessons in this booklet demonstrate the role the school building can play in educating students about the biosphere. For instance, the students at the Fortuna High School conducted a lighting and energy audit of the school and lobbied the administration to change construction plans for a new science building to install more efficient heaters. The students inform school administrators on green schools projects being conducted at other schools.[21] Fifth-grade classes at the Jacoby Creek Charter School combined the study of art, or what I would call "political art," and science. The class studied electrical usage in the school and audited plug loads in each classroom. Their work resulted in the replacement of many incandescent light bulbs with florescent and light-emitting diode (LED) lights. Learning how to use political art to persuade others to conserve electricity, the students created posters for other classrooms. They also wrote and produced a play.[22] Dressed in capes adorned with a lightening bolt, the students at John F. Kennedy elementary school investigated the school building looking for energy waste. Their findings led to major changes in the school's energy use.[23]

The Alliance to Save Energy distributes other environmental lessons centered on the school. For instance, how much of the earth's surface is needed to sustain the lives of students in a class or schools is the focus of the lesson How Big Is Your Footprint, which integrates a range of subjects from math to environmental science. Developed by David Casey for the Analy High School in the West Sonoma County Union High School District, the lesson teaches students how to calculate the impact of personal choices on the environment using online Web sites. The lesson recommends two Web sites for calculating an ecological footprint.[24] It begins with the classic progressive technique, similar to John Dewey's lessons, of asking students to investigate how much food a small farm produces. First, the students use math to determine the size of a small farm and the standard unit, the acre, used in the United States to calculate land size. The students must explore agriculture, home construction, energy sources, and geology to answer the following questions: "Could one acre provide all the food needed for one person? What about providing the materials needed to build a home? What about heating costs? Could the farm provide energy for equipment?"[25] All these questions lead students to the final question of calculating the ecological footprint of the school's students:

> What is the average number of acres to provide for the needs of our students? What is the greatest amount? What is the least amount? Suppose this number of acres were to be translated into the number of planet Earths needed if everyone on the planet lived as a member of the class does. What would be a reasonable number?[26]

Why Is It Hotter When I Wear Black in Summer Than When I Wear White? is a lesson that combines the study of science, math, and language arts. Jeff Saks created it to be used in California's Bemis Elementary School for a one-week unit, with the findings to be presented to the local school board. Using art supplies, calculators, thermometers, and journals, students applied the scientific method to determine the heat absorbent values of colors. To create a hypothesis to be tested by students, the class voted on what colors they thought were the most or least absorbent of heat. They then tested the class hypothesis by placing thermometers in different colored envelopes made of construction paper. The envelopes were placed in the sun, and after one hour, the thermometers were checked and the temperatures recorded in the class journal. After a week of data collection, a graph was made of the findings. The students decided, living in a warm climate, that it would be best to paint the school's roof white, which the school board proceeded to do.[27]

Besides the use of the school plant for environmental lessons, architects Peele and Malone advocate flexible classroom arrangements that enhance the ability of teachers to plan different types of lessons instead of just having contained age-graded classrooms. As an example, they describe Portland's Alpha High School, which has mixed-use spaces with movable walls allowing teachers to change room configurations for a wide variety of learning activities. Recalling the classic progressive shibboleth "learning by doing," the two architects emphasize the importance of flexible learning spaces: "We also know that people learn more effectively by 'doing'. Such learning can occur within a school, or within the community, workplace, or family. Finding creative opportunities outside of the actual school building can save on the amount of new construction that is required."[28] There are many sources of information on green schools that can serve as plans for new and renovated buildings and as sources for lessons. In the United States, the Northeast Sustainable Energy Association distributes an 11-page resource guide, which includes topics such as High Performance Green Schools, Renewable Energy and Schools, Daylighting, and Indoor Air Quality.[29] In England, The National Energy Foundation promotes green schools and environmental education programs.[30] The Alliance to Save Energy is working globally to encourage green schools in such countries as Armenia, India, Brazil, Bulgaria, China, Indonesia, Philippines, Mexico, Russia,, Thailand, Sir Lanka, and the Ukraine.[31] In addition, environmental nongovernment organizations, such as Green Peace and the World Wildlife Fund, are the second largest in global numbers after human rights nongovernment organizations. Between 1953 and 1993, the number of international environmental groups leaped from 2 to 90, making them the fast-growing sector of the global civil society.[32] Those nongovernment organizations are pressuring governments to build environmentally sound buildings, including school buildings.

Therefore, school buildings and grounds should contribute to the "capabilities" of teachers to plan lessons for indoor and outdoor settings. They can be included in lessons, with students examining the relationship between buildings and grounds and the impact of the school plant on the biosphere. Students can participate in planning and maintaining environmentally sound school sites. The central focus of planning new school buildings, which ideally would include staff and students in the planning process, should be to create environmental conditions that promote the health and happiness of the community.[33]

THE SCHOOL, HEALTH, AND THE COMMUNITY

Eating and health facilities are important parts of the school plant. They could be planned by the school and local community. The eating facility would provide and teach the school, community, and staff about healthful foods. Community planning would help to ensure that food provided by the eating facility would reflect local tastes. A student committee, as part of their learning activities, could be responsible for monitoring current information on human nutrition and health. Immunization programs would be included in plans for school health facilities. Currently, the World Health Organization (WHO) operates immunization programs, which also provide needed nutrients to local populations. For instance, WHO combined a campaign to eradicate polio with vitamin A therapy. The organization reports that in some geographic areas, vitamin A deficiency is

> the main cause of preventable blindness in children. We now also know that vitamin A plays an important role in strengthening the body's resistance to infection, and that children who are vitamin A deficient suffer an increased risk of death and illness, particularly measles and diarrhea. Studies have shown that improving the vitamin A status of deficient children aged 6–59 months dramatically increases their chances of survival by
>
> - reducing all causes of mortality by 23%
> - reducing measles mortality by 50%
> - reducing diarrheal disease mortality by 33%.[34]

Severe cases of vitamin A deficiency are prevalent in parts of Africa, South and Central America, the Indian subcontinent, Viet Nam, and island areas of the South Pacific. Moderate and mild deficiencies exist in China and countries of the former Soviet Union.

A school-based food and vitamin program is the easiest way to correct vitamin deficiencies. Accordingly, WHO recommends that vitamin A supplements be given during National Immunization Days (NIDs). Because these only occur once a year, WHO suggests that other means be found to provide continuing vitamin supplements: "Vitamin A distribution linked with NIDs can and should complement and strengthen these routine activities. This is important because in areas where VAD [vitamin A deficiency] is a problem, children need vitamin A regularly every four to six months, and NIDs provide only one dose per year."[35] In addition, WHO recommends that children eat foods rich in vitamin A such as milk, liver, eggs, yellow and orange fruits, and vegetables. School eating facilities can serve foods fortified with vitamin A by the addition of synthetic vitamin A to sugar, vegetable oil, and wheat flour.

A school-based food and vitamin program also could be used to correct other global nutritional problems, particularly iron and iodine deficiencies. Iron deficiency anemia affects large parts of the world's population including 57% of the Southeast Asia population, 46% of the African population, and 45% of those living in the Eastern Mediterranean.[36] Iodine deficiency "is the greatest cause of preventable brain damage in childhood."[37]

The largest percentage of school-age children affected by iodine deficiencies are in Europe, Africa, and the Eastern Mediterranean.[38] The best method of treating iodine deficiency, according to WHO, is to feed children foods fortified with iodine. Obviously, a school-based food program would be a good way to ensure that all children eat foods fortified with iodine.

Besides initiatives for vitamin supplementation, the United Nation's World Food Programme conducts a global school feeding initiative to provide students with a balanced diet and as an incentive for children to attend school. In school, they receive needed health care. The 2005 World Food Programme's *Global School Feeding Report* explains: "School meals offer hope. A school feeding programme gives poor families an incentive to enroll their children in school. It provides children with the nutrition and energy they need to focus and concentrate in class. In many cases, the programme becomes a catalyst for a host of other health and education initiatives."[39] Working with the United Nations International Children's Emergency Fund (UNICEF) and local governments, the World Food Programme created what it calls an Essential Package of heath education and hygiene assistance, which includes, depending on the location, take-home food rations, deworming treatment, latrine installation, kitchens, schools, gardens, clean water systems, HIV/AIDS and malaria prevention education, and teacher training in health issues.[40] In 2004, the World Food Programme operated school feeding programs in 72 countries, feeding 16,574, 460 children, with 8,845,766 children between the ages of 6 and 12 years receiving deworming treatment.[41]

Quality education depends on the health and nutrition of children. Sick children suffering from anemia and lacking essential vitamins cannot fully engage their minds and bodies in learning. A school-based eating and vitamin program is essential for both the health of the child and the possibility of students living a long life. As part of their learning, students should participate in planning a school-based food, vitamin, and immunization program, and they should be given the responsibility of continually investigating current research on nutrition and diseases.

HUMANITY FLAG: GLOBAL CERTIFICATION

The speed of information and travel makes it possible to have global forms of school certification that are not controlled by nation-states. School certification provides information about the school program to parents, students, and the community. Currently, nation-states use certification to force schools to conform to government policies, particularly those supporting the human capital educational model. Using compulsory education laws, the nation-state can force students to attend state-certified schools with the objective of fostering economic growth. I do not object to compulsory laws as a means of forcing parents and communities to attend to the education of their children and to fulfill the 1948 Universal Declaration of Human Rights:

> Article 26:
>
> 1. Everyone has the right to education. Education shall be free, at least in the elementary and fundamental stages. Elementary education shall be compulsory.[42]

Although the Universal Declaration of Human Rights does support compulsory education, it does not give direct support to human capital forms of education. In fact, paragraph 2 of Article 26 clearly calls for educational goals that are more akin to the goals of a long life and happiness than to education used for training workers for the global economy. The educational goals of full development of the personality, freedom, protection of human rights, global toleration of differing racial and religious groups, and peace could be considered as supportive or nested within my proposed global curriculum.

> Article 26
>
> 2. Education shall be directed to the full development of the human personality and to strengthening of respect for human rights and fundamental freedoms. It shall promote understanding, tolerance and friendship among all nations, racial or religious groups, and shall further the activities of the United Nations for the maintenance of peace.[43]

The writers of the Universal Declaration of Human Rights also recognized that the nation-state could use education to thwart the goals of freedom, human rights, toleration, and peace, as exemplified by the school systems of nations defeated during World War II, namely Nazi Germany, fascist Italy, and nationalistic Japan. Paragraph 3 of Article 26 provides an escape from the requirement of forced attendance by nation-states at schools that glorify war, neglect human rights, demand unquestioning obedience, and spread hate. Paragraph 3 recognizes the necessity of dissent to the educational dictates of a nation-state that violates the welfare of humans.

> Article 26
>
> Parents have a prior right to choose the kind of education that shall be given to their children.[44]

Global nongovernment organizations provide differing forms of school certification. An example and model of how this type of certification might look is the Foundation for Environmental Freedom's Eco-Schools program. This program awards global schools Green Flag certification for meeting the following requirements:

> Green Flag Certification Requirements: The Green Flag certification is awarded to schools which have successfully followed the Eco-Schools methodology, adapting its application to meet their specific needs and achieving their own determined concrete objectives. With its participatory approach, involving pupils themselves in both activities and decision-making processes. Fostering ties with local authorities, organizations, businesses, and indeed pupils' families, Eco-Schools provides a platform for school-based community development.[45]

The Foundation for Environmental Education (FEE) demonstrates how global nongovernment organizations form and expand. The organization was initially founded as a nongovernment environmental organization in 1983 as the Foundation for Environmental Education in Europe. In 1985, the organization, in partnership with the European Commission, began certifying the quality of beaches in 10 European countries in what it called the Blue Flag Campaign. In 1994, it launched its Eco-Schools Campaign. In the 1990s, the organization dropped "in Europe" from its name as it expanded to countries outside of Europe. In 2003, the organization signed a memorandum of understanding with the United Nations Environment Program (UNEP), which, according to the memorandum, "formalizes long-standing relationship between UNEP and FEE and provides a framework for long term cooperation on areas of common interest relating to education, training and public awareness for sustainable development globally."[46]

In 2005, there were 14,000 registered Eco-Schools, 4,000 of them certified as Green Flag holders in countries around the globe including Bangladesh, Brazil, Chile, Kenya, Morocco, New Zealand, Russia, South Africa, and Turkey. The organization now divides schools into regional areas such as Eco-Schools in Africa, America, Asia, Europe, and Oceania.[47]

To be certified with a Green Flag, a school must meet seven requirements. First, a participatory Eco-School Committee must be created involving students, school staff, parents, and other community members. Second, the Eco-School Committee must make an assessment of the environmental impact of the school. Third, an action plan must be developed to correct any problems found in the environmental assessment. Fourth, the Eco-School Committee is required to monitor and make any needed adjustments to the action plan.

The fifth requirement affects the school's curriculum. Instead of a detailed and specific curriculum requirement, Eco-Schools issue general guidelines to be acted upon by the local school. This approach is similar to one I suggest for the global core curriculum. Curriculum certification for a Green Flag requires

- Classroom study of themes such as energy, water, and waste
- Whole-school involvement in initiatives such as saving water, recycling materials, and preventing litter
- Integration of environmental education into all areas of study.

The sixth requirement is that the school, including students and staff, must promote the idea of sustainability to the local community through action, posters, displays, and press coverage. Finally, as a seventh requirement, the school must create its own 'Eco-code.'[48] Thus, earning the Green Flag requires cooperative work, investigation of environmental conditions, and activism to improve the quality of the environment.

I am using the Green Flag program as a model for global certification by a nongovernment organization that could provide information to the community, parents, and students. Similar to the Green Flag certification, I can imagine a global organization that awards a 'Humanity Flag' for complying with the following requirements.

Humanity Flag Certification

1. Adoption of a global core curriculum designed to promote long life and happiness as an important part of the school's total curriculum.
2. A school bureaucracy that reduces hierarchy among school staff and reduces the effect of the bicycle syndrome.
3. Student and staff capabilities enhanced through involvement in planning lessons.
4. Holistic learning as the guiding principle in planning most school lessons. School lessons would include
   a. Teaching students the political, social, and economic conditions that have decreased and increased human life spans and subjective well-being
   b. The use of problem-solving methods, including the use of imagination, to create conditions that promote a long life and happiness
   c. Helping students understand the complex relationships between humans and the rest of the biosphere
   d. Giving students the tools to change the world
   e. Developing an ethical responsibility to protect happiness and lives of others.

5. Achievement of optimal learning experiences as a guiding principle in planning school lessons.
6. Participation of students and staff in monitoring the environmental impact of the school plant, including the impact on student, staff, and community health.
7. Students and school staff use of a planned program for collecting and distributing information to school and community members about research related to increasing the longevity and subjective well-being of humans.
8. Maintenance of a healthy meal program, with students monitoring research findings on healthful foods.
9. Cooperation with the World Health Organization in providing for the immunization of students, staff, and possibly other community members, and providing nutrients lacking in the diet of the local population.

THE GLOBAL SCHOOL NESTED IN A WORLD OF RESOURCES

Information technology changed the global map of education, making it possible for small schools anyplace in the world to use the Internet to access lesson plans, educational games, and other information. In addition, the Internet helped to propel global nongovernment organizations, particularly human rights and environmental organizations, into ideological competition with the influence of nation-states over local schools.[49] These global organizations are continually providing new models for lesson plans and educational materials, including books. Of course, use of these rich and free global resources requires access to the Internet.

Internet access is an important part of maintaining a global school. Although Internet usage is global, many countries lack the financial resources to provide Internet access for schools. Therefore, a major effort should be made by an international organization such as the United Nations to ensure Internet access for all schools. The United States government's Central Intelligence Agency publishes the *World Factbook* (available online), which shows the unevenness of global Internet use. The *2005 World Factbook* provides only the number of national Internet users and not the percentage of the population using the Internet. However, these numbers are suggestive of the unevenness of usage (Table 5.1).

In the Central Intelligence Agency's rank order of Internet users, the first is the European Union followed in order by the United States, China, and Japan. Calculations based on Central Intelligence Agency figures show that a little more than 9% of the world's population are Internet users.[50] Of course,

TABLE 5.1
Numbers of Internet Users by Selected Countries

Country	*No. of Internet Users by Year*
Afghanistan	1,000 (2002)
Albania	30,000 (2003)
Argentina	4.1 million (2002)
China	94 million (2004)
Congo, Democratic Republic of the	50,000 (2002)
European Union	230,097,055 (2005)
Georgia	150,000 (2003)
Japan	86.3 million (2005)
Laos	15,000 (2002)
Mongolia	220,000 (2004)
Namibia	65,000 (2003)
Norway	2.288 million (2002)
Russia	6 million (2002)
Singapore	2.31 million (2002)
Sierra Leone	8,000 (2002)
Taiwan	13.8 million (2005)
United States	159 million (2002)

Source: Central Intelligence Agency. (2006, January 10). *The world factbook—field listings—internet users.* Available at: www.odci.gov/publications/factbook/fields/2153.html. Accessed.

this calculation may distort the actual percentage of users because many people use the same Internet access. The fact that the major players in the global economy have the highest Internet users—European Union, United States, China, and Japan—may be considered a sign indicating the importance of the Internet for participation in the global economy. However, for the purposes of a global school system, Internet usage is essential, and maximum effort must be made to ensure Internet access for all schools.

When Russia assumed the Group of Eight Presidency in 2006 (G8 countries represent about 66% of the world economy), Russia's President Vladimir Putin issued a statement stressing the importance of educational Internet use as part of a plan for world economic development. Although in complete disagreement with educational goals of this book, Putin expressed the G8's desire to expand Internet usage as a method of increasing global educational opportunities. Expressing the usual human capital education goals, Putin wrote: "In a postindustrial information society, education becomes a prerequisite for success in the daily life and a major input into economic development."[51] Regarding Internet usage in education, Putin asserted: "It is necessary to make more efficient use of the most advanced resources, including the Internet and other newest means of information and knowledge distribution, in the field of education."[52] With the backing of the G8, there may be greater global opportunities for schools to have Internet access, which, although G8 leaders think in terms of the Internet's contribution to economic development, opens the opportunity for global schools to tap into educational resources that will help fulfill the goal of a long life and happiness.

An important idea stressed by President Putin is that the Internet may contribute to greater global social cohesion. Although it is important for local cultures to influence the content and methods of global education, the Internet does provide a means for achieving understanding between members of differing cultures. This is important in a world experiencing mass movements of populations. As President Putin states: "In the conditions of growing mobility of world population and steady increase in migration, the problem of integration into a different cultural environment acquires special importance. Obviously, it is education that makes possible mutual social adaptation of various cultural, ethnic, and confessional groups."[53] The upgrading of the information systems and access to the Internet will help educators to confront the problem of cultural conflict resulting from the mass migration of populations. "Hence," Putin writes, "special attention should be paid to upgrading education systems for the attainment of these goals (social cohesion and economic development) both in developed and developing countries."[54]

While disagreeing with the economic goals of the G8 and Putin for education, I agree that the Internet is both an important source of education for the global school and a means of social cohesion as users connect and gain knowledge of other cultures. Through the Internet, students from around the world can participate in global projects. For instance, many of the lessons used as examples in this volume are taken from Web sites. For example, the United Nations Environment Program's textbook, *Tunza: Acting for a Better World,* can be downloaded from the Internet for free.[55]

Although the textbook is written for youth who may or may not be in school, I am evaluating its potential for use in schools. Klaus Toepfer, Executive Director of the United Nations Environment Program, explains how *Tunza* serves as both an environmental handbook and as a guide for action: "The purpose of this book is to inform youth about some of the most significant issues that affect the environment today and to show how young people around the globe can participate in promoting positive change in these areas."[56]

As a textbook approach dedicated to educating and stimulating youth to engage in environmental action, *Tunza's* format is a model for a free Internet textbook that can be used to educate students to be active in working for a world that maximizes human life and happiness. As a textbook, *Tunza* follows the classic progressive model of holistic education by weaving together basic knowledge and theory with practice and calls to action. Using a textbook format, the reader is first introduced to acronyms and abbreviations in Get Used to These Terms! as well as a history of youth involvement in environmental projects, beginning with the 1971 First International Youth Conference on the Human Environment. The remainder of the textbook is divided into three parts. Part I, Preparing for Action, sets the stage for preparing students to be activist. It contains sections on Youth Action, The Action Toolbox, and The Role of Youth. Part II, "Our World Today" provides knowledge about the context of current environmental issues in a section entitled The Global Economy and one entitled Population. The final part, Part III, Taking Up the Challenge, provides material on how youth can work to improve the environment in sections entitled Atmosphere, Freshwater Resources, Oceans and Coasts, Land and Food, Urbanization, Biodiversity, Forests, and Energy. The book concludes with a list of resources including useful Web sites. Using typical textbook methods, each chapter contains an overview, boxes highlighting examples of youth activities and environmental events, and tips for actions indicated by bullets.

The Action Toolbox section in *Tunza* provides students with a guide to accessing information from schools and universities as well as government and nongovernment organizations, and to using the Internet. The book recommends that in addition to relying on established sources, students should do their own research within their own communities. The holistic approach of *Tunza* has students learning research methods, the interrelationship of humans with the biosphere, and environmental and community conditions. This holistic approach is reflected in *Tunza*'s recommended community research activities. These activities can be adapted to a variety of concerns. In Tunza's Part I, students are given examples of activist youth, such as South Africa's Aquateens Environmental Club, which works to solve environmental problems under the banner of what they call the "three elements of learning." The three elements in this example are used to teach the reader the basic elements of an activist pedagogy including the social nature of knowledge, the importance of individual experience, and the use of knowledge to solve problems:

- Knowledge is shared
- Each individual experiences the environment
- Information is used to solve an environmental problem.[57]

The textbook explains to students the importance of establishing objectives in pursuing action projects and provides what the book calls Ten Easy Steps on How to Set up a Project. These steps can easily be adapted to other curricular goals including human rights, health and longevity, and subjective well-being. It is a model for preparing activist students of any age. The book also suggests that students take action to change their schools by investigating the number of environmental courses offered, finding out exactly what is taught in these courses, working to add environmental courses to the curriculum if none are offered, ensuring the environmental news appears in the school newspaper, and conducting research to identify and solve environmental problems and to provide information to local newspapers.

Tunza's Part II, Our World Today, presents knowledge that is necessary for understanding current environmental conditions. Using a holistic approach, Part II opens with a discussion of the global economy and its relationship to the rest of the biosphere. Besides discussing multinational corporations and trade, the section explores the impact of inequality of wealth between nations by discussing the question: Who controls the global economy? The effect of industry on the environment, biodiversity, and sustainability also are discussed. The last section of Part II is devoted to the problem of population growth, distribution of resources, sustainability, and protection of the biosphere.[58] In the context of holistic education, all these topics open doors for students to learn science, math, history, economics, and sociology.

Part III, Taking Up the Challenge, is devoted to specific environmental problems, which of course have a direct effect on the health and longevity of humans. Each section describes the various aspects of the problem. In keeping with the tenor of the book, a part of each section is devoted to taking action. For instance, the first section of Part III is devoted to the atmosphere, and includes topics such as acid rain, organic pollutants, smog, ozone layer, UV-B exposure, and climate change. The Taking Action part of the Atmosphere section is divided into individual and organizational actions. Individual activities include buying environmentally friendly products, using environmentally friendly forms of transportation, reducing energy consumption, taking proper care in disposing of old refrigerators, and planting and caring for trees. Individual students are urged to communicate their feelings and research findings on atmospheric problems to the general public, government officials, and the popular media. In organizations, students are encouraged to investigate energy consumption in their schools, promote the use of clean energy, and do research on local causes of atmospheric destruction.[59]

Tunza exemplifies the free Internet resources available for local schools and the role that these types of textbooks play in putting students in contact with other Internet resources and organizations. Throughout the text, there are recommended Web sites for gathering information and making contacts. *Tunza* is a model of a holistic textbook designed to create an ethical obligation among students to work for the improvement of their world. Also, unlike most textbooks, *Tunza* provides investigations that will help students change the world.

CONCLUSION: MAKING SCHOOLS HEALTHY AND HAPPY LEARNING COMMUNITIES

With a Humanity Flag indicating global certification, my prototype for global school organization would embody what is known about conditions that foster human welfare and optimal learning experiences. I am stressing the word "foster" because human life spans and happiness can never be guaranteed. The best that can be done is to create conditions that will nurture human welfare. Also, my prototype should be continually reinvented as new understandings are gained about the human condition.

Therefore, on the basis of current research, my prototype for a global school organization emphasizes a decrease in the stress caused by the bicycle syndrome and inequalities of power between staff members. Teachers' capabilities or ability to practice what they value about their profession is enhanced through teacher involvement in the hiring of administrators, the grouping of students for learning activities, and the planning of lessons. Small schools can reduce the stress of bicycling caused by large hierarchical and bureaucratic organizations, and they can foster the growth of social networks. In summary, my prototype of a global school is organized to maximize the opportunities for staff to experience subjective well-being and working conditions that contribute to a long life.

School buildings and grounds should be conducive to learning and the nurturing of student, staff, and biosphere health. The planning of new school buildings and landscapes as well as discussions about existing buildings and landscapes provide learning opportunities, or what has been referred to as "Eco-education." Participation in planning helps the community, school staff, and students to understand the effect of buildings and landscaping on the biosphere and, consequently, on the environmental health of the community. School buildings and grounds should contribute to the health and happiness of the staff, students, and community. The planning of school interiors should emphasize multiple use so that teachers can plan large and small group activities for indoor and outdoor settings. Schools should be the location for immunization programs and the distribution of nutrients needed to ensure the healthy growth of children. Students and staff should be involved in planning healthful food programs. The Internet should be used to access lessons, learning games, research, and other information, and to create contacts so that students can participate with students around the world in social change. Global non government certification can be created under my proposed Humanity Flag accreditation system.

In the chapter 6, I match this prototype of global school organization with a prototype of a global school textbook. As prototypes, these proposals are not perfect. They are meant to stimulate debate about how education can contribute to a long life and happiness for the world's peoples.

NOTES

1 A good example is the Houston public schools, which have admitted to cheating by teachers and administrators to achieve higher student test scores. In 2006, this situation was exasperated by the school system linking student test results to increases in teacher pay. See Ralph Blumenthal, "Houston Ties Teachers' Pay to Test Scores" (January 13, 2006), *New York Times on the Web* http://www.nytimes.com/. Retrieved on January 13, 2006.

2 Office for Standards in Education (OFSTED), "Small Schools: How Well Are They doing? A report by OFSTED based on the data from inspections and national test results," http://www.ofsted.gov.uk/publications/index.cfm?fuseaction=pubs.summary&id=837. Retrieved on February 9, 2006.

3 Kathleen Cotton, School Size, School Climate, and Student Performance (Portland: Northwest Regional Educational Laboratory, 1996), p. 8.

4 "Research on Small Scale," *Human Scale Education,* http://www.hse.org.uk/research/research1.html Retrieved on February 9, 2006.

5 Cotton, p. 13.

6 Ibid., p. 14.

7 Suzie Boss, "Big Lessons on a Small Scale," *Northwest Education: Winter 2000: Think Small Making Education More Personal* (Portland: Northwest Regional Educational Laboratory, 2000). Retrieved on February 9, 2006 from http://www.nwrel.org/nwedu/winter_00/textonly/1.html.

8 Human Rights Education Network can be at the Human Rights Education Associates on Web site http://www.hrea.org/. The World Wildlife Fund's educational lessons can be found at http://www.panda.org/news_facts/education/index.cfm Educational programs associated with the Earth Charter can be found at http://www.earthcharter.org/. Education lessons can be found at North American Association for Environmental Education, http://eelink.net/pages/EE-Link+Introduction and the Globe Program at http://www.globe.gov/globe_ flash.html.

9 Cotton, pp. 2–3.

10 Ibid., p. 8.

11 Ibid., p. 8. Regarding the affect of small schools on student learning, see Valerie Lee and Julia Smith, "High School Size: Which Works Best and for Whom," *Educational Evaluation and Policy Analysis* (Autumn, 1997), pp. 205–227.

12 "HSE Background," *Human Scale Education, http://www.hse.org.uk/about/background.html.* Retrieved on January 21, 2006.

13 Ibid.

14 "HSE Principles," Human Scale Education, http://www.hse.rg.uk/about/principles.html. Retrieved on January 28, 2006.

15 Katherine N. Peele and Sara Malone, "Schools That Sustain," *Learning By Design* (2002), pp. 1–2. Retrieved from http://www.asbj.com/lbd/2002/inprint/sustain.html on February 2, 2006.

16 Ibid., p. 3.

17 Ibid., p. 3.

18 Ibid., pp. 4–5.

19 Ibid., p. 5.

20 California Green Schools, *Students Leading the Way 2004–2005: Energy Saving Success Stories from California* (Washington, D.C.: Alliance to Save Energy, 2005), p. 5.

21 Ibid., p. 14.
22 Ibid., p. 15.
23 Ibid., p. 18.
24 Recommended Web sites are www.mec.ca/apps/ecoClac/ecoCalc.jsp and www.earthday.net/footprint/index.asp.
25 David Casey, "How Big Is Your Footprint?" *http://www.ase.org/section/_audience/educators.* Retrieved on February 5, 2006.
26 Ibid.
27 Jeff Saks, "Why is it hotter when I wear black in summer than when I wear white?" *http://www.ase.org/section/_audience/educators.* Retrieved on February 5, 2006.
28 Peele and Malone.
29 "Green Schools Resources," Northeast Sustainable Energy Association, http://www.nesea.org/buildings/greenschoolsresources.html Retrieved on February 3, 2006.
30 "The PowerEd Website—Renewable Energy for Schools," The National Energy Foundation, http://www.nef.org.uk/powered/index.htm.Retrieved on February 9, 2006.
31 Alliance to Save Energy: Creating an Energy-Efficient World, http://www.ase.org/. Retrieved on December 2, 2005.
32 Margaret E. Keck and Kathryn Sikkink, *Activists Beyond Borders: Advocacy Networks in International Politics* (Ithaca: Cornell University Press, 1998), pp. 10–11.
33 Northeast Sustainable Energy Association, http://www.nesea.org/buildings/info/; Alliance to Save Energy: Green Schools, http://www.ase.org/section/program/greenschl; Designing Sustainable High Performance School Buildings, http://schoolstudio.engr.wisc.edu/hps.html.
34 Department of Vaccines and Other Biologicals and Department of Nutrition for Health Development, "Distribution of vitamin A during national immunization days: A 'generic' addendum to the field guide for supplementary activities aimed at achieving polio eradication, 1996 revision" (Geneva: World Health Organization, 1998), p. 8.
35 Ibid., p. 9.
36 World Health Organization Statistical Information System (WHOSIS), "Table: Estimated prevalence (%) of anaemia (1990–1995) by WHO Region based on haemoglobin concentration," www3.who.int/whois. Retrieved on February 15, 2006.
37 Bruno de Benoist, Maria Anderson, Ines Egli, Bhi Takkouche, and Henrietta Allen, editors, *Iodine States Worldwide: WHO Global Database on Iodine Deficiency* (Geneva: World Health Organization, 2004), p. 1.
38 Ibid., p. 12.
39 World Food Programme, *Global School Feeding Report 2005* (Rome: World Food Programme, 2005), p. 4.
40 Ibid., p. 6.
41 Ibid., p. 11.
42 "Universal Declaration of Human Rights, 1948," *Basic Documents on Human Rights Third Edition* edited by Ian Brownlie (New York: Oxford University Press, 1992), p. 26.
43 Ibid.
44 Ibid.
45 "Eco-Schools: A Contribution to Local Agenda: An International Programme for Environmental and Sustainability Education, Management, and Certification," *Partners and Sponsors of the Eco-Schools International Coordination,* www.eco-schools.org/partners/partners.htm. Retrieved on January 6, 2006.
46 "About FEE," www.fee-international.org/AboutFEE. Retrieved on January 28, 2006.
47 "Eco-Schools: International Dimension," www.eco-schools.org/countries/countries.htm. Retrieved on February 13, 2006.
48 "How Eco-Schools Work," *www.eco-schools.org/aboutus/howitworks.htm.* Retrieved on February 12, 2006.

49 I explore the impact on education of global nongovernment organizations in Joel Spring, *How Educational Ideologies Are Shaping Global Society: Intergovernmental Organizations, NGOs, and the Decline of the Nation–State* (Mahwah: Lawrence Erlbaum Associates, 2004).

50 Central Intelligence Agency, *The World Factbook–World–People,* http://www.odci.gov/cia/publications/factbook/geos/xx.html. Calculation is based on an estimated world population of 6,446,131,400, with a total number of Internet users being 604,111,719. Retrieved on January 16, 2006.

51 Vladimir Putin, "The Upcoming G8 Summit in St. Petersburg: Challenges, Opportunities, and Responsibility," *The New York Times* (March 1, 2006), p. A6.

52 Ibid.

53 Ibid.

54 Ibid.

55 United Nations Environment Program, *Tunza: Acting for a Better World* (Nairobi: The United Nations Environment Program, 2003). This publication is available on the Internet at the Web site for the United Nations Environment Programme's Children & the Environment http://www.unep.org/Tunza/children/.

56 Ibid., p. v.

57 Ibid., p. 18.

58 Ibid., pp. 48–68.

59 Ibid., pp. 70–79.

Chapter 6

Humanity: A Prototype Textbook for a Global Core Curriculum

This text embodies the paradigm for a global core curriculum proposed in Chapter 3. It is meant to be used in a prototype global school flying the Humanity Flag. As a prototype textbook, teachers should adapt its contents to differing ages and local cultures. Similarly, the suggested lessons in the book are to serve as examples for teachers who might change them to meet their own needs, or as inspiration for teachers creating their own lessons.

As a prototype, *Humanity* is not meant to dictate the actions of teachers. The subjective well-being of teachers depends on maximizing their "capabilities" to plan and develop their own lessons. To avoid cultural domination, the book assumes that the interpretation of the text and lessons will be made by teachers with knowledge of local cultures. Readers are asked to think about topics, such as the environment and community relations, in the context of local culture or cultures. In addition, local school people are expected to adapt, change, and expand *Humanity* and its lessons to meet the needs of students with differing reading abilities and knowledge.

TABLE OF CONTENTS: *HUMANITY: A PROTOTYPE TEXTBOOK FOR A GLOBAL CORE CURRICULUM*

Textbooks can sometimes defeat the goal of holistic education through categorization, chapter divisions, and isolated topics. I try to overcome this potential problem by highlighting throughout *Humanity* the interconnection between issues and the human condition within the broader biosphere. Text and lessons demonstrate the interdependence of individual welfare with that of the community and the larger world. In addition, prototype lessons are holistic, utilizing reading and vocabulary skills while integrating knowledge and methodologies from science, math, geography, geology, history, economics, sociology, and politics. For instance, each chapter begins with a vocabulary list: Words That Help Us Understand. These vocabulary lists, like the rest of the prototype's content, will have to be adapted by teachers to the reading ability and knowledge of the student. The chapters provide a holistic picture of issues related to health, the environment, social relations, consumer economics, human rights, and politics. Multiculturalism is emphasized in chapter sections that ask students to think about how people in differing cultures view the topic, and in student research projects related to local cultural attitudes.

Each chapter covers a topic related to known social conditions that foster individual longevity and happiness. The textbook is not intended to cover issues of personal mental health. The goal is a textbook designed to create a world in which people have an equal opportunity to live a long and happy life. I use the phrase "known social conditions" because of ongoing research in these areas that will require updating of the content and lessons in *Humanity*. Consequently, teachers and students are encouraged to use the Internet to update the textbook's contents. Throughout the book are examples and suggestions for student activities to improve conditions in the school and community. Students are urged to contact and join activist organizations. The book also recommends Web sites where students can engage in appropriate learning games and exercises. The following is the table of contents for *Humanity:*

Humanity: A Prototype Text for a Global Core Curriculum

Table of Contents

Chapter 2. Does Everyone Have Enough to Eat?

A. Words That Help Us Understand

B. What in the World Do We Eat?
   1. Drawing a World Map of Hunger
   2. Researching Student and Community Eating Habits
   3. Are There Missing Nutrients?

C. Let's Get People Some Healthy Food
   1. Food Force
   2. School Feeding
   3. Examples of Aid for Food and Nutrient Shortages
   4. The World Food Program's "Essential Package"

Chapter 3. Our Neighbors

A. Words That Help Us Understand
B. Let's Get Along With Others: Cooperation and Trust
C. Who Has the Money and Power?
D. Race and Gender

Chapter 4. What Do We Want and What Do We Need?

A. Words That Help Us Understand
B. What Is a Want and What Is a Need?
C. How Does Advertising Make You Want to Buy More Things?
D. Can We Buy Things Without Hurting the Biosphere?

Chapter 5. Human Rights and the Protection of Life and Happiness

A. Words That Help Us Understand
B. Children's Rights
C. Universal Declaration of Human Rights
D. Protecting Rights in Your Community

Chapter 6. Choosing a Life That You Want

A. Words That Help Us Understand
B. Identifying the Life I Want to Live and How to Live It

THE WORLD WE LIVE IN

Chapter 1, The World We Live In, is designed to give students the knowledge and skills for active work to ensure environmental conditions that support a long and happy life. The United Nations Environment Programme's (UNEP) *Tunza: Acting for A Better World* (discussed in chapter 5) provides basic information for this chapter's subsections on The Air We Breath, The Water We Drink, and The Land We Live On.[1] In my prototype for a global school, I emphasized the importance of Internet resources for education. *Tunza* exemplifies this type of resource. What happens if *Tunza* disappears sometime in the future from the UNEP Web site? The teacher and students then must search for other sites. If my goal is maximizing teacher capabilities, then the teacher should be actively involved in updating *Humanity*. In preparation for Making Our Community a Healthy Place, students should study the following sections in *Tunza*'s Part III: Taking up the Challenge: Atmosphere, Freshwater Resources, Oceans and Coasts, Land and Food, and Urbanization. These short chapters introduce students to the effect of health on various forms of environmental pollution. Students with basic literacy skills might be directed to *Tunza for Children*.[2] The section called Pachamama[3] contains simply written units on air, water, and land pollution.

Holistic education is central to environmental education. The use of *Tunza* or other environmental materials provides an opportunity for reading instruction. Understanding environmental pollution also requires learning math, science, geology, and the social sciences. Reading about global pollution issues and understanding these issues are initially passive. The active side of learning occurs when students are asked to investigate their local community for any possible environmental problems.

Students are introduced to holistic thinking about the environment in the Chapter 1 section Thinking Within the Biosphere. The goal of this section is to have students think about themselves, other living creatures, and the earth as part of an interrelated whole. Students are given a short history of science, including a discussion of Vladimir Vernadsky's 1926 book, *The Biosphere,* in which he criticizes Western science for trying to understand nature by breaking it down into smaller and smaller parts.[4] Students learn that Vernadsky caused a revolution in Western science by declaring: "Basically man cannot be separated from it [biosphere]; it is only now that this indissolubility begins to appear clearly and in precise terms before us .... Actually no living organism exists on earth in a state of freedom."[5] They learn about Vernadsky's argument that "all organisms are connected indissolubly and uninterruptedly, first of all through nutrition and respiration, with the circumambient material and energetic medium."[6]

A simple lesson in biodiversity can occur in the school's garden. As I argue in chapter 4, my prototype for a global school is an "eco-school" or "green flag school" in which the school itself becomes a site of environmental studies including learning about the biosphere. As part of participation in school landscaping or work in the school garden, as discussed in chapter 4, students study the growth of plants and their interdependence with other elements of the biosphere. Like all lessons in *Humanity*, this lesson, Plant a Seed and Chart the Biosphere, is meant to be an example that the teacher can adapt or change according to the age of the students and the local environmental and cultural conditions.

Lesson: Plant a Seed and Chart the Biosphere

1. Students plant seeds on the school grounds or in the school garden.
2. Students study the factors promoting or inhibiting the growth of their plants and the effect on the plants in the surrounding environment:
    a. Water
    b. Sun and shade
    c. Soil
    d. Insects and animals
    e. Air Quality
3. Students create a drawing that illustrates the interaction of their plants with the preceding factors.
    a. Illustrated on one side of the drawing are the elements that the plant uses to grow.
    b. Illustrated on the other side of the drawing are the elements that the plant gives back to the biosphere such as food for insects and animals, possible shelter for insects and animals, chemicals released into the air, and elements released into the soil.
4. In the final part of the lesson, students are asked to chart the life cycle of at least one insect or animal that is benefited by their plants. Ideally, students would identify insects that eat their plants and draw their life cycles by asking the following questions:
    a. What does the insect need from the biosphere to grow and live?
    b. Are there other insects or animals that depend for their food on eating these insects?
    c. What happens to the insect if it dies without being eaten?
5. Students complete a final drawing, again illustrating the interaction of their plants (no. 3 in the lesson) with the environment, but connecting the plant to the life cycle of a dependent insect or animal (no. 4 in the lesson).

a. At this point, one option for the teacher is to introduce the idea of the importance of biodiversity. The World Wildlife Fund offers a number of lessons on the importance of biodiversity.[7]

6. If the teacher has the paper and the time, the class or groups of students could prepare an illustration in which students continually branch out from their plants to other elements of the biosphere, such as from their plant to the life cycle of an insect to a bird that eats that insect to an ever-increasing illustration of the biosphere's complexity.

Modeling California's Green Schools Program, students might continue their study of the biosphere by studying the energy consumption of their school or the school's building materials. What is the source of the energy and building materials? How did these sources of energy and building materials develop? What elements in the biosphere were utilized to create these sources of energy and building materials? What effect does using these forms of energy and building materials have on the biosphere? The following lesson, My School Is Part of the Biosphere, is an example of a holistic lesson that uses reading and comprehension skills, geography, science, art, and mathematics, which the teacher should adapt to the culture and abilities of the students.

Lesson: My School Is Part of the Biosphere

1. The teacher and students should decide whether they want to study a school's energy supply or one of the materials used in its construction.
2. Students should investigate the source of the energy or the building material. For instance, an energy source could be traced to a power plant supplying the energy, and then the source of the plant's energy and resources could be explored. The same could be done for a building material.
3. On a world map, the students should identify the possible origins of the school's energy from its natural sources to its conversion into energy for the school. The same could be done for the building material selected by the student.
4. As in the lesson, Plant a Seed and Chart the Biosphere, students should draw the life cycle of the school's energy or building material.
5. Using drawings from step 4, the class should work together on a large mural of the complex interrelationships within the biosphere of the school's energy or building material. One can imagine the complexity of tracing something such as wood used as a building material to the various environmental factors that nurtured its growth as a tree

and its relationship to forest life, the energy sources for harvesting and transporting the tree, the impact of harvesting the tree on the life of the forest, the source and environmental impact of the plant that mills the lumber, and the energy and consumption of other materials needed to transport the lumber to the building site.

The last section of Chapter 1, Making Our School and Community a Healthy Place, is designed to teach students an ethic of responsibility to ensure that others have an opportunity for a long life and happiness. The students can investigate the environmental impact of their school and community as eco-sites. In the following lesson, I have used *Tunza's* recommendations for student environmental research.

Lesson: School and Community Environmental Research Project

1. Have students investigate their school and community and make a list of all environmental problems. Possible methods of investigation include the following:

    a. Have students observe the school staff and other students for the duration of one week. Direct students to record in a notebook if any member of the school community behaves in an environmentally unfriendly manner. Discuss the notebook with the school staff and other students at the end of the week to clarify the issues.
    b. Have students walk through the school marking on a map any areas of pollution.
    c. Have students observe their family's behavior for the duration of one week. Direct students to record in a notebook if any family member behaves in an environmentally unfriendly manner. Discuss the notebook with household members at the end of the week to clarify the issues.
    d. Have students walk through their neighborhoods marking on a map any areas of pollution.
    e. Have students examine the state of the animals and plants in their community looking for signs of pollution.
    f. Have students check to see the results of any possible monitoring of the local community by environmental organizations.

2. Students should choose a problem from their notes that they can realistically investigate and solve.
3. Have students determine the scope of the problem they have chosen by reading relevant sources.

4. Have students plan activities to remedy the environmental problem they have chosen by answering the following questions:
   a. What is the cause of the problem?
   b. What needs to be done, by whom, where, how and when?
   c. What will it cost to undertake their activities?
5. Have students get the school staff and students or the local community involved.
6. Students should plan specific actions to solve the problem. For example, they could suggest ways the school could save on energy or organize a cleanup campaign of a local stream.
7. Have students keep a good record of all activities by means of photos, letters, newspaper cuttings, and the like.

Realistically, teachers must help students to choose a feasible project that can be carried out in their school and community as noted in step 2 of the preceding lesson. When I presented a similar lesson for discussion with my college classes in New York City, there were of concerns about the safety of students wandering the streets making maps of environmental problems. Also, teachers must advise students on realistic approaches in planning to solve an environmental problem. Teachers and students should evaluate the appropriateness for their school and community of the methods recommend in *Tunza's* A Toolkit For Action, which includes contacting appropriate government officials and the media, leafleting, and educating the public through displays and posters.[8]

In summary, The World We Live In, presented in Chapter 1, with its accompanying lessons uses a holistic approach to teach language arts, science, math, art, and geography to help the student understand how to maintain a healthy environment that will be supportive of long life and happiness. The text and lessons are designed to encourage students to think about life as part of an integrated and interacting biosphere. Involvement of students and teachers in school and community activities to solve environmental problems teaches an ethic of responsibility to maintain environmental conditions conducive to the health and happiness of humans.

DOES EVERYONE HAVE ENOUGH TO EAT?

Chapter 2, Does Everyone Have Enough to Eat, touches upon an essential condition for long life and happiness by introducing students to how the body uses food as well as the types of foods and nutrients needed for a healthy body. This science-based discussion integrated into an economic and geographic discussion on the global distribution of food will raise issues about why some countries face the problem of obesity, whereas others face famine. Obviously, the sophistication of the discussion on disparities in world food supply would depend on the reading level and knowledge of the students. Because my prototype is for students with basic literacy skills, the text uses maps to show the unequal distribution of food and nutrients. Lengthy discussions on the economics of the food supply would be reserved for more advanced learners. To feel a part of worldwide concern about hunger and proper nutrition, students are encouraged to make Internet visits to the United Nations' World Food Programme, the World Health Organization, and Oxfam.[9] These organizations have linkages to other organizations fighting world hunger.

All levels of learners can engage in household and community research on family and community eating habits and potential eating problems. Food diaries are the easiest way for students to study family and community eating habits. For a week, students are asked to keep a diary of what they and their families eat. Students conduct a community survey or encourage community members to keep food diaries. Diaries and community surveys are evaluated according to known standards of nutrition. Lessons guide students in planning any community action regarding healthful eating. Like other holistic lessons in *Humanity*, teachers must adapt the following lesson to the local culture, particularly local and religious eating preferences. Also, teachers must help students determine the nutritional value of local foods.

What in the World Do We Eat?

This second section of Chapter 2 is based on the following holistic lesson designed to introduce students to world, local, and personal nutritional issues. It is important for the teacher to adapt this lesson to local foods and eating preferences.

Lesson: What in the World Do We Eat?

1. Have students prepare a large global map of hunger and nutrition using the World Food Programme's Hunger Map.[10]
2. Students should indicate on the classroom map, using percentages from the World Food Programme's Hunger Map, the percentage of undernourished people in their country and immediately surrounding countries. Even in well-nourished countries such as Argentina, Australia, the United States, and member nations of the European Union, approximately 2.5% of the population is undernourished.
3. Students should keep a food diary of what they eat for one week. An alternative, if individual food diaries are too difficult to maintain, is

for the teacher to ask every day what the students ate the previous day and to list the daily food intake by the class.

4. After a week, the class should construct a chart showing the class's daily consumption of nutrients for the week. This could be an average made from the diaries or the class data kept by the teacher.
   a. This part of the lesson depends on the local diet. The teacher must help students convert local diets into nutritional values.
5. Students should determine their own caloric requirements. This can be done by visiting a number of Web sites such as ExRx Fitness Calculators at http://www.exrx.net/Calculators/CalRequire.html.
6. Based on the nutrient chart of local diets, students should determine whether they are undernourished.
   a. Are there enough calories in their diets?
   b. Do they suffer from protein energy deficiency because they lack of macronutrients such as carbohydrates, fats, and proteins?
   c. Are there deficiencies of iron, vitamin A, zinc, and iodine in their diets (see discussion in chapter 4).
   d. Students should check the World Food Programme's Web site, which lists consequences for humans of deficiencies in marcronutrients, iron, vitamin A, zinc, and iodine.
7. Students should investigate the nutritional value of food served in the school's food programme and determine its contribution to students' nutrition.
8. Students should return to their map of world hunger and select for investigation one country in which undernourishment affects more than 20% of the people.
9. Teacher helps students investigate why that country has such a high rate of undernourishment.

The lesson What in the World Do We Eat? ideally would be completed in a school with Humanity Flag certification that requires: "a healthy meal program with students monitoring research findings on healthy foods" and "cooperation with the World Health Organization … [in providing] students, staff, and possibly other community members … nutrients lacking in the diet of the local population." Therefore, just as the textbook *Humanity* considers school buildings and grounds as eco-sites, it also considers them also as nutritional and immunization sites. Students and staff are involved in planning a healthful school menu. This planning process allows the school menu to reflect student and staff food tastes. A sad part of school cafeteria history was the effort by 19th-century developers of school cafeterias in the United States to use the school lunch program to wean immigrants away from their traditional foods. The Anglo-Saxon American leaders of the school cafeteria movement simply dismissed immigrant food tastes, particularly Italian and Greek tastes, as unhealthy and hoped that they could educate immigrant children to eat bland American food. This was part of a broader program of cultural domination aimed at using the schools to strip immigrants of their native cultures and replace these cultures with Anglo-American culture.[11] In the context of *Humanity*, the goal, unlike that of U.S. food reformers, is to promote healthful eating within the framework of local food practices.

Let's Get People Some Healthy Food

This section of Chapter 2 is designed to teach students how they might help to ensure that they and their community have access to nutritional food. As a Humanity-certified institution, the school already has in place a school feeding and immunization program.

Lesson: Let's Get People Some Healthy Food

1. After reviewing the Hunger Map in the previous lesson, students are asked to play the World Food Programme's educational game, Food Force.[12] In the game, players are told: "A major crisis has developed in the Indian Ocean, on the island of Sheylan. We are sending in a new team to step up the World Food Programme's presence there and help feed millions of hungry people."[13] On Sheylan, a combination of drought and civil war has left a starving population. As a rookie in the Food Program's team, the player must complete six missions. The first involves the location of villagers displaced by war and famine. The second mission exemplifies a holistic lesson on food aid, in which the player must determine the right nutritional balance in a diet of rice, oil, beans, sugar, and salt (iodized). Players must practice their math skills by keeping the proper nutritional balance below 30 cents a day. The result is a complicated set of calculations integrating dietary requirements with monetary costs. This is similar to the calculations required for mission four, in which the player must buy supplies from around the world using a limited budget that includes transportation costs.
2. Students are asked create a nutritional calculator similar to the one in Food Force for their own school lunch program, which balances cost with the nutritional value of the various foods served by their school. Note: As students in a Humanity School, they are already involved in planning a healthful school lunch program.
3. Students should be working with the *Humanity* school's immunization program to determine what nutrients are needed for the healthy development of local children. The next part of the lesson depends on the nutritional condition of the students

4. If students are well nourished, then they should learn how they can help undernourished school children by investigating United Nations International Children's Emergency Fund (UNICEF) and the World Food Programme's Essential Package of their global school feeding program.[14]
    a. Students should be told to access the How to Help section of the World Food Programme's Web site as well as the Individuals section. From there, the students should follow the link to School Feeding.[15] Working through the World Food Program, students in affluent communities could in 2006 give $10 so that a school could buy plates, bowls, and cups for school canteens; $34 so that a child could be fed at school for one year; $110 to feed a class for a month, $250 for a school latrine; and $500 for a school vegetable garden.
5. If students in the class are undernourished, they should also access the School Feeding program to see what aid they might be eligible to receive.
    a. Students can help plan a school garden to help supply needed nutrients.
    b. Students can investigate other possible sources of food and vitamin aid.
6. Students should do research, as part of the World Food Programme's Essential Package, to determine whether there is a need in their local community for take-home food rations, deworming treatments, latrine installation, or HIV/AIDS and malaria prevention education.
7. Students should plan how the school community might help to provide take-home food rations, deworming treatments, latrine installation, or HIV/AIDS and malaria prevention education.

In summary, Chapter 2, like Chapter 1, introduces students to preconditions for a long life and happiness. Using holistic lessons, the chapter has students investigate world hunger issues and nutrient issues that may exist in their own community. The activist elements in the chapter attempt to imbue students with a concern about local and world food issues. As part of a Humanity-certified school, students are directly involved in the school and community regarding food issues and immunization programs.

OUR NEIGHBORS

Chapter 3 of *Humanity* deals with the role of the social conditions that promote long life and happiness. The Chapter 3 section Let's Get Along With Others: Cooperation and Trust deals with the importance of cooperation and trust in reducing war and crime. A related issue is social inequality, particularly economic inequality, which is discussed in the section Who Has the Money and Power?, Let's Get Along With Others draws upon the work of peace educators. Central to peace education is the United Nations Educational, Scientific, and Cultural Organization's (UNESCO's) 1995 Declaration and Integrated Framework of Action on Education for Peace, Human Rights, and Democracy.[16] In line with the goals of this declaration, the United Nation's Cyberschoolbus provides a number of instructional units.[17]

The UNESCO 1995 Declaration emphasizes that "strategies relating to education for peace, human rights, and democracy must … be comprehensive and holistic, which means addressing a very broad range of factors."[18] The Cyberschoolbus's symbol for peace education reflect's this holistic approach. The symbol is a circle with "teacher as learner" on one side of the circle and "learner as teacher" on the other side. Around the border of the circle are the words "Human Rights, Ecological Awareness, Tolerance, Respect for Life and Human Dignity, Intercultural Understanding, Nonviolence, Social Responsibility, and Global Agency."[19] Indicative of the holistic approach, the "teacher as learner" side of the circle begins with a quote from Miles Horton: "I have a holistic view of the educative process. The universe is one: nature and mind and spirit and the heavens and the future are part of the big ball of life."[20] The "learner as teacher" side has a quote from Paulo Freire: "The teacher is no longer merely the 'one' who teaches, but one who is him/herself in dialogue with the students, who in turn while being taught also teaches."[21]

Critical Conversation Skills and Conflict Resolution

It is in this holistic spirit that the Cyberschoolbus offers lessons to fulfill the mandate in the Declaration and Integrated Framework of Action on Education for Peace, Human Rights and Democracy. These lessons can serve as models for the Chapter 3 section Let's Get Along With Others: Cooperation and Trust. For instance, one of many activities involves critical conversation skills. This lesson assumes that "peacemaking, peacekeeping, and peace-building are complex and important responses to the proliferation of violent conflict. The root of these approaches lies in the basic knowledge and commitment to the practice of nonviolence and critical thinking."[22] Through critical conversation skills, students are taught how to see the many sides of a conflict, which, it is hoped, will lead to students to apply these skills to future conflicts.

Lesson: Critical Conversation Skills and Conflict Resolution

1. Divide the students into groups of five.
2. In each group, one person acts as a storyteller; three act as detectives; and one acts as an umpire.
3. The storyteller describes a personal or observed incident involving conflict between people.

4. The three detectives listen carefully to the story for unquestioned assumptions.
5. The umpire ensures that everyone is respectful of each other.
6. In their role as detectives, the three students look for the following:
    a. Does the storyteller have any biases related to the story?
    b. What do they appear to be?
    c. What assumptions or conclusions has she or he drawn about what took place?
    d. What is stated as an assumption, and what seems to be implied or unstated?
    e. What are some alternative interpretations that could be given based on the same facts and circumstances?
7. On the basis of their analysis, the detectives offer their findings about assumptions in the story and possible alternative interpretations of the incident, which leads to a general group discussion on differing resolutions of the conflict.
8. All five students work together to understand the incident and suggest other ways of interpreting the situation.
9. The lesson ends "when all parties have had an opportunity to speak; participants should step out of their roles and discuss what took place and any new insights they gained. The group may also discuss ideas about how they might act differently if a similar conflict situation arose in the future."[23]

Who Has the Wealth and Power in My Community?

The Chapter 3 section Who Has the Money and Power? introduces readers to concepts of social inequality, which is a source of crime, war, and reduced longevity. This chapter has a local and global look at these issues. On the local level, students research their own community regarding who is considered rich and who is regarded as poor. If income statistics do not exist for the local community, then a purely subjective referential method can be used. This referential method, described in the next lesson, also yields data on who are considered the most powerful people in the local community. The lesson is designed to help students gain an understanding of wealth and power in their communities.

Lesson: Who Has the Wealth and Power in My Community?—A Referential Method

1. The class brainstorms about who is the wealthiest in their community.
2. The class creates a list of who they think are the wealthiest people in their community. The list is limited to 10 names of persons or families.

3. The class brainstorms about who has the most power in their community. In this case, power refers to those who make the most important decisions affecting the entire community. The list is limited to 10 names of persons or families.
4. The class compares the list of the wealthiest and most powerful to see if there is any connection between wealth and power in the opinions of the class.
5. Individual students are assigned to interview one person on the two lists.
6. The interviews use the "referential method", whereby wealth and power are identified by members of the community.
7. The interviewers ask each interviewee two questions:
   a. Who do you think is the wealthiest person in the community?
   b. Who do you think makes the most important decisions affecting the entire community?
8. The interviewers report their findings to the class. The class creates two lists in rank order of those most frequently mentioned as the wealthiest and those most frequently mentioned as the most powerful in the community.
9. The class then compares the two lists to determine, according to this referential method, whether
   a. There is any relationship between wealth and power in the community?
   b. There are some people on the most powerful list who are not on the wealthiest list?
10. If there are people listed as powerful who are not on the list of the wealthiest, then the class should investigate the source of this power. For example, are these people elected officials, religious leaders, teachers, wise persons, or the like?

Hunger Banquet

The next lesson is on global differences in wealth adapted from an Oxfam International lesson called the Hunger Banquet.[24] The objective is for students to explore the conditions and feelings related to differing levels of wealth. The Hunger Banquet deals with global conditions regarding differences in wealth. The one problem with the Hunger Banquet lesson is that students are mainly passive except when forming income groups and standing when called on by the teacher or group leader.

Lesson: Hunger Banquet (adapted from Oxfam)

1. Divide students into three income groups based on global income distribution: 15% high-income, 30% middle-income, and 55% low-income.

2. Have the high-income group stand, the middle-income group sit at their workplace, and the low-income group sit on the floor.
3. The teacher or a student reads the following statement: "Everyone on earth has the same needs. However, we are born into different living conditions. Some people have more, whereas others have less. No one income group in this room represents one country. All countries have these income groups."
3. The teacher or a student stands near the high-income group and reads descriptions of how children live in this income group in different countries.[25]
4. The teacher or a student stands near the middle-income group and reads descriptions of how children live in this income group in different countries.[26]
5. The teacher or a student stands near the low-income group and reads descriptions of how children live in this income group in different countries.[27]
6. The teacher or a student tells the entire group: "This activity shows how people with different incomes live around the world. How do we end poverty?"

As I mentioned previously, student passivity is a drawback to the Hunger Banquet lesson. However, the lesson is global and multicultural. The Hunger Banquet is a transitional lesson from the lessons on critical conversations and Who Has the Wealth and Power in My Community to the following lesson, The Lives of the High-Income, Middle-Income, and Low-Income Groups in My Community.

The Lives of the High-Income, Middle-Income, and Low-Income Groups in My Community

After considering the global impact of economic differences in the lesson Hunger Banquet, students turn their attention to the meaning of wealth in their own community. In the next lesson, critical conversation techniques are combined with the lesson Hunger Banquet. The lesson assumes that there are all levels of income in the community. If the incomes of everyone in the community are similar, then the students must use the characters in the Hunger Banquet as the basis of comparison.

Lesson: The Lives of the High-Income, Middle-Income, and Low-Income Groups in My Community

1. After the Hunger Banquet lesson, the class is divided into four groups: high-income, middle-income, and low-income groups, and detectives.

2. The high-income, middle-income, and low-income groups write a story about the daily life of a child living in their community at the income level of their group. For instance, the low-income group writes a story about the daily life of a child from a low-income family in their community.
3. Each group selects a group member to read the story to the class.
4. The detectives listen carefully to these stories for any assumptions or possible misrepresentations.
5. After each group has presented its story, the detectives present their opinions about the assumptions and misrepresentations they found in the stories.
6. All the students then participate in a dialogue about the lives of different income groups in their communities.

Variation for a Single-Income Community

1. After the Hunger Banquet lesson, the class is divided into four groups.
2. Three of the groups are assigned to write about the daily life of a child in their community and compare it with the lives of the children in the Hunger Banquet.
3. Each group selects a group member to read the story to the class.
4. The detectives listen carefully to these stories for any assumptions or possible misrepresentations.
5. After each group has presented its story, the detectives present their opinions about the assumptions and misrepresentations they found in the stories.
6. All the students then participate in a dialogue about the lives of different income groups in their communities and the world.

Our Neighbors: Race and Gender

The last section of *Humanity's* Chapter 3, Race and Gender, focuses on social inequalities caused by differences in race and gender. In this section, students are asked to explore these issues within their own school and community. The first task is to determine the definition of race in the local community. As a socially constructed concept, the term can be used to divide people of differing skin colors or, as is the case in Singapore, different ethnic groups. Consequently, the issue of inequality between races might in some localities include inequality between ethnic groups and, in some situations, between religious groups. After arriving at a locally meaningful concept of race, the students then are asked to explore whether race is a factor in the local community determining who has the power and who are the rich and the poor. For instance, Trinidad–Tobago has a large population of

African and Indian descents. Each group is represented by a political party, and each is vying for political power. However, those of African ancestry complain that those of Indian ancestry control the wealth of the islands. In Japan, ethnic Koreans tend to have less wealth and power than native Japanese. Therefore, initial discussions about race or ethnic group must be guided by local concepts and traditions. Teachers are asked to adapt the following research questions to local social circumstances.

Community and School Research on the Meaning of Race

Similar to other prototype lessons, this lesson will have to be modified and adapted by teachers to local cultural conditions. This lesson is designed to determine local attitudes about race and ethnicity, and eventually, in a later lesson, the relationship of these factors to local attitudes about power and wealth. Before beginning the lesson, teachers should discuss with students concepts of race, ethnic groups, and religion and their applicability to local social conditions. On the basis of this dialogue, teachers and students can develop a research project in which students ask community members and other students whether there are differences in wealth and power among different racial, ethnic, and religious groups.

Lesson: Community and School Research on the Meaning of Race

1. Have students plan a survey to determine how the local community defines the concept of race or ethnicity. As part of this survey, students initially will want to find the answers to the following questions:
   a. Are ethnic differences stressed by local community members rather than race?
   b. Are religious differences stressed by local community members rather than race?
2. After the initial survey, the students decide the answers to the following questions:
   a. If ethnic differences are more important than racial concepts in the local community, then what are the community's different ethnic groups?
   b. If religious differences are more important than racial or ethnic groups in the local community, then what are the community's different religious groups?
3. Using a referential method (see Who Has the Wealth and Power in My Community lesson on the referential method), students continue their survey to determine whether members of the community feel

that a particular locally defined racial, ethnic, or religious group has more power and wealth than other groups?

4. Using a referential method, the students survey other students to determine whether they feel that racial, ethnic, or religious groups are treated differently in the local school.
5. The students discuss their findings and whether there could be changes in the local community and school that would increase equality of treatment and power between racial, ethnic, or religious groups.

Community and School Research on Gender

Possible inequalities in power and wealth based on gender must be understood in the context of local traditions. Although international organizations such as the World Bank and Education for All have made the education of women a high priority, there is sometimes little respect for local traditions and family structures. Equality between genders is an important human rights issue, but this equality will sometimes undermine local family structures without providing any alternatives. There should be some transition from local family structures that reduce the power and wealth of women to structures that support equality of power and wealth. The danger is that the combination of undermining traditional family structures and the exodus from rural to urban areas may result in urban ghettos filled with single-parent families without any support from a social network. Consequently, students are asked to research gender in the framework of community attitudes. The following research questions will have to be modified by teachers according to their knowledge of the local community and customs.

Lesson: Community and School Research on Gender

1. Have students plan a survey to determine how the local community feels about gender differences. In planning the survey, students should seek answers to the following questions.
    a. Do local people feel that there are differences in wealth between males and females in their community?
    b. Do local people feel that there are differences in power between males and females in their community?
2. Have the students analyze the behavior in their own families to determine whether boys and girls are treated differently.
3. Have the students survey other students to determine whether boys and girls are treated differently in their school or not.
4. The students discuss their findings to determine whether there could be changes in the local community, families, and school that would increase equality of wealth and power between genders.

Teachers will be able to create interesting research projects for their students using the preceding questions as a guide. Teachers might create a lesson in which students ask family members about which gender has the formal and informal power within their families. Reports of family responses on gender issues would generate important discussions about gender equality. Similar research projects could be conducted in the school and community leading to further discussion of gender equality and what might be done to improve gender equality.

Community and School Research on Sexual Orientation

In some cultures and religions, issues regarding gay, lesbian, and transsexual humans are extremely sensitive. However, equality for people with differing sexual orientations has become an important global human rights issue. For situations in which local religions and customs make sexual orientation an explosive issue, the teacher must develop a research project that is sensitive to local beliefs or decide whether the local community considers it appropriate or not for younger students to explore issues of sexual orientation.

Lesson: Community and School Research on Sexual Orientation

1. Have students plan a survey to determine community and student attitudes about gay, lesbian, and transsexual humans. This survey should try to answer the following questions. (Teachers must help students organize a community survey of attitudes that is sensitive to local traditions. Also, teachers must decide whether the local community considers this to be an appropriate research project for younger students or not.)
    a. Do gay, lesbian, and transsexual community and school members hide their sexual orientation?
    b. Is there any evidence that gay, lesbian, and transsexual people are discriminated against in the community and school?
2. The students discuss their findings about community and student attitudes about gays, lesbians, and transsexuals.
3. The students formulate a plan to increase social equality for gay, lesbian, and transsexuals in their school and community. (Again, the teacher must be sensitive to local and particularly religious attitudes in supervising this part of the lesson.)

For religiously oriented teachers and students, the idea of social equality or even recognition of differences in sexual orientation might be a difficult topic. In fact, it might result in a discussion of social equality versus freedom to hold religious beliefs. Again, I stress the importance of the teacher adapting this lesson to local religious and community traditions.

Social Inequalities in My Community—Who Has the Wealth and Power?

In the previous lessons, students were asked to gather research information on differences in wealth, power, race, ethnic affiliation, religion, gender, and sexual orientation in their local community. I remind the reader that power is being defined as influence over decisions affecting the local community and a referential method is being used to determine who has the wealth and power in the local community. In the next lesson, Social Inequalities in My Community—Who Has the Wealth and Power? students consolidate the information from these previous lessons into a single table This exercise is important because of the role that social equality plays in fostering conditions supportive of subjective well-being and longevity.

Lesson: Social Inequalities in My Community—Who Has the Wealth and Power?

1. Using data collected in the previous lessons on wealth, power, race, ethnicity, religion, gender, and sexual orientation, the students complete Table 6.1. This table will represent the extent of social inequality in the students' community. To simplify the project, the students are asked to use a rating scale ranging from 1 (most wealthy or powerful) to 2 (least wealthy or powerful). It is assumed that any group not rated as 1 or 2 is in the middle of the local community's wealth and power structure.
2. In constructing Table 6.1, the students will have to decide whether racial, ethnic, or religious divisions are important in their local community.
3. The number of rows in Table 6.1 devoted to these groups will depend on their number in the local community. For instance, if race is an important division within the local community, then one row might be labeled Black, another row White, another row mixed, and so forth. If ethnic groups are important, then there should be a row for each ethnic group. If religion is an important division within the local community, then one row might be labeled Hindu, another row Moslem, another row Buddhist, and so on.
4. Led by the teacher, the students engage in a dialogue about the implications of Table 6.1 for social equality within their community, including health issues related to differences in power and wealth.
5. The students discuss what changes might take place in their community to increase equality of wealth and power between the groups.

TABLE 6.1
Social Inequalities in My Community: Who Has the Wealth and Power

Social divisions in local community: the relative importance and numbers of these division will vary with the community	*Wealth: '1' (most wealth) and '2' (least wealth)*	*Power (influence over local community decisions): '1' (most power) and '2' (least power)*
Racial group (if this is important for the local community)		
Racial group (add more rows or delete racial category based on local conditions)		
Ethnic group (if this is important for the local community)		
Ethnic group (add more rows or delete ethnic category based on local social organization)		
Religious group (if this is important for the local community)		
Religious group (add more rows or delete religious category based on local social organization)		
Females		
Males		
Gay, lesbian, and transsexual		

WHAT DO YOU NEED AND WHAT DO YOU WANT?

Humanity's Chapter 4, What Do We Want and What Do We Need, focuses on the interrelated problems of consumption, social inequality, and the environment. The issue of environmental destruction is central to increasing longevity. Status can be related to the use of consumer items as status symbols, or what often is referred to as conspicuous consumption. Conspicuous consumption can highlight social inequalities.[28] Furthermore, as discussed in chapter 2 of this book, status has a direct effect on health and longevity. In contrast to conspicuous consumption, sustainable consumption refers to the purchase of products that do not result in a depletion of natural resources.

Critical advertising studies are central to understanding the deleterious effect of a consumer-oriented society. Advertising is the driving force in an industrial-consumer system. By creating desires for new products, redesigned products, or both, advertising can put humans on a consumer treadmill in which the desire to consume one product is quickly replaced by a desire to consume another. Advertising-driven consumption also can deplete resources and foul the environment. Advertising depends on tapping into or creating human unhappiness and dissatisfaction. If people felt satisfied with their lives and the products they own, then they might not be tempted by advertising to buy new products. A goal of advertising is to make people dissatisfied with their lives or to make them believe that the purchase of a product will be transformative. Advertising might be used to convince the viewer trapped in a city that the purchase of a four-wheel-drive vehicle will open wildernesses for them. The advertising promises that the vehicle will provide escape to the freedom of unpopulated mountains and forests. Faced with crowded highways and others seeking a similar escape, the purchaser's advertising dream is never satisfied and her or his frustration is directed by advertising to other products that promise psychological relief. Advertisers try to convince the public that purchases of clothing, cosmetics, cars, appliances, food stuffs, and other products will enhance sexuality, increase their community status, guarantee the finding of a mate, or fulfill any other desires.[29] The false allure of advertising and its play on human unhappiness is captured in the title of Kathy Peiss's history of the cosmetics industry: *Hope in a Jar: The Making of America's Beauty Culture.*[30]

Section B, What Is a Want and What Is a Need, opens with helping children make a distinction between needs and wants using Betty Reardon's lesson, Wishing a World Fit for Children—Understanding Human Needs[31] and a lesson requiring students to distinguish between their own needs and wants. These lessons were discussed in the chapter 3 section this book: Human Rights and Subjective Well-Being: Global Core Curriculum for Young Children. These two lessons set the stage for an exploration of advertising and its role in turning wants into needs. The reader will recall that Reardon's lesson has children reflect on the needs of children as the first step in differentiating needs and wants for all humans. In the second lesson, students create lists of their personal needs and wants, with a recognition of the often thin line between a want and need. Is playing a sport a want or a need? One person might argue that sports are a need because they provide the exercise necessary for health and well-being. Others might argue that exercise can occur in other venues besides organized sports. Therefore, sports are not a necessary need, but can be a means for fulfilling a real human need for physical activity. Both lessons include the question of how the world could be changed to ensure that all human needs are fulfilled. Both lessons are holistic, requiring students to practice writing while learning about physiology, nutrition, disease, and geography.

Making Exercise a Consumer Item

The following lesson at the end of Section B is designed to stimulate students to think about how needs can be incorporated into a consumer culture in which advertising tries to promote the consumption of more products. For instance, sports might not be a necessary form of exercise if community members walk to school and work and engage in physical activity at work or in doing household chores. On the other hand, sports might be considered a necessity for people living sedentary urban lives in which work involves sitting at a desk and in which cars and public transportation replace walking. Of course, sports can be fun. The following is a holistic lesson requiring students to learn about the human body and human caloric requirements, and to practice basic arithmetic calculations along with understanding the problems of human exercise and urban living.

Lesson: Making Exercise a Consumer Item

1. The students should maintain a physical activity diary in which they list the different forms of physical activities in which they engage during one day.
2. Teachers will help students calculate their caloric needs. There are Web sites that provide calculators for estimating caloric needs, particularly the Web site ExRx Fitness Calculators.[32] Teachers also can find other materials that can be used in estimating human caloric intake and output.
3. Using the same or similar Web sites, teacher-provided caloric charts, or both, the students compare their caloric intake with their caloric needs.
4. The students determine whether they need more physical activity or not to match their caloric intake.
5. After applying these calculations to themselves, students are asked to calculate the daily caloric intake and output of an adult urban office worker who does not exercise and who drives to work and to stores but seldom walks. ExRx Fitness Calculators allows users to calculate

caloric needs by age, weight, height, and types of daily activities. For instance, students could be asked to calculate the caloric requirements for our sedentary urban worker using the following statistics or any others provided by the teacher.

a. Age 30 years
b. Male
c. Weight 180 pounds
d. Height 70 inches
e. Hours of activities

    i. Resting: sleeping, reclining (10 hours)
    ii. Very light: seated and standing activities, painting trades, driving, laboratory work, typing, sewing, ironing, cooking, playing cards, playing a musical instrument (13 hours)
    iii. Light: walking on a level surface at 2.5 to 3 mph, garage work, electrical trades, carpentry, restaurant trades, housecleaning, child care, golf, sailing, table tennis (1 hour)
    iv. Moderate: walking 3.5 to 4 mph, weeding and hoeing, carrying a load, cycling, skiing, tennis, dancing (0 hours)
    v. Heavy: walking with load uphill, tree felling, heavy manual digging, basketball, climbing, football, soccer (0 hours).

6. Students next imagine this urban worker eating a large breakfast, lunch, and dinner based on the tastes of the students. Students then calculate the difference between the caloric intake of our imagined big diet and the caloric requirements of this urban office worker.
7. Students next calculate how much moderate and heavy physical activity is required to balance the food intake and caloric expenditure of our sedentary urban worker (I am assuming that the caloric content of our imagined diet exceeds the caloric expenditure of our urban worker.)

The preceding lesson suggests that our urban worker needs either more strenuous activity or a reduction in food intake to balance caloric intake with output. This lesson leads into Section C, How Does Advertising Make You Want to Buy More Things?

How Does Advertising Turn Needs That Can Be Fulfilled for Free Into Products to Buy?

In the next lesson, an urban worker can choose to balance caloric intake and output by doing things that are free or to spend money consuming products and services. The goal in this lesson is to help students understand how needs can be achieved without the consumption of products or with a minimum of products that might be needed for sports.

Lesson: How Does Advertising Turn Needs That Can Be Fulfilled for Free Into Products to Buy?

1. Have students list all the things the urban worker in the preceding lesson could do either to expend more energy or to reduce caloric intake without spending money on products, such as walking fast, weeding and hoeing, carrying a load, or eating less.
2. Have students list all the things the urban worker in the preceding lesson could do to expend more energy while spending only a minimum amount of money on the basic equipment needed for individual and team sports such as running, soccer, basketball, baseball, and the like.
3. The teacher collects and distributes magazines to students that contain advertisements for exercise and sports equipment, exercise gyms, sports clothing, diets, and nutritional supplements for weight loss.
4. The students cut out these ads and place them on a table for display to the class.
5. Working together, the students estimate the cost of purchasing these products. Information on the cost of gyms often can be gained from a gym's Web site.
6. Each student examines the advertisements and creates a list of "hidden persuaders" in the ads inciting purchase of these products. Besides the promise of exercise and weight loss, the "hidden persuaders" might include
   a. Attracting a boy- or girlfriend
   b. Meeting new friends
   c. Adventure and escape from ordinary life
   d. Personal beauty
7. On the basis of the students' lists of hidden persuaders, the students and teachers discuss methods used by advertising to persuade people to purchase products and services to meet a need (in this case, overconsumption of food and lack of exercise) that could be achieved for free or at minimal cost.

Critical Advertising Studies

The preceding lesson on How Does Advertising Turn Needs That Can Be Fulfilled for Free Into Products to Buy" provides the background for a more general study of advertising. In what is called "critical advertising studies," the student learns how advertising attempts to create a desire within people to purchase products. In Toward a Critical Theory of Advertising, John Harms of Southwest Missouri State University and Douglas Kellner of the University of Texas argue: "In a democratic society, individuals would freely determine their needs and desires and would resist being molded by institutions which mainly wish to manipulate and exploit them."[33] Instruction in critical advertising studies would help people to resist the seductive power of advertising to control human emotions and channel those emotions toward the consumption of products. Harms and Kellner hope that "in a rational society, information would be made readily available to individuals through databases concerning any product they might wish to buy. A computerized information system would thus eliminate the need for advertising."[34] The promise of critical advertising studies is that "in a world without advertising perhaps individuals could finally attempt to discover and determine what they really wanted to be and to discern for themselves what kind of a world they wanted.[35]

As indicated by Harms and Kellner, advertising has become a pervasive method for manipulating needs and desires. It is estimated that in affluent countries such as the United States, children reaching their senior years will have spent a total of three years watching commercials.[36] The United States' Public Broadcasting System reports a 2002 poll that found American teenagers can get their parents to buy an advertised product by making an average of nine requests.[37] How much advertising children are exposed to in other countries is unclear. However, with the march of industrial-consumerism it would appear that much of the world may eventually be engulfed in various forms of advertising from flashing street signs to television. I was surprised to find advertising appearing even on the passenger straps hanging on a monorail in Kuala Lumpur, Malaysia, and in the crosswalks on streets in Singapore.

Lessons on Advertising and Media Literacy

Lessons on media literacy often include an analysis of advertising. This is exemplified by the United States' Public Broadcasting System's Media Literacy: Getting Started: Activity Ideas for Language Arts, Social Studies, Math Science, and Health.[38] In the section of the lesson on Health, students are asked to analyze the sexual content, gender bias, and portrayal of families in media guided by question: "Are certain products like alcohol or tobacco targeted to specific ethnic or gender groups?"[39] Also, students are asked: "What techniques do pharmaceutical ads use to popularize their products?"[40] To answer this question, students are told to compare "the slogans, actors, settings, and plots of advertisements for different medicines."[41] Under Liberal Arts, students are asked "count the ads they see or hear for a whole day. This might include billboards, flyers left on car windshields, and logos on clothes. As students share results, ask them to define what's advertising and what's not: A label on a sweater? A name on a mailbox at a private residence? Together, create a definition for 'advertisement'."[42] Under Math, students study fractions and percentages by determining the ratio of ads to news in their local papers, and in Science, students test products to determine whether they live up to the promises of their ads. In Social Studies, students study political campaign advertising.

The PBS Kids' Don't Buy It: Get Media Smart Web site provides opportunities for students to understand advertising tricks by designing ads, such as Food Advertising Tricks, Create Your Own Ads, Design a Cereal Box, What's in an Ad?, and Be the Ad Detective. For instance, Design a Cereal Box provides an online game that introduces players to advertising methods. In the first step, players are asked to choose a color for the cereal box they are designing. Players are told that red makes people feel that they can make choices, orange makes people hungry, blue calms people, and yellow makes people feel energized. The next step requires selection of a character for the box, with players being informed that some kids might like a worm and that a superhero cartoon character works because little kids like fantasy characters. A soccer figure would appeal to girls, whereas a football (American style) player would appeal to boys. The player then chooses a name for the cereal they think will attract attention. Players are told that they should make the cereal name short and easy to remember. In the next step, players must choose a descriptor from four choices: Outrageous Crunch!, Delicious and Nutritious!, New and Improved!, and Tastes Like Cardboard! The player is informed that each descriptor will project a different image of the product, with Outrageous Crunch! making the cereal seem exciting, Delicious and Nutritious appealing to parents, and New and Improved! appealing to people who like new things. In the next step, players choose a prize to be included in the box such as a sports trading card to appeal to boys, a princess figure to appeal to girls, or tattoos to appeal to both boys and girls. In the concluding screen, players are told to make sure their cereal box is placed on a lower shelf in a supermarket so that kids can beg their parents for it.[43]

Recognizing the importance of critical advertising studies, the International Reading Association and National Council of Teachers of English also offer critical advertising lessons under the general title of media studies on their Web site Read·Write·Think.[44] One lesson, Critical Media Literacy: Commercial Advertising, creates critical awareness among students for the impact of advertising by investigation of hidden messages in advertising.[45] The lesson opens with a general discussion about students' television viewing habits and any magazines they might read. Then students are told that they will be "cultural investigators" of mass media. While watching television, students record the content of the advertisements appearing on the screen. Working in groups, students create categories and place the ads in these categories on large chart paper. The same process is followed using ads from magazines distributed in class. Students should do their own interpretations of ads without the teacher providing any interpretive ideas. For instance, students could be asked to analyze ads looking for themes and patterns. Any conclusions about themes or patterns are decided on by the students. The teacher then asks the students how ads might influence their peer culture. In the final activity, the students are asked to review and discuss as a group the patterns and themes they found in ads, write about how advertising affects their peer culture, and discuss the following questions: What do they always see in television ads? Magazine ads? Which medium does the best job with accurate representation?[46]

The PBS Kids' Don't Buy It: Get Media Smart Web site offers insight into advertising methods, and Critical Media Literacy: Commercial Advertising creates an awareness of the effect that advertising has on culture. However, I believe that critical advertising studies must look more closely at the manipulation of desires and needs by advertisers. *Humanity* recommends that teachers try some variation on the following lesson.

Lesson: Critical Advertising Studies

1. The class collects and displays a variety of advertisements by
   a. Examining magazines distributed in class
   b. Writing descriptions of television ads
   c. Writing descriptions of ads appearing on billboards or in other public places.
2. Students discuss these ads looking for answers to the following questions:
   a. Does the ad associate the product with an emotion, such as happiness and joy?
   b. Does the ad imply or promise that the use of the product will result in some transformation of the viewer, such as they will become stronger, win friends, or the like?
3. Students design a public billboard that advertises their school using the techniques discovered in their analysis of advertising.
   a. The billboard should be designed so that most viewers will desire to send their children to the school.
   b. The class reviews the PBS Kids' Don't Buy It: Get Media Smart Web site and the lessons Create Your Own Ads and Design A Cereal Box.[47]
   c. Students consider how their ad will appeal to particular emotions.

   d. Students consider how their ad will suggest to viewers that school attendance will transform children's lives, such as enabling them to get a better job than their parents or a nicer home, and so on.
4. The design is put on display for review by all members of the school community, including students and teachers.

Sustainable Consumption: Can We Buy Things Without Hurting the Biosphere?

The Chapter 4 section of *Humanity*, Can We Buy Things Without Hurting the Biosphere, is designed to impress upon students the importance of sustainable consumption for protecting the biosphere and protecting the life and happiness of humans. Teaching for sustainable consumption was an outgrowth of the 1997 International Conference Environment and Society: Education and Public Awareness for Sustainability held by UNESCO in Thessaloniki, Greece. The Declaration of Thessaloniki states: "In order to achieve sustainability, an enormous coordination and integration of efforts is required in a number of crucial sectors and *rapid and radical change of behaviors and lifestyles, including changing consumption and production patterns* [my emphasis]."[48] The report of the Conference, *Educating for a Sustainable Future: A Transdisciplinary Vision for Concerted Action,* emphasizes the importance of ethical human responsibility to ensure sustainability in its sections on Ethics, Culture and Equity: Sustainability as a Moral Imperative and Towards a Common Ethic.[49] Sustainability, or what is called "sustainable development," is defined by the 1992 United Nations' Conference on Environment and Development as "development that meets the needs of the present without compromising the ability of future generations to meet their own needs."[50]

Educating for a Sustainable Future develops the concept of sustainable consumption in a section called Shifting to Sustainable Lifestyles: Changing Consumption and Production Patterns, which calls upon educators to change global behaviors:

> The effectiveness of awareness raising and education for sustainable development must ultimately be measured by the degree to which they change the attitudes and behaviors of people, both in their individual roles, including those of producers and consumers, and in carrying out their collective responsibilities and duties as citizens.[51]

Educators are called upon to transform consumerism into "sustainable consumption," which is explained by the report: "Sustainable consumption does not necessarily mean consuming less. It means changing unsustainable patterns of consumption by allowing consumers to enjoy a high quality of life by consuming differently."[52]

The goal of educators supporting sustainable consumption is to have students think about the environmental effect of their purchases. The sustainable consumer "insists upon purchasing products that are kind to the environment."[53] According to *Educating for a Sustainable Future,* consumption should be guided by the principle of eco-efficiency. The consumer is to be taught to evaluate purchases according to their eco-efficiency. "Eco-efficiency," the report contends, "calls for better management of existing processes or products to reduce waste, use less energy and facilitate reuse and recycling."[54] The consumer should be taught to ask: Does the manufacturing process for a product reflect a concern about reducing the use of resources? Can the product be recycled? What are the environmental consequences of the consumption of a product?

A Counting Lesson on Biodegradability

A kindergarten teacher in my class developed a holistic lesson designed to have young children begin thinking about sustainable consumption and, at the same time, learn their numbers. She brought to class a variety of plastic containers and bottles with numbers indicating the degree of biodegradability. These numbers are located inside recycling symbols found frequently on the bottom of plastic containers. The teacher had students find the numbers on the plastic containers and arrange the containers in a row from 1 to 10. Using the placement in the row, the teacher taught the students how to count to ten and to read the numbers by checking the biodegradability number on the container. While the students were learning their numbers, the teacher explained how plastic could hurt the environment and the importance of checking the numbers on plastic containers. An ethical dimension was added to the lesson when students were urged to tell their parents about the meaning of the numbers and to have their parents check the numbers when shopping.

A useful guide to help teachers develop a similar lesson can be found in the 2002 UNESCO and UNEP publication *YouthXChange: Training Kit on Responsible Consumption.*[55] This publication lists the common features of sustainable consumption that can be used by teachers to conceptualize and create lesson plans. The publication identifies a number of complex issues involved in sustainable consumption:

Common Features of Sustainable Consumption

- Satisfying human needs
- Favoring a good quality of life through decent standards of living
- Sharing resources between rich and poor

- Acting with concern for future generations
- Looking at the "cradle-to-grave" impact when consuming
- Minimizing resource use, waste, and pollution.[56]

The Life Cycle of a T-Shirt

An important part of the Common Features of Sustainable Consumption is sharing world resources to ensure that all people have a standard of living that fosters happiness and longevity. This is an important theme in previous discussions about reducing social inequalities. In the publication *YouthXChange: Training Kit on Responsible Consumption,* education for sustainable consumption encompasses standard elements of other environmental education programs such as chemical and air pollution, transportation, ecotourism, reducing waste, improving energy consumption, clean water, and testing products on animals.

As reflected in *YouthXChange,* education for sustainable consumption requires an integration of environmental issues into what the United Nations Environment Programme calls a "life cycle" approach. In education, this means having students think about the environmental impact of a product's life cycle. As stated in the United Nations Environment Programme's publication *Why Take a Life Cycle Approach,* "a life cycle approach is a way of thinking which helps us recognize how our selections—such as buying electricity or a new T-shirt—are one part of a whole system of events."[57] For instance, the publication uses the example of a T-shirt's life cycle, in which a consumer thinks about the materials and energy used in making the T-shirt, the energy used for its transportation to market, the impact of its maintenance (washing), and its recycling, reuse, or disposal.

The Life Cycle approach has the potential of creating a lengthy but rewarding holistic lesson. The following is a lesson for this section of *Humanity* based on the T-shirt example.

Lesson: The Life Cycle of a T-Shirt

1. Students examine any of their T-shirts for the material used in manufacture and the country where it was manufactured.
2. Students investigate what raw materials were used in manufacturing.
   a. If natural materials, such as cotton, hemp, or silk were used, students investigate the effect on the soil of growing the material and whether any fertilizers or pesticides were used. Is cotton or hemp a more environmentally friendly material?
   b. If the t-shirt is made of synthetic materials then students should investigate the raw materials required to make the synthetic cloth and the impact of manufacturing on the environment.

3. Students locate the country of origin on a map and consider the potential use of natural resources in getting the product to a market where the student or her/his parents can buy it.
4. Students investigate the conditions of workers in the manufacturing country.
5. Students investigate the environmental impact of soaps used to keep their T-shirts clean.
6. Students consider what happens to students' T-shirts when they are discarded?

Show, Tell, and the Life Cycle

John Dewey might have been pleased at the idea of students tracing the life cycle of a product because of its holistic approach and the resulting understanding of the interdependence of society. Dewey also might have been happy with the idea of children acquiring knowledge through the study of a real social issue. However, the described approach differs from that of Dewey by emphasizing a particular educational end—in this case teaching sustainable consumption.

The traditional progressive Show-and-Tell exercise could be used for the same purpose. This is an exercise that fits nicely into holistic education and can be given an ethical direction. Again, like other lessons suggested for *Humanity*, this is a prototype that teachers should freely adapt to the age of students, available time, and local culture. Usually, Show-and-Tell is limited to younger ages, but could be adjusted for use with older ages.

Lesson: Show, Tell, and the Life Cycle

1. Have students bring to class objects that interest them and that they want to share with others.
2. Have students show their objects to the class and explain why they are interesting.
3. Have the class select one or more of the objects for a life cycle project.
4. The actual life cycle project or projects could have the following organizational variations:
   a. If the class has a common interest in one object presented for show-and-tell, then the entire class should plan a single life cycle study.
   b. If many objects are of interest, then the class could be broken into project groups.
5. If the object used for the life cycle project is manufactured, then the steps in Lesson: The Life Cycle of a T-Shirt could be followed by the class or group.

6. If the object used for the life cycle project is a natural object, such as a sea shell, flower, or rock, then the class or group should study the life cycle of that natural object and its relationship to the biosphere.

The World Wildlife Fund's *Smart Consumers: An Educator's Guide to Exploring Consumer Issues in the Environment* offers an extensive set of lessons to involve students in promoting sustainable consumption.[58] The guide recommends that students choose realistic projects to promote the idea of sustainable consumption in their communities. As examples, they suggest that students create a green shopping guide showing the options for buying environmentally friendly products, searching malls for stores selling green products, making sure the community has enough recycling bins, doing energy audits, creating a community list of green cleaning products, planting organic vegetable gardens, and organizing paper recycling centers. Students can visit the Web site for the World Wildlife Fund's sustainable consumption program: http://www.ibuydifferent.org/.

HUMAN RIGHTS AND THE PROTECTION OF LIFE AND HAPPINESS

Humanity Chapter 5, Human Rights and the Protection of Life and Happiness, introduces students to the concept of human rights and its role in protecting long life and happiness. The assumption of the chapter is that defining human rights is an ongoing process that varies over time and between cultures.[59] Also, I am defining rights as human needs for a long and happy life. This definition of rights avoids abstract discussions of rights based on religious or philosophical beliefs. By equating human needs with human rights, I am grounding human rights doctrines in tangible social conditions that can be understood by students. By considering human rights as a function of human needs, students can engage in meaningful debates about what should or should not be a human right.

Therefore, the United Nation's Convention on the Rights of the Child and the Universal Declaration of Human Rights are treated as important historical documents that can serve as guides for ongoing discussions. The chapter introduces students to the work of human rights organizations, such as Amnesty International and Human Rights Watch.[60] Students are directed to the Web site Human Rights Web to explore the work of other human rights organizations and resources.[61]

Chapter 5 makes human rights personal and of interest to students by beginning with the issue of Children's Rights. Previous lessons in *Humanity* have already considered some of the issues related to children's rights such as the need to protect the environment, health care, and adequate nutrition. Also, other lessons have distinguished between wants and needs. The next lesson is designed to translate some of these issues into rights topics and to help students make a distinction between "claim" rights and "liberty" rights. In the case of a "claim" right, humans, in this case children, have a claim against parents, civil society, institutions, and governments for not guaranteeing the provision of certain needs such as shelter, health care, and food. A "liberty" right involves freedom from outside interference, usually from governments, in pursuing in matters such as freedom of speech and assembly. A good illustration is the difference between two articles on the Convention of the Rights of the Child. Article 24 gives children a "claim right" ensuring that governments will make provisions for their health care, whereas Article 13 gives children a "liberty right" that protects them against outside interference in expressing their beliefs. This distinction is illustrated in the following quote:

> Claim right—Article 24: States Parties recognize the right of the child to the highest attainable standard of health and to facilities for the treatment of illness and rehabilitation of health....
>
> Liberty right—Article 13: The child shall have the right to expression; this right shall include freedom to seek, receive, and impart information and ideas of all kinds ....

Keeping this distinction in mind, the teacher can lead students through the following type of lesson. Of course, teachers will need to change or create a similar type of lesson based on their judgments about the maturity of their students and local cultural issues. Some of the local issues might be related to cultural expectations about the relationship of the child to the family. For instance, how do parents feel about the right of children to freedom of expression and freedom to seek information?

The Rights of Children

In this lesson, students learn to think how human rights, such as the right to other forms of knowledge and beliefs, are socially constructed in contrast to accepting the human rights' document as established truth. A real danger in teaching human rights is the possibility that students will come to venerate the 1948 Universal Declaration of Human Rights and the Convention on the Rights of the Child in the same way students are currently taught in national school systems to venerate the founding documents of their governments. This can lead to an unreasoning form of patriotism or emotional attachments. In the following lesson, teachers guide children through the process of creating their own children's rights document and then comparing it to the Convention on the Rights of the Child.

Lesson: The Rights of Children

1. Divide students into groups and ask each group to brainstorm about what children need.
2. Have each group create a list of what they think children's needs are and present these to the rest of the students for discussion to determine what is a want and what is a need.
   a. The teacher should refer back to *Humanity* Chapter 4, What Do We Want and What Do We Need?
   b. In their discussion, the students should create a list that separates needs from wants.
   c. The teacher participates in this discussion by asking questions about possible children's needs, such as: Do children need the right to freely express their opinions?
3. Students place next to each children's need on the list who or what institution will be responsible for fulfilling that need. For instance, consider the following possibilities:
   a. The class list might include children's need for food. The determination of who is responsible for providing this food might result in the following types of questions and answers:
   Who should give children food?
   Their parents!
   What if the parents don't have food for their children?
   Then neighbors and friends!
   What if they don't have enough food to feed children in the community?
   Then the government!
   What if there isn't enough food in the country to feed all children?
   Then the world must help!
   b. The class list might include the need of children to complain if they are hungry or need medical care. A discussion of who or what might keep them from complaining may result in the following types of questions and answers:
   If you need food or medical help, who would you ask?
   Our parents!
   Do your parents let you complain?
   Yes and no!
   If your family cannot provide you with food or medical care, who would you ask?
   Friends! Neighbors! Religious leader! Police! Government!
   Do they let you complain?

Maybe! Some tell us to shut up! Some don't pay any attention! Some listen!
Do you think you should be allowed to complain?
If I'm hurt ... etc.

c. The next set of questions could lead to a discussion of whether or not the students think children should be allowed to gather as a group (assemble) to complain.

4. Students should be told that children's needs can be considered children's rights.
5. The class list of needs is converted into a list of children's rights.
6. Students should compare their list of rights to the list of rights provided for in the Convention on the Rights of the Child. A plain language (simply written and abridged) version of the Convention is available on the UNICEF website.[62] This comparison should be guided by the following question and procedures:

   a. What are the differences between the class list and the Convention?

      i. Students should make three lists.

         (1) The first list should contain those things that are the same between the class list and the Convention.
         (2) The second list should include those things on the class list and not in the Convention.
         (3) The third list should include those things in the Convention but not on the class list.

   (a) For instance, students might not think of play as a need. However, Article 31 of the Convention declares: "States Parties recognize the right of the child to rest and leisure, to engage in play and recreational activities appropriate to the age of the child and to participate freely in cultural life and the arts."

7. After comparing the class list with the Convention, students discuss whether or not they agree with the rights listed in the Convention. The teacher should stress that the Convention was written by other humans and therefore is a document that is not perfect and open to interpretation and change.
8. On the basis of the original lists of needs, class discussion, and comparison with the Convention, students are asked to finalize their list and post it on the class door or a wall as their own Declaration of the Rights of Children.

Universal Declaration of Human Rights

Within the framework of considering the identification and formulation of human rights as an ongoing process, the second section of *Humanity* Chapter 5, Universal Declaration of Human Rights, introduces students to this historic document for the purpose of fostering discussion about the meaning of human rights. Students are directed to the Web site for the United Nations' Cyberschoolbus, which provides an interactive version of the Universal Declaration of Human Rights and a "plain language" version of the document.[63] The plain language version is particularly useful for young students and those with limited reading ability. The interactive version is divided by numbered articles in the Universal Declaration of Human Rights. Links from a particular article lead the viewer to both the original and plain language version of the article, along with notes, definitions, questions, and activities.

Using as a model the preceding lesson, The Rights of Children, the teacher plans a similar lesson with a focus on the needs of all humans. After refining their ideas about human needs, students compare their list to the Universal Declaration of Human Rights and discuss whether they agree or do not agree with its list of human rights. Students should post their own version of the Universal Declaration of Human Rights.

Protecting Rights in Your Community

The final section in Chapter 5, Protecting Rights in Your Community, encompasses many of the themes in *Humanity's* previous chapters, such as the condition of the environment, hunger and healthful food, inequality of wealth, sustainable consumption and use of earth's resources, and discrimination based on race, gender, and sexual orientation. These previous discussions and lessons are designed to fulfill human needs so that social conditions will foster the opportunity for all people to experience a long life and happiness. In translating human needs into human rights, students probably will touch on most of the themes in other sections of *Humanity*.

Similar to some of the other lessons in *Humanity*, the lesson Protecting Rights in Your Community asks students to look for any rights violations in their own community. Teachers in planning this lesson must be sensitive to the maturity of their students as well as local cultural standards and social conditions. Also, some of the rights problems identified by students may require remedial action similar to those related to environment, hunger, inequality, discrimination, and sustainable consumption.

Lesson: Protecting Rights in Your Community

1. Students plan how they can realistically look for rights violations in their local community using their classroom list of children's and human rights.
2. Following the agreed upon plan, the students investigate and compile a list of possible children's and human rights violations in their local community.
3. After the investigation, the students compare their lists of possible violations and discuss the following:
    a. Which of the items on these lists are real violations of children's and human rights?
    b. Which rights violations are caused by local social, economic, and political conditions?
    c. Which rights violations are a result of national or global conditions?
4. After identifying rights violations that are a result of local circumstances, the students decide which rights violations they can realistically try to remedy.
5. The students plan a course of action to remedy one or more of the rights violations they believe they can realistically tackle.
6. After the plans to correct rights violations are implemented, the class engages in an ongoing dialogue that results in a continuous revision of the action plan as it is put into practice.

CHOOSING A LIFE THAT YOU WANT

The final chapter of *Humanity,* "Choosing A Life That You Want," addresses Amartya Sen's concept of "capabilities." The reader will recall that Sen defines social equality or inequality according to "people's ability [capabilities] to lead the kind of lives they value–and have reason to value."[64] Being able to live the life that a person wants directly affects her or his feelings of subjective well-being. Also, as Sen and others have suggested, inability to live a life that one wants produces stress that has consequences for personal health and longevity.

What can schools do about capabilities? First, they can help students identify the type of lives they want to live. Second, they can provide students with the skills and knowledge that will help them live the lives they want. Finally, they can help students understand the political, economic, and social conditions that will allow them to live the lives they want.

Like so many other lessons in *Humanity*, this one requires making a distinction between needs and wants. In this case, fulfillment of needs is basic to living the life a person values. Wants go beyond the fulfillment of basic needs and include work, helping to improve the human condition, and leisure time activities. Work is simply defined as activities required to fulfill one's basic needs, such as shelter, food, and health care. Helping to improve the human condition refers to fulfilling the ethical duty to ensure that others are able to live a long and happy life. Leisure time activities refer to things a person wants to do besides the work required to fulfill basic needs.

An ideal situation might be when needs and wants are fulfilled in a single activity. As I discussed in chapter 1 this provides an opportunity for the worker to have an "optimal experience." For instance, one's work could fulfill basic needs while helping others and providing the enjoyment associated with leisure time activities. One might call this a "holistic life" with an integration of work, ethics, and pleasure. However, I risk the danger of imposing my own value for a holistic life on others by proclaiming it ideal. To my knowledge, no findings in research literature shows that a holistic life is "better" than one divided into separate activities to achieve fulfillment of needs, ethical responsibilities, and pleasure. "Better" in this sentence refers to increasing longevity and subjective well-being.

As with previous lessons, the teacher should adapt this lesson to local cultural and social conditions. Local culture is an important aspect of this lesson because of its effect on the choices made by the student and the possibility of students fulfilling their capabilities. Also, exploration of what a student wants to do with his or her life touches on important psychological issues outside the scope of *Humanity*. *Humanity* deals with the social, economic, and political conditions that foster a long life and happiness, but it does not deal directly with the internal psychological state of the individual. Of course, there is an interrelationship between internal mental states and external conditions. However, I am not considering in *Humanity* mental health issues as related to individual and group therapy and the use pharmaceutical drugs. The next lesson is meant to motivate students to think about what they would like to do with their lives.

Lesson: Identifying the Life I Want to Live and How to Live It

1. The teacher emphasizes that this lesson is only the beginning of what could be a lifelong quest to understand what type of life the students want to live and how they want to live it.
2. Have the students prepare three lists.

a. The first list should describe their needs (this could be a reflection of class work on children's and human rights).
b. The second list should describe their ethical responsibilities to others. This list could be based on previous action-oriented lessons such as the School and Community Environmental Research, Let's Get People Some Healthy Food, Community and School Research on the Meaning of Race (also lessons on gender and sexual orientation), and Protecting Rights in Your Community.
c. The third list should describe those things they would most enjoy doing in life.

3. Each of these lists is used to complete the following tables. Each of these tables will require research on the part of the student.
4. The first table, Needs and Work, will require students to list at least four types of work they would like to do to satisfy their basic needs. Students will have to do research to identify the knowledge and skills needed for each job and whether the work is available locally, globally, or both.

Table : Needs and Work

What type of work would I like to do to satisfy my needs	Knowledge and skills required for the work	Is this type of work available locally, globally, or both?
#1		
#2		
#3		
#4		

5. The second table, Meeting My Ethical Responsibilities, will require students to list at least four types of activities they would like to do to fulfill their ethical responsibilities. Students will have to do research to identify the knowledge and skills needed for each activity and whether these activities can be done locally, globally, or both.

Table: Meeting My Ethical Responsibilities

What would I like to do to help others live a long and happy life?	Knowledge and skills required for this activity	Can I engage in this activity locally, globally, or both?
#1		
#2		
#3		
#4		

6. The third table, What I'd Like To Do for Fun, will require students to list at least four types of activities. Students will have to do research to identify the knowledge and skills needed for each activity and whether these activities can be done locally, globally, or both.

What I'd Like To Do for Fun

What I'd like to do for fun	Knowledge and skills required for this activity	Can I engage in this activity locally, globally, or both?
#1		
#2		
#3		
#4		

7. For the fourth and final table, Can I Have It All?, students are asked to consider the possibility and desirability of a holistic life in which activities combine satisfying basic needs, fulfilling ethical responsibilities, and engaging in enjoyable activities.

Can I Have It All?

What things can I do that will be fun, satisfy my needs, and help others	Knowledge and skills required for this activity	Can I engage in this activity locally, globally, or both?
#1		
#2		
#3		
#4		

CONCLUSION: USING A TEXTBOOK PROTOTYPE

The purpose of *Humanity: A Prototype Textbook for a Global Core Curriculum* is to provide a guide and examples of lessons that will help to implement the proposed global core curriculum. It is important to emphasize that *Humanity* is not intended to be the only textbook or educational materials used in a global school. Also, it is not intended to restrict the capabilities of teachers in planning curricula and lessons. Teachers will need to use their own knowledge and skills to adapt *Humanity* to differing ages and cultures. Suggested lessons are examples and possibly inspirations for teachers to use in their own schools.

To avoid being a form of cultural imposition, *Humanity* relies on teachers to adapt the text and lessons to local cultural circumstances. However, *Humanity* does have the specific goal of developing and sustaining actions that will maximize the longevity and subjective well-being of humans.

NOTES

1 United Nations Environment Program, *Tunza: Acting for a Better World* (Nairobi: The United Nations Environment Program, 2003), pp. 70–122. This publication is available on the Internet at the Web site for the United Nations Environment Program's Children & the Environment http://www.unep.org/Tunza/children/.

2 United Nations Environment Programme, *Tunza: For Children,* http://www.unep.org/tunza/children/default.asp. Retrieved on March 16, 2006.

3 United Nations Environment Programme, *Pachamama.* http://www.grida.no/geo2000/pacha/welcome2.htm. Retrieved on March 16, 2006.

4 Lynton Keith Caldwell, *International Environmental Policy From the Twentieth to the Twenty-First Century: Third Edition* (Durham, North Carolina: Duke University Press, 1996), pp. 24–25.

5 As quoted in Caldwell, p. 26.

6 Ibid., p. 26.

7 World Wildlife Fund, *Marine Biodiversity Education: Oceans of Life* http://worldwildlife.org/windows/marine/oceans.cfm and *Biodiversity Education Frameworks: Key Concepts and Skills, http://worldwildlife.Org/windows/pdfs/education_framework.pdf.*Retrieved on March 2, 2006.
8 United Nations Environment Program, *Tunza* ... pp. 24–36
9 The World Food Programme Web site is http://www.wfp.org/; the World Health Organization Web site is http://www.who.int/; and Oxfam's international Web site is http://www.oxfam.org/.
10 World Food Programme's "Hunger Map," *http://www.wfp.org/country_brief/hunger_map/map/hungermap_popup/map_popup.html.* Retrieved on March 20, 2006.
11 I discuss this campaign for school cafeterias as part of cultural domination and as part of the development of home economics and the standardization of American food in Joel Spring, *Educating the Consumer-Citizen: A History of the Marriage of Schools, Advertising, and Media* (Mahwah: Lawrence Erlbaum Associates, 2003), pp. 28–62.
12 United Nation's World Food Programme, "Food Force" http://www.food-force.com/index.php/game/downloads Retrieved on February 24, 2006.
13 Ibid.
14 See World Food Programme, *Global School Feeding Report 2005* (Rome: World Food Programme, 2005).
15 The Internet address for the "School Feeding" program of the World Food Programme is http://www.wfp.org/food_aid/school_feeding/index.asp?section=12&sub_section=3.
16 "Declaration and Integrated Framework of Action on Education for Peace, Human Rights, and Democracy" (Paris: UNESCO, 1995).
17 See United Nations Cyberschoolbus, "Unit Three: Critical Thinking and Active Non-Violence," http://www.un.org/cyberschoolbus/peace/frame3_3.htm Retrieved on February 27, 2006.
18 "Declaration and Integrated Framework of Action on Education for Peace ...," p. 14.
19 United Nations Cyberschoolbus, "Peace Education ...." Retrieved on February 27, 2006.
20 Ibid.
21 Ibid.
22
23 Ibid.
24 Cyberschoolbus, "Poverty Curriculum—Introduction adapted from Oxfam International's 'Hunger Banquet',"http://www.un.org/cyberschoolbus/poverty2000/introclass.asp Retrieved on March 15, 2006.
25 See Ibid. for stories that can be used in this lesson.
26 See Ibid. for stories that can be used in this lesson.
27 See Ibid. for stories that can be used in this lesson.
28 See Michael Marmot, *The Status Syndrome: How Social Standing Affects Our Health and Longevity* (New York: Times Books, 2004), p. 86.
29 See Joel Spring *Educating the Consumer–Citizen: A History of the Marriage of Schools, Advertising, and Media* (Mahwah, New Jersey: Lawrence Erlbaum Associates, 2003).
30 Kathy Peiss, *Hope In a Jar: The Making of America's Beauty Culture* (New York: Henry Holt & Company, 1998).
31 Betty A. Reardon, *Educating for Human Dignity: Learning About Rights and Responsibilities* (Philadelphia: University of Pennsylvania Press, 1995), pp. 33–35.
32 For instance, "ExRx Fitness Calculators" at http://www.exrx.net/Calculators/CalRequire.html.
33 John Harms and Douglas Kellner, "Toward A Critical Theory of Advertising," *Illuminations*, . Retrieved on March 9, 2006.
34 Ibid.

35 Ibid.
36 "Media Literacy," *PBS Teacher Source, http://www.pbs.org/teachersource/media_lit/quiz.shtm.* Retrieved on March 9, 2006.
37 Ibid.
38 "Media Literacy: Getting Started: Activity Ideas for Language Arts, Social Studies, Math Science, and Health," *PBS Teacher Source http://www.pbs.org/teachersource/media_lit/getting_started.shtm.* Retrieved on March 9, 2006.
39
40 Ibid.
41 Ibid.
42 Ibid.
43 PBS Kids, "Don't Buy It: Get Media Smart—Design a Cereal Box" *http://pbskids.org/dontbuyit/advertisingtricks/cerealbox_flash.html.* Retrieved on March 8, 2006.
44 International Reading Association, National Council of Teachers of English, and the Marcopolo Education Foundation, "Read·Write·Think," http://www.readwritethink.org/index.asp.
45 Laurie Henry, "Critical Media Literacy: Commercial Advertising," *Read·Write·Think http://www.readwritethink.org/lessons/lesson_view.asp?id=97.* Retrieved on March 6, 2006.
46 Ibid.
47 See "Media Literacy: Getting Started: Activity Ideas for …."
48 *Declaration of Thessaloniki, International Conference Environment and Society: Education and Public Awareness for Sustainability (Thessaloniki, 8–12 December 1997)*, (Paris: UNESCO, 1997), p. 1.
49 UNESCO, *Educating for a Sustainable Future …*, pp. 36–41.
50 National Council for Science and the Environment, "Education for a Sustainable and Secure Future," *http://www.ncseonline.org/NCSEconference/2003conference/page.cfm?fid=2344.* Retrieved on December 12, 2003. Also see Lynton Keith Caldwell, *International Environmental Policy From the Twentieth to the Twenty-First Century: Third Edition* (Durham, North Carolina: Duke University Press, 1996), pp. 242–244.
51 Ibid., p. 33.
52 Ibid., p. 34.
53 Ibid., p. 34.
54 Ibid., p. 33.
55 United Nations Educational, Scientific, and Cultural Organization and United Nations Environment Programme, *YouthXChange: Training Kit on Responsible Consumption* (Paris and Nairobi: United Nations Publication, 2002).
56 Ibid., p. 7.
57 United Nations Environment Programme, *Why Take A Life Cycle Approach* (Paris: United Nations Environment Programme, 2004), p. 6.
58 World Wildlife Fund, *Smart Consumers: An Educator's Guide to Exploring Consumer Issues in the Environment, http://worldwildlife.org/windows/education_guides.cfm#3.* Retrieved on March 3, 2006.
59 For an example of cultural issues and human rights, see my study of the cultural issues involved in the education rights Article 26 of the Universal Declaration of Human Rights in JoelSpring, *The Universal Right to Education: Definition, Justification, and Guidelines* (Mahwah, N.J.: Lawrence Erlbaum Associates, 2000).
60 Amnesty International, http://www.amnesty.org/and Human rights Watch http://www.hrw.org/. Retrieved on March 29, 2006.
61 "Human Rights Web," *http://www.hrweb.org/resource.html.* Retrieved on March 29, 2006.
62 Plain and abridged version can be found at UNICEF, "Rights Under the Convention on the Rights of the Child," http://www.unicef.org/crc/index_30177.html. Retrieved on March 30, 2006.

63 United Nations Cyberschoolbus, "The Interactive Declaration," http://www.un.org/cyberschoolbus/humanrights/declaration/index.asp.
64 Amartya Sen, *Development as Freedom* (New York: Anchor Books, 2000), p. 18.

Chapter 7

Conclusion: *Koyaanisqatsi: Life Out of Balance*

Necks chained, making it impossible to see the reality behind them, dwellers in Plato's cave sit and analyze the meaning of reality's shadows cast on the wall in front of them.[1] The heavy chains reach to the rocky floor, sometimes clanging against it when wearers take a deep breath or gasp at the profundity of their analysis of the passing shadows. Gazing at the shadows, school leaders spend endless years fruitlessly debating how schools can contribute to economic growth, provide equality of economic opportunity, and eliminate poverty. Clusters of conservatives, liberals, critical theorists, Freireians, Marxists, libertarians, constructivists, ethnographers, sociologists, policymakers, philosophers, learning theorists, developmentalists, curriculum planners, pedagogues, and statisticians drag their chains into the cave's nooks and corners, debating how schools can more equitably process students for the global economy. The noise is often deafening as learned educators shout their solutions and clank their chains on the cave's floors while wandering between groups trying to decide if they are liberal statisticians, conservative ethnographers, or adherents to some other combination of academic discourse. Sparks fly off dragging chains as school people rush with hands out to gather research funds that occasionally fall from the cave's ceiling as governments and businesses shove their largesse through the cracks in the ground above. A drought in the rain of research money causes waves of discussion about how to better serve the masters above.

A film flashes onto the cave's wall showing an assembly line of rush hour commuters streaming endlessly down escalators onto the crowded floor of New York City's Grand Central Station, where they run bobbing and weaving through the throng to a train home. A rush hour scene of packed trains and buses, clogged highways, and frayed nerves pans out in the world's major cities—cities bloated by rural-to-urban migration, with China experiencing the world's greatest internal migration. The film is Godfrey Reggio's 1982 documentary *Koyaanisqatsi: Life Out of Balance,* accompanied by the pulsating beat of Philip Glass's minimalist music.[2] Based on Hopi prophecies, the movie's images show technological advancement putting humans out of balance with nature and reducing them to raw material for processing by the industrial machine.

Koyaanisqatsi stirs the cave dwellers into a new frenzy of speculation, with many staring at the ceiling looking for research grants from their masters. "I can determine causality, find correlations, determine reliability, and ascertain standard deviations of this raw human data," shout statisticians to the ceiling as they start counting those being spit out at the bottom of the escalators. "Put me in the crowd," say the ethnographers, "and I'll tell you their stories." A group of sociologists bang their chains on the cave's walls chanting, "Inequality! Inequality! Inequality!" One learned-looking sociologist in a nondescript black skirt and shirt proclaims, "The trains go to suburbs differentiated by income and school quality. A rich suburb means good schools. Commuters had unequal educational opportunities, which are now reproduced in the commuter train they take." Wearing all black leather and neck chains decorated with little metal emblems depicting Che Guevara, Mao, Marx, Castro, and Foucault, critical theorists ask the ceiling for money to buy consciousness-raising banners to liberate commuters to overthrow their masters and create dialogical schools.

The masters laugh as they shove more money through the cracks in the ceiling. Obedient to authority, educators lift their chains in praise of businesses and governments so willing to support the creation of equal schools so graduates have equal chances to buy more and more goods. Equal schools implant equal desires to serve the whims of the masters. Lifting their arms in supplication to the ceiling, learning theorists propose measuring lifelong learning skills: "As jobs change, people must learn new competencies." The plan is to build mazes with food carts requiring commuters descending onto Grand Central's floor to find new paths to their trains. Each day, trains will be assigned to new tracks, and carts will be moved to create new mazes. Certain commuters will be tracked to determine their learning curves. One learning theorist pontificates, "We'll determine tolerable levels of frustration caused by change. Free markets, technological development, global movement of factories and workers make people anxious like the commuters getting to their trains. Schools could be conveyor belts of children running mazes and learning lifelong skills for economic change." Clanging their chains, developmentalists express concern that plans are being based on adults dashing to trains: "Starting with preschool and working up to adolescence, the reaction of each age group to change should be calculated. Sending preschool kids down an escalator into a world of changing mazes and train gates to reach home could develop lifelong tolerance to economic change. That'll be our school design!"

Policy wonks strain to turn their heads to see reality, but the long arms of businesses and governments dangling through the cracks in the ceiling grasp their neck chains and force them to look only at the glory of economic growth and equality of opportunity to earn and buy. In their minds, *Koyaanisqatsi* is the educational ideal. Out come the flow charts. Out come the measuring sticks. Escalators speed children to the school's central hall. Train gates become classes. Take a train to a career for the global economy, then on to a suburb where people are likeminded consumers. Prepare kids for lifelong learning by exchanging food cart mazes with academic hurdles of curriculum and course requirements, high stakes tests, indifferent administrators, bicycling teachers, boredom, and unreasonable and unjustified rote learning. "Now they'll live with any business and corporate bureaucracy," shouts one policymaker. "We can get them all bicycling to authority." The money comes raining through the cracks in the cave's ceiling.

WHAT DOES THE GLOBAL ECONOMY WANT?

Bicycling to authority is what's needed by the global economy. Entry level jobs require only a solid ninth-grade education along with a good work ethic, timeliness, and good attendance habits concludes Paul E. Barton, a senior associate of the Educational Testing Service, after analyzing 20 million job openings projected by the U.S. Bureau of Labor statistics. Most entry level workers are trained on the job. Citing economists Richard Murnane and Frank Levy as well as the U.S. Chamber of Commerce, Barton reasons that employers are mainly concerned with "soft skills,"and that these skills are not correlated with the results of paper and pencil tests.[3] The U.S. Chamber of Commerce considers "soft skills" to be "basic employability skills (attendance, timeliness, and work ethic, etc.)."[4]. Because of "inadequate basic employability skills,"69% of companies reporting to the U.S. Chamber of Commerce rejected applicants as hourly production workers.[5] In 2005, the National Association of Manufacturers reported that "basic employability skills" and technical skills were put highest on the list of employment requirements by manufacturers. Next were "reading/writing/communication skills."[6]

While employers complain about the education of their workers, Michael J. Handel, professor of sociology at Northeastern University, points out that "it is unclear whether they are dissatisfied mainly with workers' cognitive skills or rather with their effort and attitude."[7] Obviously, professional jobs, such as engineering, science, medicine, and accounting require extensive schooling. What about well-paying white collar jobs? A number of studies show that for this group, the needed academic skills are equivalent to the reading and math skills required for success in the first year of college.[8] Again, the occupational skills for these white collar workers are learned on the job. This is not surprising. Imagine a person applying for an entry level white collar job in a publishing company. Schools did not teach the candidate to perform the actual tasks required by the company. On the other hand, schools did teach basic reading, writing, and math skills. Therefore, the company must teach the employee how to do specific tasks required in a publishing firm and rely on his or her ability to learn. In the end, the new employee retains his or her job by learning the company tasks and bicycling to authority—working hard, following orders, and being punctual. For most occupations, schooling is more about learning obedience to authority than about learning actual job skills.

LIFE IN BALANCE

It would be arrogant to suggest that the Koyaanisqatsi-like crowds spewing into Grand Central are unhappy, and that their lives are out of balance with nature. On the other hand, are educators trapped by their narrow focus on economic growth and consumption? Can educators turn their backs on their masters and ask about human happiness rather than how to get more research money? Chains broken, the educators turn to see a world of limited natural resources, environmental destruction, extreme wealth contrasted with life-threatening famine and health conditions, happiness threatened by status competition, longevity shortened by lack of capabilities and bicycling, and limits on what economic growth can provide for personal and national happiness.

Seeing the reality of economic growth, the educators look anew at the conveyer belts of commuters dodging and weaving their way to trains. Statisticians descend onto the station's floor measuring the subjective well-being and age of the commuters to determine conditions that foster happiness and longevity. Ethnographers wander through the crowds collecting stories of distress and jubilation. Sociologists study which trains are taking riders to suburbs with high and low rates of subjective well-being and longevity. Critical theorists storm across Grand Central's immense hall holding aloft banners of smiley faces dialoging with the crowd about the social conditions that foster the good life. Learning theorists plan optimal educational experiences to help the homeward bound enhance their capabilities. Developmentalists shout at the waves of people trying to get on their trains to the good life: "Remember, children have the right to happiness and a long life."

And the policy wonks? They start designing schools that foster the happiness, longevity, and the pleasure of optimal learning experiences for students and staff. The schools have a reduced hierarchy and little bicycling between the school staff and between students. Conditions are created for holistic lessons that contribute to optimal learning experiences and teach the place of humans in the biosphere. Policymakers plan for students and staff to monitor the environmental impact of the school plant, including the impact on student, staff, and community health. They promote student activism as preparation for assuming an ethical responsibility to work for the long life and happiness of all. Capabilities of teachers and students are maximized by cooperative lesson planning. Different "ways of seeing" are embedded in cultural lessons.

With chains removed and perspectives broadened from the maddening focus on economic growth and consumption, the cave dwellers no longer look at the ceiling for the money of their masters to fall. With new light in their eyes, educators see that their happiness and long lives are dependent on the lives and happiness of all humans and the condition of the biosphere. They assume the ethical responsibility to protect the life and happiness of all, support human rights, and protect the biosphere. Without their chains, educators help others plan global schools that free students from conveyor belt processing into a work and buy society. In the new paradigm, students actively participate in increasing their capabilities and fostering conditions for a long life and happiness.

NOTES

1 In W. H. D. Rouse's translation of Plato's Republic Socrates opens the parable of the cave with the following description which I have modified for my purposes: "Imagine mankind as dwelling in an underground cave with a long entrance open to the light across the whole width of the cave; in this they have been from childhood, with necks and legs fettered, so they have to stay where they are. They cannot move their heads around because of the fetters, and they can only look forward, but light comes to them from fire burning behind them higher up at a distance. Between the fire and the prisoners … is a low wall … bearers carrying … all sorts of articles [cast shadows on the wall in front of the prisoners] … What do you think such people would have seen of themselves and each other except their shadows, which the fire cast on the opposite wall?" Plato, The Republic in Great Dialogues of Plato translated by W. H. D. Rouse (New York: The New American Library, 1956), p. 312.

2 *Koyaanisqatsi: Life Out of Balance* directed by Godfrey Reggio and written by Ron Fricke, Michael Hoening, Godfrey Reggio, and Alton Walpole (New Cinema and Island Alive, 1983).

3 1. Paul E. Barton, *High School Reform and Work: Facing Labor Market Realities* (Princeton, New Jersey: Educational Testing Service, 2006), pp. 4-5.
4 Ibid., p. 2
5 Ibid., p. 3.
6 Lynn Olsen, "Ambiguity About Preparation for Workforce Clouds Efforts to Equip Students for Future," *Education Week* (24 May 2006), p. 20.
7 Ibid., p. 18.
8 Ibid., p. 18

Author Index

L

M

N

O

P

R

S

U

V

W

Y

Subject Index